Windows XP®
Weekend Crash Course®

Windows XP®
Weekend Crash Course®

John R. Nicholson

WILEY

Wiley Publishing, Inc.

Windows XP® Weekend Crash Course®

Published by
Wiley Publishing, Inc.
10475 Crosspoint Boulevard
Indianapolis, IN 46256
www.wiley.com

Copyright © 2003 by Wiley Publishing, Inc., Indianapolis, Indiana

Published simultaneously in Canada

ISBN: 0-7645-4223-0

Manufactured in the United States of America

10 9 8 7 6 5 4 3 2 1

1B/RX/QZ/QT/IN

About the Author

John R. Nicholson is a professor of Computer Information Systems at Johnson County Community College in Overland Park, Kansas. He has been using Microsoft Windows since Version 1 was introduced, and has been an authorized beta tester of every version of Microsoft Windows and Microsoft Office since 1994. He is a Microsoft Certified Professional in both Windows NT and Windows 2000. John is author of more than a dozen computer-related books, translated into over 20 languages. Recent books include *Inside Dreamweaver UltraDev 4* (2001), which he co-authored with his son Sean, and *Teach Yourself Outlook 98 in 24 Hours* (1998), which he co-authored with his daughter Rebecca. He has four children and seven grandchildren. When he isn't chained to his computer, John watches nearly every movie ever made, loves theater, and collects old radio shows from the 1920s through the 1960s. He can be reached at jnichols@jccc.edu.

Credits

Senior Acquisitions Editor
Sharon Cox

Development Editor
Sara Shlaer

Production Editor
Felicia Robinson

Technical Editor
Todd Meister

Copy Editor
Maggie Warren

Editorial Manager
Mary Beth Wakefield

Vice President & Executive Group Publisher
Richard Swadley

Vice President and Executive Publisher
Bob Ipsen

Vice President and Publisher
Joseph B. Wikert

Executive Editorial Director
Mary Bednarek

Project Coordinator
Nancee Reeves

Graphics and Production Specialists
Beth Brooks
Jennifer Click
Sean Decker
LeAndra Hosier
Heather Pope

Quality Control Technician
Angel Perez
Carl William Pierce
Charles Spencer

Permissions Editor
Carmen Krikorian

Media Development Specialist
Kit Malone

Proofreading and Indexing
Publication Services

This book is dedicated to my son Matthew A. Nicholson, who is currently serving in Saudi Arabia while his wife and two babies wait patiently at home. May he return safe, sound, and soon. Thanks for helping defend our country, Matt. We all miss you and love you. And a special thanks to all the soldiers, sailors, airmen, and others who responded when our country called.

Preface

Welcome to *Microsoft Windows XP Weekend Crash Course*. It may seem impossible to master a program as rich and powerful as Windows XP in such a short time, but if you are dedicated and motivated, I'll help see you through in record time. I have been using Microsoft Windows since Version 1 (even though it didn't become popular until version 3, several years later), and have been teaching it for over a decade. Beginning with the first session, you will receive an overview of Windows XP that is used as a building block for future sessions.

This book is designed to be completed over a fairly intense weekend. Some sessions may actually require more than 30 minutes of your time. For example, the time required to complete Session 2, "Installing Windows XP," will vary from computer to computer, depending on the speed of the hardware, the amount of RAM, and whether or not you need to format your hard drive as part of the installation process. So if you already have Windows XP installed, you might just hit the highlights of that session. If you are beginning from scratch, it might take as long as 90 minutes. Whatever time you require, whether it is more or less than the suggested time, take it. The purpose of this book is to teach you basic and intermediate tasks related to Windows XP, *not* for you to stick strictly by the suggested session times.

This is *not* a book on how to use Microsoft Office, even though that may be the application you are going to use most often. Instead, this book concentrates on accessories and options available when only Windows XP is installed. It is also *not* a book on how to use Windows XP to connect to a domain network. To do this, you need to have a server and server software, which is beyond what this book covers. However, networking (sharing local resources between computers) is covered in Session 14.

Who Should Read this Book

This book is for beginning to intermediate users of the Microsoft Windows XP operating system. It covers both the Professional and Home Edition. The text notes features where the two operating systems differ. Basically, most tasks that you can do with the Professional version can also be accomplished with the Home Edition. The book is structured in such a way that each session is independent of the other, so if you are familiar with a particular topic, you can skip it and move to the next. This book is structured for the home or small business user who does not want to invest the extra money required to set up a domain network. If you fall into any of the following categories, this book will help you reach your goals.

- **Beginners** who want to learn the basics of Windows XP.
- **Intermediate users** who want to learn more than the basics of XP, and may need to assist other users in setting up their computers.
- **Individuals** who want to learn the tips and shortcuts of Windows XP.
- **Small business technical users** who want to learn to share a single resource, such as a printer.

How to Use this Book

This book can be used in one of three ways. First, you can work through it from Session 1 to Session 30. This is the suggested way to use the book if you haven't had much experience with computers or with the Windows XP operating system. The way the book is laid out is conducive to completing all 30 sessions in a single weekend (from Friday evening through Sunday afternoon).

The second way to use it is to simply read and complete the sessions you need to brush up on. You are the best judge on what you need to learn. Since each session is independent of all others, you need not work through sessions you are already familiar with just to get to the topics you want to cover. Simply select the topics, read them, and complete the hands-on exercises in the sessions.

The final way to use the book is as a reference book. Although not specifically designed as a reference manual, the index is thorough and you will be able to pick a topic from a session and work through the hands-on-exercises to gain the knowledge you need. Since there are over 100 specific hands-on-exercises in the book, you should find one that meets your specific needs.

The writing style of this book is friendly. You won't find a lot of technical jargon, and if technical terms are needed, they are defined at the point they are introduced. This means that you should be able to jump into any of the sessions and pick up at the point you need to learn.

Overview

The book is divided into six parts, each containing four to six sessions. Each session will take approximately 30 minutes to complete.

Friday Evening

In the first four sessions, I discuss the differences and similarities between Windows XP Professional, Windows XP Home Edition, and previous versions of the Windows operating systems. Next, I move to installation of Windows XP, discussing what an operating system is and how best to install it. In the third session, you learn some introductory information about the Windows XP operating system in particular, along with some quick tricks to make you feel more at home with Windows XP. Your first evening is rounded out by exploring the Windows XP Help and Support Center. By this time, you should have a basic idea of what Windows XP is, and how it will help you keep efficiency at a maximum level.

Saturday Morning

Saturday morning will really begin to tax your brainpower; so make sure you get plenty of sleep and rest the night before. I guide you in an overview of the XP control panel, the basic and advanced accessories included with Windows XP. Next, you move on to basic and advanced desktop customization. You finish the morning by exploring the basics of files and folders, and how they are used with Windows XP.

Saturday Afternoon

You begin Saturday afternoon, by extending your knowledge of advanced file and folder options. The My Documents folder and its subfolders are discussed at length. One of the most important aspects of working with any operating system is the ability to print. This session takes you through installing, configuring, and sharing a single printer that can be used by multiple computers. Next, I'll give you an overview of networking, and discuss the differences between a domain network and a workgroup. I'll show you how to develop a workgroup, allowing multiple computers to share a single resource. And in the final two sessions, you will have an opportunity to cover basic and advanced Internet Explorer options. Internet Explorer is supplied with Windows XP and is used to surf the Internet.

Saturday Evening

By Saturday evening, you'll probably be pretty overloaded with all of the information you have gained throughout the day, so I keep the number of sessions to four. You'll learn about managing your computer, what to do to prevent disasters, and how to recover from one when it does happen; you'll learn to use Outlook Express as your e-mail and newsgroup reader client. For the grand ending on Saturday, you'll get to have a little bit of fun talking to your friends in real time using Internet Messenger.

Sunday Morning

Sunday morning hopefully finds you recovered from a previously intense day. I begin by explaining how to master multimedia in Windows XP. Then we'll cover a more technical topic about adding and configuring hardware. Sharing resources is the next topic on the list, one that can save you or your company a lot of money. The ability to use Task Manager is one of the major things that separate the person with technical know-how from those who just putter on the computer. To round out the morning, you'll get a chance to look at auditing the efficiency of your computer.

Sunday Afternoon

As you begin the last part of the book, you learn to add users and give them rights to perform specific tasks on the operating system. In a very important chapter, you learn all about viruses and what they can do to your computer if you are not fully protected. You then learn some basic troubleshooting techniques that should help you keep your maintenance costs down. I wind up with a session on "Where to Go from Here," outlining other free and moderately priced resources to help in your continued growth toward becoming very proficient in Windows XP.

Appendixes

The appendixes include the answers to the Part Review questions and a listing of what is contained on the Web site.

The Companion Web Site

The companion Web site for this book, located at www.wiley.com/compbooks/Nicholson, contains several useful resources. If you are unfamiliar with the hardware side of computing, there is a reference section available to give you an introduction to computer hardware. There is also a self-assessment test that allows you to test your knowledge of beginning and intermediate Windows XP topics. The companion Web site also contains a list of resources to keep you up-to-date with new Windows XP changes, places from which to download Windows-associated files, and miscellaneous Windows-based Web sites.

Layout and Features

The time symbols in the margin show you where you are in your lesson. You may wish to allow a few extra minutes for each session, rather than rushing past something you do not understand. Although I have carefully planned the time so that the work can be completed as promised, you should work at the pace that is best for you.

Also scattered throughout the sessions are hints, tips, and relevant information about addendum topics and concerns. You'll find these items illustrated with the margin symbols shown below.

This symbol means that the accompanying information is important for broadening your awareness of Windows XP features, procedures, or perhaps Windows glitches in general.

This symbol adds information to the material you are studying, or provides an alternative method or a time-saving suggestion.

This symbol is your warning of common errors that you might make while working with a technique.

This symbol indicates where you can find more information on the current subject elsewhere in the book.

This symbol refers you to this book's companion Web site for more information.

The symbol ⇨ indicates a menu path. For instance, if you see File ⇨ Save, it means select the File menu, and then select Save. Text that the reader is to type into the computer is presented in **boldface** font

Ready, Set . . .

One little weekend — such a small amount of time to invest for so much knowledge. *Go* get it!

Acknowledgments

One amazing team of people made this book possible. I have never worked on a project this efficiently, with so many people delivering so many pieces of a puzzle right on time, every time. It's the only way it could have worked, but it is still like watching a miracle.

My acquisitions editor, Sharon Cox, prepared the course with efficiency and clarity. Thank you for this. Sara Shlaer, my project editor, is a master of keeping me on task in order to meet the deadlines required for a book such as this. You allowed me to concentrate on my writing, keeping the critical comments to a minimum during the first draft of the book.

As the book approached publication, I worked closely with Felicia Robinson, the production editor. She was a great help in gathering the various parts of the book and putting them together. This book is not only made up of 30 sessions, but has nearly as many additional pieces that had to be put together into a format recognizable as a book.

To my oldest son, Sean R. Nicholson, who was so helpful in the preparation of the first draft of this manuscript. Without his help, this book would not have such a high quality of information in so many different sessions.

Kate Chase provided critical time-sensitive editing on the final third of this book. Kate, I can't tell you how much I appreciate your help with this book. Without your help, I wouldn't have been able to meet the deadlines.

To David Fugate, my agent, and all the wonderful folks I have worked with at Waterside Production, Inc., over the last 10 years. David has been unflagging in negotiating a deal I could live with.

Finally, to my family, both the blood relatives and all the children who have grown up over the years in our houses. Particularly to Amanda, who has been a best friend to my youngest daughter, Molly. The night before writing this, Amanda graduated from nursing school, and I couldn't have been more proud of her if she were one of my biological children. One thing I have learned over the years is that family comes in many shapes and sizes; they have their own problems, but are always willing to take time to listen to my problems. A man can't ask for anything better than that.

To my wife, Pamela, for the encouragement required to write books. She allowed me to work the odd hours without complaint, and for that, I am truly grateful. She has a wicked red pencil, but the end product is much stronger for her editing.

Although they are all on their own now, my kids, Rebecca, Sean, Matthew, and Molly, as well as my seven grandchildren, have had a dramatic influence on what I have been able to accomplish. The years that they stood firmly behind what I was doing, regardless of the cost to them, allowed me to build a wonderful career and a happy life. Kids who can have that effect on a parent's life are special, very, very special.

Contents at a Glance

Contents

Windows XP®
Weekend Crash Course®

☑ **Friday**

☐ Saturday

☐ Sunday

Part I — Friday Evening

Session 1
Introducing Windows XP

Session 2
Installing Windows XP

Session 3
Windows XP Operating System and Time-Saving Tips

Session 4
Letting Windows Help You

PART

I

Friday
Evening

Introducing Windows XP

Session Checklist

✔ Introducing new and redesigned Windows features

✔ Understanding the differences between Windows XP Professional and Home Versions

✔ Buying Windows XP at a discount

30 Min. To Go

Microsoft Windows XP is the newest addition to the Windows home and small business line of operating systems. (It's also a very popular operating system in large businesses, as I discuss in Session 14.) It is very stable, and the computer seldom has to be completely restarted. In this session you'll find out what an operating system is, what it does, and why you need one. You'll take a brief look at some of the new features in Windows XP, along with some redesigned features from previous versions of Windows.

What Is an Operating System?

The operating system is the most important program that runs on a computer. Every general-purpose computer must have an operating system to run other programs. Operating systems perform basic tasks such as recognizing input from the keyboard, sending output to the display screen, keeping track of files and directories on the hard drive, and controlling peripheral devices such as disk drives and printers. In order for a computer to accept input in the form of keyboard commands or mouse commands, an operating system must be loaded and functional.

Session 3 covers the Windows XP operating system in more detail. For an introduction to computer hardware, see the companion Web site for this book at www.wiley.com/compbooks/nicholson.

Microsoft Windows

Microsoft Windows is the most popular operating system in use today. Microsoft has offered many versions over the years, some more popular than others. Although Versions 1 and 2 did exist (introduced in 1985 and 1987, respectively), they were only used by people who wanted a graphical user interface (GUI). They were not stable and were unacceptable for most home or business use. The following list points out some of the major strengths and weaknesses of various versions of Windows.

- **Versions 3.0, 3.1, and 3.11:** Version 3.0 (1990) of Windows was the first widely popular GUI-based operating system. Although Windows 3.0 was quite unstable, having to be restarted several times a day, most users were willing to sacrifice stability for ease of use. Users just saved their work every few minutes in case the system crashed.

  One of the main drawbacks of Version 3.0 was that it could not run on a local area network (LAN). The introduction of Version 3.11 remedied this problem. In its various incarnations, Version 3.x was popular for several years.

- **Windows 95 (1995):** The introduction of Windows 95 launched one of the world's largest marketing campaigns. Windows 95 went on sale at midnight, and computer stores all over the United States had pajama parties with thousands of dollars worth of gifts given away at each store. Windows 95 was a major upgrade in terms of ease of use, stability, and software availability at the time of introduction. Since the introduction of Windows 95, each new version of Windows has been an incremental upgrade rather than the giant leap from Version 3 to Windows 95.

  While earlier versions of Windows allowed you to switch between programs, *multitasking* was not available. Multitasking is the ability of an operating system to work on more than one application at the time. For example, you could use your computer to play a game, download a file over the Internet, and listen to music all at the same time. The introduction of multitasking drove a need for updated hardware, increased random access memory (RAM), and even larger displays (so that you could see more applications on the screen at one time).

- **Windows 98 (1998) and ME (2000):** Following Windows 95, Microsoft released Windows 98, Windows 98 Second Edition (SE) (1999), and Windows ME. Each of these releases included increased stability and many bells and whistles. Although few users upgraded their existing machines to these versions, new computers came with the upgraded versions already installed.

  Home versions of these Windows operating systems were designed primarily to run games and other multimedia applications. The systems designed for business use were less capable of working with multimedia applications and played few of the popular games. They were designed to run powerful word processors, spreadsheets, databases, and programs that were designed specifically for a company.

- **Windows NT 3.1 (1993) and Windows NT Workstation 4.0 (1996):** Most large businesses have standardized on Windows NT for several years. Version 3.51 was extremely popular and the introduction of Version 4.0 resulted in a business standard that has lasted for many years. In all likelihood, the popularity of Windows NT for business use will continue for many additional years. Standardization on Windows 4.0 was a combination of three things: increased stability, all the perceived features that businesses wanted, and certification by Microsoft [Microsoft Certified

System Engineer (MCSE)] helped ensure that Network Administrators were properly trained.

- **Windows 2000 (2000):** Windows 2000 can be thought of as Windows NT version 5. It took nearly 3 years after the release of Windows 2000 to standardize on that operating system. The release of Windows 2000 was delayed for several months while Microsoft attempted to develop a version that could be used equally well at home and at the office. Eventually, Microsoft changed direction and released Windows 2000 to the business sector and Windows ME to home users. Windows 2000 was an incredible upgrade to the business community. In fact, it was so large that it took businesses several years to fully adapt to it. Moving to 2000 was a large investment in hardware, software, and training. While 2000 looked basically the same on the surface, it was immensely more powerful, and thus more complex. Since most business didn't want to spend the money for a complete upgrade, many decided to remain with NT.

All About Windows XP (Well, Almost)

Microsoft has tried for years to develop a Windows-based operating system that could be used equally well at home, in a small business, or in a large business. The constraining factor has been that home users wanted games and multimedia. Prior to the introduction of Windows XP, this simply was not practical. Games and multimedia applications wanted to take direct control of the central processing unit (CPU), Random Access Memory (RAM), sound card, and video card, among other pieces of hardware, rather than allowing the CPU to assign rotating use of hardware facilities. For example, one application may set aside a specific area of RAM for use and, while multitasking, another application tries to overwrite data in memory, because it uses the same area of RAM. These collisions caused computer crashes.

In Windows NT and Windows 2000, Microsoft set up a gatekeeper that does not allow any application direct access to the hardware. This results in a much more stable system, a priority of nearly all businesses. The release of Windows 2000 was well overdue (Microsoft had announced release dates as early as 1999), mostly because of Microsoft's attempts to release an operating system that would work with games and multimedia and remain as stable as the operating systems used in businesses. Finally, in about mid-2000, Microsoft released the Windows 2000 operating system for businesses and the ME version of Windows for home use. Windows 2000 was moderately successful, but Windows ME was a fiasco, one of the least stable systems since Windows 3.0.

Windows XP (2001) is what Microsoft has been wanting for many years: An operating system that is stable enough for businesses, and yet capable of handling games and multimedia applications. Windows XP is only a client-operating system. There is no version of XP capable of actually running a network. (Microsoft Windows 2003 Server, released in the third quarter of 2003, is the successor to Windows 2000 Server.) One of the ways that Microsoft was able to accomplish this feat was to convince game and multimedia developers that XP was the operating system of the future, and would be shipped on all new home and non-server business computers. If the game and multimedia developers didn't develop for XP, they would be missing a huge market share in the near future. Today, most new software is specifically designed to run on the XP operating system.

**20 Min.
To Go**

New and improved Windows XP features

Windows XP offers many improvements over previous versions of Windows. Take a look at just a few of these.

Visual design

The default Windows XP color scheme is brighter and bolder than in previous versions of Windows. The desktop is less cluttered, the buttons and windows display a 3-D realism, and the icons are sharper. Icons used to be available only in 32×32 pixels (a pixel is the distance between like-colored dots on a monitor), but are now available in three different sizes, including the jumbo 48×48 pixel size. You can change the icons to the larger size by following these steps:

1. Right-click any open area of the desktop. In the context menu, click Properties to show the Display Properties dialog box (shown in Figure 1-1).

Figure 1-1 *The Display Properties dialog box allows you to modify the way various objects are presented on the screen.*

2. Click the Appearance tab.
3. Click the Effects button.
4. Click Use large icons to place a checkmark in the box.

The small square to the left of each option is called a check box. Check boxes are examples of *toggles*. A toggle is a feature with two states, on and off. In the case of check boxes, the option is toggled on or off by clicking the check box. A checkmark means the option is on, no checkmark means the option is off.

5. Click OK twice.

To revert to regular-sized icons, repeat the above steps, making sure there is no checkmark in the Use large icons check box.

When you first install Windows XP from scratch, you will notice the desktop is uncluttered. In fact, this is one of the negatives for users of previous versions of Windows. The icons they expect to see aren't there. A few clicks of the mouse will display those icons for users who are lost without them.

1. Right-click any open area of the desktop, and click Properties on the pop-up menu to show the Display Properties dialog box (shown in Figure 1-2).

2. Click the Desktop tab.

3. Click the Customize Desktop button.

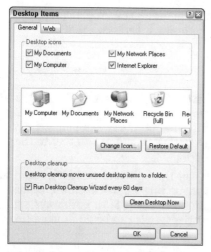

Figure 1-2   *The General tab of the Desktop Items dialog box is used to select which desktop icons will be displayed by default.*

4. In the Desktop icons pane of the General tab, make sure that any icons you want displayed have a checkmark next to them.

5. Click OK twice.

User switching

In previous versions of Windows, if you wanted to change users you had to log off and then load the settings for the new user. In Windows XP, multiple user settings can be held in memory at the same time. To switch between users, simply click Start ➪ Log Off. Figure 1-3 shows the revamped Start menu. Notice the left column shows your commonly used and most recently used programs, while the right column displays the options commonly seen in earlier versions of Windows.

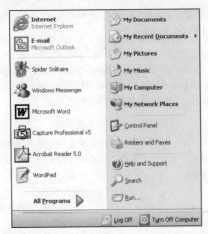

Figure 1-3   *The redesigned Start menu allows you quick access to commonly used programs as well as the ability to log off quickly to switch between users.*

Internet Connection Firewall

Today, there are three basic ways that home users connect to the Internet. The first is through a device called a *modem*. A modem allows you to connect to the Internet using your regular telephone line. You are only connected to the Internet when you actually dial your Internet Service Provider (ISP). This is a relatively slow way of connecting to the Internet, but much less costly than the other two options.

The other two options are connecting to the Internet through your cable television service (cable), or connecting through specialized telephone wire run between the nearest telephone switching site and your house [digital subscriber line (DSL)]. Both ways are expensive compared to using a standard modem, but the speeds can be 20 or more times faster using cable or DSL.

 In reality, cable and DSL connections also require modems. However, when we talk about connecting to the Internet through a modem we are normally talking about using a standard telephone line for the connection.

In the case of a cable or DSL connection, your computer is constantly connected to the Internet. This exposes your computer to the possibility of being *hacked*. Hacking is when an unauthorized person attempts to gain control of your computer for purposes of stealing data or causing malicious damage. One step that can be taken to deter hackers is placing a hardware or software *firewall* between your computer and the Internet. All messages entering or leaving the computer pass through the firewall, which examines each message and blocks those that do not meet the specified security criteria. Although a hardware firewall is always considered to be more effective than a software firewall, it is considerably more expensive. To save Windows XP users from having to invest additional money for basic security, Microsoft has included a software Internet Connection Firewall (ICF) that can be used without additional charge.

Internet Connection Sharing

Although Internet Connection Sharing (ICS) has been available in every edition of Windows since the Windows 98 Second Edition, the version included in Windows XP streamlines the setup process and adds the capability for remote users to start and stop a dial-up connection on the host PC. The purpose of ICS is to allow multiple computers to connect to the Internet through a single Internet connection at the host computer.

 Since the ICF is not very effective and in reality the ICS tends to be difficult to actually get to work, many users bypass both features and invest about $100 to purchase a router. The router not only gives the advantage of better, programmable security but makes hooking multiple computers to the Internet a matter of plugging in a few connections.

Windows Media Player

Although Windows Media Player has been available in many versions of Windows, it has been greatly enhanced in version 8, included with Windows XP. Figure 1-4 shows the latest version of Windows Media Player.

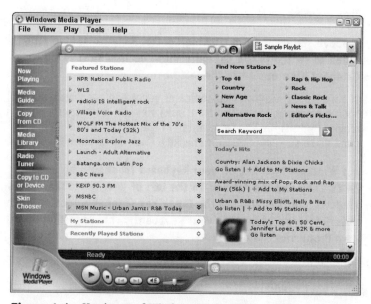

Figure 1-4   *Version 8 of Windows Media Player allows you access to online multimedia material, hundreds of radio stations, as well as the ability to copy to and from CDs.*

 Many users prefer RealPlayer from Real One Networks or Apple's QuickTime, particularly to view streaming media over the Internet. However, it's a good idea to have all three applications available on your computer since some Web sites offer multimedia material only for a specific player.

A few final words about Windows XP features

Some of the Windows XP features are most helpful to those users new to computers, while others will appeal to more experienced users. Similarly, some sections of this book are especially useful for readers setting up their first computers, while other parts provide detailed information for readers migrating to XP from other operating systems. If you're new to computers, I suggest moving forward chapter by chapter. If you're already familiar with another Windows system, you may prefer to jump around as you explore the new and updated features of XP.

**10 Min.
To Go**

Windows XP Professional or Windows XP Home Edition?

Windows XP comes in two basic variations: Windows XP Professional and Windows XP Home Edition. If Windows XP has already been installed on your computer and you're not sure which version you have, here's a quick way to tell.

1. Start your computer.
2. Click Start ⇨ Control Panel ⇨ Performance and Maintenance ⇨ System. This displays the System Properties dialog box. On the General tab, under System, the first line tells you that you are using Windows XP; the second tells you the version you are using.

> **If in step 2 above you went from clicking Control Panel to seeing all of the icons, you need to switch to the Category View. Do this by clicking the Switch to Category View option in the left pane.**

If you do not see a left pane in the window, that indicates you are in the Classic view. The text and figures in this book correspond to the Common Tasks view. To correctly set the Control Panel view, click Tools ⇨ Folder Options. On the General tab in the tasks area, click Show Common Tasks in folders and make sure the option is checked. Click OK to close the window.

> **If you have a Windows logo key on your keyboard (it should be located between the Ctrl key and the Alt key, to the left of your spacebar), press and hold the Windows logo key and tap the Break key (probably located at the right of the very top row of keys on your keyboard). This immediately brings up the System Properties dialog box.**

Following are some significant differences between Windows XP Professional and Home Edition. If you need the functionality of the extra features, buy Professional; otherwise, the Home Edition should satisfy your needs.

Cost

After checking a dozen online stores, I found the Home Edition consistently costs about $100 less. This price difference is the same whether you are buying the full retail or the upgrade-only package. There is no difference in functionality between the full retail version and the upgrade-only version. The only difference is that if you purchase the upgrade-only edition, you will be required to supply, during the installation, the original CD from the previous version of Windows in order to install the upgrade edition of XP. Otherwise, the two versions are identical.

If you are upgrading to Windows XP Home Edition from an older version of Windows you must have the original CD for Windows 98, Windows 98 SE, or Windows Me. (CDs from earlier versions of Windows do not allow you to install the upgrade-only version of XP.) If you are upgrading to Windows XP Professional, the original CD for any of the previous versions will work, as well as the CD from Windows NT 4 Workstation, Windows 2000 Professional, or Windows XP Home Edition. Because this is a book for beginner and intermediate users, rather than Network Administrators, upgrades from Server software are not discussed. Additional information can be found at www.microsoft.com.

Remote desktop

Windows XP Professional provides the Remote Desktop feature, allowing you to access your computer from any other Windows-based computer. Remote Desktop is not just a program that allows you to download files from other computers, but actually allows you to work on the remote computer. For example, you could connect to your work computer from your home office and what you would see on your home monitor would be identical to what you would see if you were at work.

Remote Desktop works best when the two computers are connected by modems. Although it can work through an Internet connection, you must be able to see the IP addresses for both computers. Explaining IP addresses is beyond the scope of this book. For additional information, contact your network administrator.

Network size

In general, Windows XP Professional is the operating system of choice for client computers on a large network. Home networks and small local area networks would probably not benefit from the extra money invested in the Professional version of Windows. Most of the advanced networking features for multiple PC environments would simply be wasted on a small network or a lone desktop machine.

Getting Windows XP at a Discount

Your computer cannot start without an operating system. One of the ways that some businesses may try to save money is by selling you a computer either without an operating system or one that includes a *pirated* version of the operating system. Pirated means that a legal license to include the operating system has not been purchased by the seller. One of the ways that you can make sure you have a legal copy of the operating system is to check for the license that comes with the original CD.

If you are a student or a teacher, you may find it less expensive to purchase a computer without an operating system and then purchase Windows XP at an educational discount.

Protecting sensitive files

One of the major features available in XP Professional that is lacking in the Home version is the ability to encrypt individual files and folders. The Professional version contains a feature called the Encrypting File System (EFS). EFS allows you to encrypt your files and folders for added security against theft or hackers. Restricted File Access is an additional feature found only in Professional, allowing you to restrict access to selected files, applications, and other resources.

Recovery from catastrophic failure

The capability to back up and recover data from a total system failure is more robust in XP Professional than in the Home version.

CPU

The Home Edition of Windows XP is only capable of handling a single 32-bit CPU and a single video display terminal. Professional can work with two CPUs at the same time (of course, your motherboard must be designed to accept two CPUs). This makes processing much faster. Professional can also handle the 64-bit Intel Itanium processor (again, this greatly increases the speed of processing in the computer).

Video display

Windows XP Professional is capable of using up to 10 video display terminals (monitors) at one time. You can stack monitors (for example, three wide by three high) and display a single desktop across all nine monitors. Or, if you have a spreadsheet with many columns, you can set Professional to display different sets of columns on each monitor. You can also display a different file or application on each monitor. Realistically, most users barely have room for one monitor on their desktop, but if you are in a special situation, this option is available for your use.

To use two monitors, you don't need any special hardware. You need a video card with dual connections, or two separate video cards. To use more than two monitors, you will require special video hardware. For more information, go to www.microsoft.com and search for *dualview*.

Done!

REVIEW

- Microsoft Windows XP is an operating system. Operating systems perform basic tasks, such as recognizing input from the keyboard, sending output to the display screen, keeping track of files and directories on the hard drive, and controlling peripheral devices such as disk drives and printers.

- All versions of Windows beginning with Windows 95 are capable of multitasking.

- The visual design is one of the most apparent changes to Windows XP.

- Windows XP comes in two editions: Professional and Home Edition. The Professional edition provides several features not included in the Home Edition, including remote use, greater networking capability, and some security features.

- You can install the full retail version of Windows XP, or upgrade from an older Windows operating system to XP.

QUIZ YOURSELF

1. Which version of Microsoft Windows was first able to operate on a network? (See *Microsoft Windows* section.)

2. What is a business's primary concern when considering an operating system? (See *Microsoft Windows* section.)

3. Which feature in Windows XP makes it more attractive to home users than previous business-oriented versions of Windows? [See *All About Windows XP (Well, Almost)* section.]

4. In previous versions of Windows, screen icons were only available in a 32×32 pixel size. What is the largest size screen icon available in Windows XP? (See *Visual design* section.)

5. What does a modem allow you to do? (See *Internet Connection Firewall* section.)

6. How can you tell if you have the XP Professional or Home Edition? (See *Windows XP Professional or Windows XP Home Edition?* section.)

7. What feature, found in XP Professional but not in XP Home Edition, allows you to protect sensitive files and folders ? (See *Protecting sensitive files* section.)

Installing Windows XP

Session Checklist

✔ Identifying the hardware requirements for Windows XP

✔ Collecting necessary data before installing XP

✔ Upgrading from an existing operating system

✔ Performing a full Windows XP installation

✔ Activating Windows XP

30 Min. To Go

Installing Windows XP can range from a fairly simple, nearly fully automated installation experience to a complex manual installation. In any case, you need to count on anywhere from 1 to 2 hours in order to do a complete installation. Since this session only lasts 30 minutes, I'll give you some instructions and you can take it from there. The less RAM that you have, the slower your CPU, the slower your hard drive, and the slower your compact disc–read-only memory (CD-ROM) drive, the longer the installation will take.

I'll give you some hints to make the installation go more smoothly as well as ways to ensure a stable performance throughout the time you use Windows XP. You'll take a look at the advantages and disadvantages of installing Windows XP from scratch versus installing it on an existing system. But first, you need to take a look at what kind of hardware is required before you should even consider installing Windows XP.

Windows XP Professional and Home Edition Hardware Requirements

Microsoft Windows XP, as with nearly all software, has three sets of hardware values you should consider:

- The minimum required hardware
- The recommended hardware suggestions
- The real-world hardware suggestions

If you haven't had much experience with computer hardware, you might want to check out the hardware article on this book's companion Web site at www.wiley.com/compbooks/nicholson**. It offers a brief overview of basic computer hardware components.**

The minimum required hardware

Microsoft always sets a minimum required hardware value for each of its software applications. Without this hardware, the program won't even install. It's similar to saying that the minimum requirements to paint the outside of a house are a bucket of paint and a 1-inch-wide paintbrush. Indeed, you might be able to accomplish your task, but you wouldn't be able to do anything else with your life, not to mention the frustration level and the inability to reach high places.

The rule here is, whenever reading the minimum hardware requirements for a piece of software, disregard it. Given these requirements, the software probably won't do what you need it to do.

According to Microsoft, Windows XP Professional and Home Edition *require*:

- 233-MHz CPU
- 64-MB RAM (some features may be limited)
- 1.5 GB available hard drive space
- Super VGA (800×600) or higher video adapter and monitor
- CD-ROM or DVD drive
- Keyboard and Microsoft (or Microsoft-compatible) mouse

The recommended hardware suggestions

Using Microsoft's recommended hardware suggestions, Windows XP will run, but you might find it slow. If you want to run more than one application at a time, you probably need to consider additional hardware. Microsoft *recommends*:

- 300-MHz CPU. Intel Pentium/Celeron family or AMD K6/Athlon/Duron family
- 128-MB RAM
- 1.5 GB available hard drive space

- Super VGA (800×600) or higher video adapter and monitor
- CD-ROM or digital video disc (DVD) drive
- Keyboard and Microsoft (or Microsoft-compatible) mouse

Real-world suggestions

A 550-MHz CPU should be plenty. Strangely, upgrading from a 550-MHz CPU to a 1-GHz CPU, all other things remaining the same, will result in about a 10 percent overall increase in performance. RAM, however, is a different story. If you can only afford a faster CPU *or* more RAM, buy more RAM. All computer professionals will tell you that RAM is the cheapest way to increase speed on your computer.

In some cases, you may have sufficient RAM, but other problems may be slowing your computer. If adding additional RAM doesn't result in increased speed, you may be looking at an overhaul of your motherboard, RAM, hard drive, hard drive controller, video card, and other hardware. In a case such as this, consult a professional to determine if a new computer would be better than upgrading your current one.

Like RAM, you can't have too much hard drive space. Buy the largest drive you can afford. Buying a computer is a tradeoff. You can seldom buy exactly what you want, so you need to buy some less expensive parts. Again, unless you know exactly what you are doing, consult a professional (usually not the salesperson) before you buy.

Before Installing Windows XP

If you already have a Windows operating system (OS) on your computer, you'll need to make a couple of decisions before you install Windows XP. Will your system work better with the Professional version or the Home Edition? And should you upgrade your current OS, or perform a full installation? These sections guide you through those questions.

Assessing your current system: caveat emptor

There is no difference between the installation instructions for Windows XP Professional and those for the Home Edition. While that makes the installation itself easier, you might want to do some homework before purchasing either version of Windows XP. If you just bought a brand-new computer, you should be fine with either version. If you have one that's a few years old and has been upgraded over time, you should make sure that your hardware is compatible with XP. Microsoft suggests that you look at its Hardware Compatibility List (HCL), located at www.microsoft.com/whdc/hcl/search.mspx. The HCL is purported to identify hardware manufacturers and model numbers that are compatible with XP. Although this sounds good in theory, it doesn't work very well. If your hardware is on the HCL, Microsoft warns that it still may not work in your particular computer. If your hardware isn't on the HCL, Microsoft notes that the hardware may be too new to have been added to the list, or it might not have worked with a particular computer setup that they were using for testing.

CompUSA has set up a site for testing your hardware at www.pcpitstop.com/xpready/default.asp. This is a free site, and although it will tell you if your computer meets the minimum and will offer suggested requirements for running Windows XP, it really can't do much about checking your individual pieces of hardware (for example, an older modem). Another fact that you might want to consider is that many of your games and multimedia programs will no longer run under Windows XP. Also, many of your utility programs, such as virus protection, disk health, and anti-spam programs will probably require replacement.

The bottom line is that if you own a lot of older software applications, as well as hardware, and you are unsure of its compatibility with XP, you might want to remember your reasons for upgrading to XP. Windows XP is a highly stable operating system and should last you for several years, so the investment in new equipment should be well worth the price.

Should you upgrade or perform a full installation?

The next choice you have to make is whether to upgrade (that is, install XP with the current operating system in place) or perform a full installation (delete the current operating system and all data from the hard drive, replacing it with Windows XP). Upgrading an existing operating system is nearly always easier than formatting your hard drive and starting from scratch. The disadvantage is that your computer will be more likely to crash on a regular basis.

According to Microsoft, if you already have a qualified Windows operating system on your hard drive you can simply run the XP installation program and upgrade the operating system to XP, leaving all your programs and settings intact. You don't have to back up your data first (although it's a really, really good idea to do so anyway).

The other option is to back up all your data, format your hard drive, install Windows XP, reinstall all of your applications, and reinstall your data. While a full installation may sound daunting, it's really a much better option than upgrading. Installing Windows XP over an existing operating system will, in the long run, result in a system that crashes intermittently. That means you must have access to all of your applications as well as having some way of backing up your data. (In Windows you cannot back up your applications. You must install them from the original disks. But you can back up the data within those applications.)

A full installation requires a lot more time in preparation. You need to make sure you identify all your data files, write down the information about your e-mail accounts (and back up the data for those programs), and record any information about getting onto the Internet. If you are on a network, you will also have to record the network settings. If you are performing a full installation, it's a good idea to have someone guide you that has done it before. If you don't have a friend helping you out who knows what he or she is doing, you may need to hire a professional to perform a full installation. That can be very expensive.

 Wiley Publishing, Inc. and the author of this book take absolutely no responsibility for steps you take in making changes to your hard drive. For your information, Microsoft doesn't either. There are just too many things that can go wrong.

I seriously recommend you do a full installation of Windows XP. However, some users just want to upgrade their operating system, so I provide instructions on both options. Now that you know what you're getting into, let's get started with the installation.

Upgrading an Existing Operating System

Although you are not *required* to back up your data before upgrading from another Windows OS to Windows XP, it's always an excellent idea to back up your hard drive before making any significant changes to it.

 If you are going to upgrade an existing operating system, it is still critical to back up your data. For additional information on backing up your hard drive, refer to Session 18.

In theory, upgrading an existing operating system should be an easy task to accomplish. As with all things technology-related, there are no guarantees. This section details the steps to follow for upgrading an eligible operating system to Microsoft Windows XP. If you are upgrading to Windows XP Home Edition, you must have the original CD for Windows 98, Windows 98 SE, or Windows ME. If you are upgrading to Windows XP Professional, the original CD for any of the previous versions will work, or you can upgrade from Windows NT 4 Workstation, Windows 2000 Professional, or Windows XP Home Edition.

 Before beginning the installation, you need to identify your CD-ROM drive on your computer and determine its letter designation (such as D: drive). Next, you need your copy of Windows XP, including the Product Key (normally located on the disc case, not on the disc itself). The Product Key is a combination of 25 letters and digits, arranged in five groups of five. Once you have this information, you can begin the installation.

20 Min. To Go

1. Insert the Windows XP CD-ROM in the drive. After a few seconds, the Welcome screen appears, as shown in Figure 2-1.

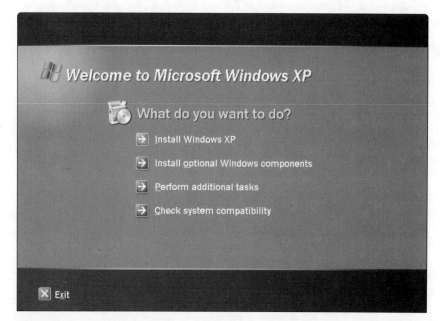

Figure 2-1 *The Welcome screen allows you to begin installing Windows XP or perform other related tasks.*

If nothing happens, double-click My Computer and double-click the icon for the CD-ROM drive. If that does not cause the installation program to begin, the root directory folders and files should be displayed. Find the file named Setup.exe and double-click it.

2. Click the first option, Install Windows XP, to begin the installation process. The Welcome to Windows Setup dialog box (see Figure 2-2) is displayed. From this screen, you can choose to Upgrade (Recommended) or Perform New Installation (Advanced).

Figure 2-2 *In the Welcome to Windows Setup dialog box, you can choose to upgrade your existing operating system or do a complete installation of Windows XP.*

3. Click Next to display the License Agreement. This is also referred to as the End User License Agreement (EULA). This outlines your legal responsibilities, and if you haven't already read it, now would be a good time to suffer through it.

After reading the EULA (a portion of which is displayed in Figure 2-3), you must click the I accept this agreement option button. By default, neither option button is selected, and the Next button is not available. If you click the I don't accept this agreement option, you are taken to the screen ending the Setup Wizard. In other words, if you don't agree to Microsoft's terms, you don't get to install the software.

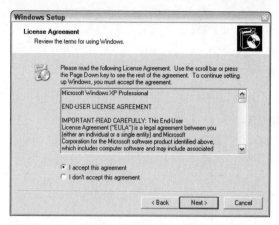

Figure 2-3   *Microsoft requires that you agree to its lengthy legal contract before you can continue installing Windows XP.*

4. The next dialog box requires you to enter your 25-character Product Key (as shown in Figure 2-4). When you have finished, click Next.

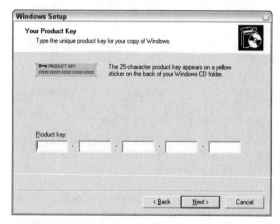

Figure 2-4   *The Product Key screen allows you to enter the Product Key found on the original CD-ROM case. This number is* not *found on the CD.*

When inputting the characters, you do not need to press Tab or insert the hyphen to move between the empty blocks. Just enter the 25 characters exactly as they are shown.

5. Click Next to display the Get Updated Setup Files dialog box (shown in Figure 2-5). If you have an Internet connection already set up, Windows downloads the updated files needed to bring your version of Windows XP up to date.

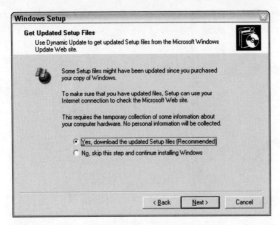

Figure 2-5 *The Get Updated Setup Files will save you update time later, but may take more time now than you are willing to invest in getting your computer up and running.*

If you have a modem, rather than a cable or DSL connection, you might want to wait until later to update your copy of Windows. Downloading the files can take quite a while without a fast connection.

6. Click either the Yes or No option button, and click Next to continue. At this point, things may seem to stall for a few seconds or longer, and then the computer restarts automatically.

7. Now go to lunch or take a long, hot bath. Don't interfere with what's going on. Windows is preparing to begin the installation, and it will take quite a while. (Depending on many variables, the time could be from 1 to 2 hours.)

8. Once the computer is finished doing its initial installation, you'll see a setup screen displayed. Clicking Next (now located at the lower-right of your screen) takes you to the Windows Activation screen. In theory, you are supposed to be able to run your upgraded software for 30 days before activation is required. In reality, the screen might say 0 days before activation must take place. If you have a connection to the Internet already established, you can choose to activate your copy of Windows XP now. If not, you will have to choose the option button that says you wish to do it later. In either case, the Product Key for your new software may not work. (See the sidebar *What Can I do if My Product Key Doesn't Work*? for additional information.)

9. Next, Microsoft asks you if you're ready to register over the Internet. It assures you that no personal information will be collected during the registration process. Microsoft also states that registration is optional, not mandatory. Click either the Yes or No button and click Next to continue.

10. Enter the information you want to supply to Microsoft and click Next. Hopefully, you will get a message stating that you have activated your copy of Windows, registered your copy of Windows with Microsoft, and that your computer is configured to access the Internet.

What Can I Do if My Product Key Doesn't Work?

If you change four or more critical items (such as certain hardware devices) on your computer, or if you try to install Windows XP on a second computer, you may get an error message that the Product Key has already been registered. You will be given a phone number to call, or an Internet address to log on to. You must have Windows open and have the Product Activation dialog box displayed. The support assistant will ask for a number that will be displayed. Based on that number, he or she will give you a 42-digit number to input into your computer to reset the number of major changes you can make to four.

If you are using a pirated copy of Windows XP, when you attempt to upgrade to Service Pack 1, you will not be allowed to do so. You will have to purchase a legal copy in order to keep your software updated. In Windows Help and Support, you can search for Product Activation for additional information.

11. Clicking the Finish button will display your programs and Desktop as it appeared under your previous operating system.
12. Remove the original CD from your drive, replace it in its original case, and file it in a safe place for future use.

Performing a Complete Installation of Windows XP

10 Min. To Go

Performing a complete installation of Windows XP requires formatting your hard drive. This is a major commitment, but worth it in the long run. The results will be a much more stable operating system.

Formatting your hard drive destroys all data stored on it. Not only does the operating system need to be installed, but all of the applications need to be reinstalled. Then the data needs to be reinstalled. If you have a second hard drive in your computer, you should also format it, using the New Technology File System (NTFS).

Remember that performing a complete installation of Windows XP requires you to back up any data you want saved, since formatting the drive results in a loss of all data and applications already installed. For more information on backing up your data, see Session 18.

If you are going to do a fresh installation of the operating system, the first few steps will be the same as for upgrading. Steps 1 through 4 above are identical, except in step 2, where you choose Perform New Installation (Advanced). After entering the Product Key, you are taken to the Setup Options dialog box (shown in Figure 2-6). Click Next to continue.

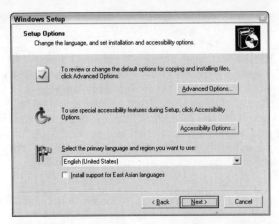

Figure 2-6 *Changes to the Setup Options dialog box should be avoided unless you know specifically what you are doing.*

After clicking Next at the Setup Options dialog box, the computer reboots into the DOS mode. No graphics are displayed. At this point, you are asked if you want to install Windows XP.

1. In the DOS Setup window, press Enter to continue with the XP installation.
2. At the next Setup dialog box, Windows will recognize that you already have an operating system. Since you want to do a clean installation, press Esc.
3. In all probability, Windows will recognize a partition that is nearly the size of your hard drive, and a smaller one. Make sure the larger partition is highlighted. Press Enter to continue the installation.
4. A new screen is displayed, and you are reminded that partitioning the drive will erase everything on it. To continue, press L. Windows will take several minutes examining your disk.

Pressing L deletes the partition, and *all* of your data is destroyed. Make sure this is really what you want to do.

5. Press Enter to continue. The Format screen is displayed. Choose to format the drive as NTFS. This is the filing system designed specifically for Windows 2000 and XP. It is more secure than FAT or FAT32.

Since you want a complete format, choose Format the partition using the NTFS file system. Do not choose the Quick Format option. The Quick Format option will not check each sector for integrity. A complete format checks integrity, and reads and writes to each sector to make sure that each one is good.

6. Press Enter to begin the formatting. This will probably take about a half hour, depending on the size and speed of your hard drive. Again, Windows pretty much proceeds on its own.

If you are using the Upgrade Edition of XP, at this point you will be asked to insert the CD from a qualified earlier Windows Edition. You can use a Windows 98, 98SE, Me, or 2000 disc.

7. Eventually, the Regional and Language Options dialog box is displayed. From here, you can set the time on your computer, change the language, and perform other regionally related tasks. If you are in the United States, just click Next to continue.

At any later time, you can display the Regional Settings dialog box by opening the Control Panel and selecting it.

8. In the Name and Organization dialog box, enter your name and organization. Click Next.

9. At the Computer Name and Administrator dialog box, you will probably want to change the computer name to something that makes sense to you. Leave the Administrator password blank for now.

Entering an Administrator password now can cause serious problems later on if you forget it. There are programs that can recover it, but they cost several hundred dollars. Usually, using a screen saver with a password is enough to keep general users away from unauthorized access.

The computer name should only contain letters, numbers, and hyphens. No spaces or underscores should be used. It should be no longer than 15 characters.

10. Click Next. In the Modem Dialing dialog box, you must enter an area code before the Next button becomes available, even if you are not using a modem. Click Next.

11. In the Date and Time dialog box, make sure your time and date settings are correct. Click Next.

12. In the Network Settings dialog box, choose Typical Settings. You can always add, modify, or delete modules later.

13. In the Network Settings dialog box, unless you have network experience, leave the computer as part of WORKGROUP. Again, this can be changed later.

14. Take another break while Windows copies the required files to your computer.

Don't be surprised if Windows automatically adjusts your screen resolution. Just click OK, since that's the only thing you can do anyway. If your mouse doesn't work, just press Enter. Click OK at the next screen.

15. Next, Windows asks you to spend a few minutes setting up your computer. Click Next to continue.

16. At the Connection Wizard dialog box, you can choose the option of connecting your computer to the Internet through a home or small business network, or connecting directly to the Internet. You can change this setting later. You can also choose to skip this step. Click the appropriate button.

17. In the Windows Activation dialog box, you are asked to activate your copy of Windows. You can either do it now, or have Windows remind you every few days. You have 30 days from the day the operating system is first booted to activate your product. To activate it now, click Yes and Next for the current and following screens. If you don't want to register now, click Skip, and Windows will remind you every few days.

18. In the registration information dialog box, enter the appropriate information and click Next, or click the Skip button.

19. If this is the first time you have used the Activation number, everything should continue normally. If you get an "Online activation could not be completed" message, you can still use Windows XP for up to 30 days. Click Next to continue.

 If the Activation sequence is not completed, you can choose the Activate Windows option from the Start menu.

20. At the Who Will Use This Computer dialog box, you can set up accounts for up to five users. By default, your full name (as entered earlier) is entered as the account name. You may want to shorten it to a name you normally go by. When you have completed filling out the account names, click Next.

21. At the Thank You screen, click Finish to complete the installation.

Activating Windows XP After Installation

As mentioned earlier, you have 30 days from installation to activate your Windows XP Product Key. If you did not choose to activate your computer during the installation process, you can do that over the Internet or by telephone. To begin the activation process, click Start ⇨ All Programs ⇨ Activate Windows. Once activation is successful, the Activate Windows option is removed.

Activation over the Internet

You cannot proceed to the next screen until you choose whether or not you also want to register with Microsoft. There is no obligation to do so, and if you did so during the installation process, there is no reason to duplicate the information. Choose the appropriate option and click Next. You are again allowed to try to activate the product over the Internet. If this doesn't work, a toll-free support number for the activation code is displayed on the screen.

Activation using the telephone

Using the telephone to activate Windows XP is broken down into four simple steps.

1. Find your location.
2. Call the toll-free number.
3. Provide the customer service agent with the 50-digit code found on your screen. These are broken down into eight groups of six numbers each, with an extra two numbers tagged on at the end.
4. Type the 42-number confirmation ID given to you by the customer service representative. Double-check it. Click Next to proceed. Click Finish.

Finalization of Windows XP installation

One of the benefits of Windows XP, according to Microsoft, is that the desktop (the main area where you work) is uncluttered. That is an understatement. The only icon you find on the desktop is the Recycle Bin in the lower-right corner. Don't despair, however. In Session 3, you'll start to get an idea of how you can modify your desktop to meet your specific preferences.

Done!

REVIEW

- There are three sets of hardware values to be considered before deciding to upgrade to Windows XP: minimum, recommended, and real-world.
- The same set of instructions is used to install Windows XP Professional and Windows XP Home Edition.
- Upgrading an existing operating system doesn't require you to reformat your hard drive and reinstall everything, but your computer might be more susceptible to intermittent crashes if you don't.
- Regardless of the type of installation you perform, you should always back up your data first.
- Your Product Key, used for activating Windows XP, is found on the plastic case your CD-ROM came in.
- You have 30 days from installation to activate Windows XP.

QUIZ YOURSELF

1. What is the recommended RAM for Windows XP? (See *The recommended hardware suggestions* section.)
2. Is it easier to upgrade an existing operating system or perform a clean installation? (See *Should you upgrade or perform a full installation?* section.)
3. If you want to upgrade from a previous operating system to Windows XP Home Edition, which operating system versions are eligible? (See *Upgrading an Existing Operating System section.*)

4. Where can you find the Product Key? (See *Upgrading an Existing Operating System* section.)

5. How long can you use Windows XP without activating it? (See *Upgrading an Existing Operating System* section.)

6. What are the restrictions on naming your computer? (See *Performing a Complete Installation of Windows XP* section.)

Windows XP Operating System and Time-Saving Tips

Session Checklist

✔ Defining common Windows XP terminology

✔ Demonstrating how the desktop can be modified

✔ Using the Windows Logo and Ctrl keys to save keystrokes

**30 Min.
To Go**

Windows (with a capital W) is Microsoft's operating system; windows (with a lower-case w) is an area of the screen used to view information. In this session, you will learn some new vocabulary associated with Windows XP and how to identify desktop objects that you will use on a regular basis. We will wrap up with some tips on making your Windows experience a little easier.

Windows XP Terminology

Windows XP uses terminology similar to previous versions of Windows. But if this is your first introduction to Windows, you're going to need to know the basic terminology. Start by taking a look at the Windows desktop.

The Windows XP desktop

As mentioned in Session 2, the Windows XP desktop is free of clutter when first installed. Figure 3-1 shows the default Windows XP desktop.

The desktop consists of the entire working surface, with the exception of the bar running along the bottom of the window. This bar is generically known as the *task bar*. The Start button is at the left edge of the task bar. According to Microsoft's philosophy, everything should begin by clicking the Start button, even shutting down the computer.

In the lower-right corner of the desktop is a small picture of a trash can. A picture such as this, which represents a feature, function, or application, is called an *icon*. This particular icon is the Recycle Bin. It is a place for temporarily storing deleted files, folders, and icons so that you can get an item back if you find out that you should not have deleted it. The picture of the clouds and rolling hills is called a *background*.

 By default, the task bar is locked in the Home Edition, but not in XP Professional. An unlocked task bar can be dragged to another position on the screen.

Figure 3-1   *The default Windows XP desktop is uncluttered, but everything you need is still quickly available.*

Populating the desktop with common icons

Some users complain that the desktop is too sparse. I'll show you how to add a few basic icons to your desktop to make using your computer a little easier.

1. Right-click any empty area of the desktop. Choose Properties. The Display Properties *dialog box* is displayed.

 A dialog box is a window with one or more related tabs that shows current settings and allows you to change them.

2. Click the Desktop tab.
3. Click the Customize Desktop button in the lower-left corner. Your screen should appear similar to the one shown in Figure 3-2.

Figure 3-2 *The General tab of the Desktop Items dialog box allows you to place the four most commonly used icons on your desktop.*

4. Place a checkmark in the My Documents, My Computer, and Internet Explorer check boxes. Remember, clicking a check box once places a checkmark in it, activating the option; clicking it again removes the checkmark.

5. Click OK twice. Your desktop should now be similar to the one shown in Figure 3-3.

Figure 3-3 *Three commonly used icons have been added to your desktop. Double-click any of these to run the program.*

Displaying the Quick Launch bar

The Quick Launch bar is used to launch an application with a single click instead of the customary double-click. By default, the Quick Launch bar is not activated. When activated, the Quick Launch bar is located directly to the right of the Start button. To activate the Quick Launch bar, follow these steps:

1. Right-click any empty area of the task bar. Make sure there is no checkmark next to Lock Taskbar. If there is, click it to turn it off.

2. Right-click any empty area of the task bar. Choose Properties. The task bar and Start Menu Properties dialog box are displayed.

3. Click Show Quick Launch to place a checkmark in the box. Click OK. Your task bar should be similar to the one shown in Figure 3-4, but may show a different number of icons.

Figure 3-4   *The Quick Launch bar is displayed just to the right of the Start button.*

4. You will be using the My Documents folder on a regular basis, so you'll want to add it to the Quick Launch bar. To do so, point the mouse cursor at the center of the My Documents icon, press the left mouse button, drag the icon onto the Quick Launch bar, and release the left mouse button. (This is called dragging and dropping and works in nearly every Windows application.) Your Quick Launch bar should now be similar to the one shown in Figure 3-5.

Figure 3-5   *The Quick Launch bar icons are partially hidden.*

5. If you see double right-pointing arrowheads to the right of the last icon on the Quick Launch bar, as in Figure 3-5, it indicates that some icons on the bar are hidden. To display all the icons, drag the vertical bar directly to the right of the arrowheads a little further to the right.

6. Click once on the My Documents icon in the Quick Launch bar. The My Documents folder opens immediately.

You can reposition the Quick Launch icons by dragging them left or right. You can delete one by right-clicking it and choosing Delete. The icons are actually shortcut routes to the applications, not the applications themselves, so you will not be deleting the actual application or folder.

Tips Time

One of the nice features of Windows XP is that it is very flexible in completing tasks. Shortcuts to completing a task in fewer steps are often called *tips* or *tricks*. For example, if you want to display the Display Properties dialog box, you can click Start ⇨ Control Panel ⇨ Appearance and Themes ⇨ Display. But you have already learned a shorter method for displaying the Display Properties dialog box, in the *Populating the desktop with common icons* section. You simply right-click any empty area of the desktop and click Properties.

The rest of this session gives you some tips on reducing the number of keystrokes required to complete an action or shows you how to accomplish a task that Microsoft doesn't even mention in the Help file. As you read through these shortcuts, you might want to keep a list of ones you think you will use often.

Many tips and tricks require you to edit the registry. This is an advanced topic and you should refrain from editing the registry unless you have the systems files duplicated or if you don't mind doing a fresh install on your computer.

Using the Windows logo key

The Windows logo key (if you have a newer keyboard) is located in the lower-left area of most keyboards, adjacent to the Ctrl key. (The icon on the key looks like a four-pane window.) On some keyboards, there is an identical key on the lower-right portion of the keyboard, near the spacebar. Using the Windows logo key in conjunction with other keys can save many keystrokes. Table 3-1 shows you just a few of the more common keys that may save you work.

Table 3-1   *Shortcuts Using the Windows Logo Key*

Key combination	Result in Windows XP
Windows Logo Key alone	Opens the Start menu
Windows Logo Key + D	Minimizes all open windows. Repeating the command reverses the action.
Windows Logo Key + E	Opens Windows Explorer (*not* Internet Explorer)
Windows Logo Key + F	Opens the File Search window
Windows Logo Key + L	Locks the workstation (if you have Windows XP password protected, any user will have to input the password to continue)
Windows Logo Key + R	Opens the Run window
Windows Logo Key + U	Opens the utility manager (for setting Accessibility Features)
Windows Logo Key + Ctrl + F	Opens the Search dialog box
Windows Logo Key + Break	Opens the System Properties window
Windows Logo Key + F1	Opens the Help and Support Center window

**10 Min.
To Go**

Using the Control key

The Control (Ctrl) key is another often overlooked method of completing tasks quickly. Table 3-2 lists some of the more commonly used key combinations.

For additional information about shortcut key sequences, press Windows logo key + F1 to open the Help Support Center window. In the Search box, type keyboard shortcuts and press Enter. From the Suggested Topics area double-click *Windows keyboard shortcuts overview*.

Table 3-2   *Shortcuts Using the Control (Ctrl) Key*

Key combination	Result in Windows XP
Ctrl Key + A	Selects all objects in the active window
Ctrl Key + C	Copies the selected object or objects for later pasting
Ctrl Key + F	Displays the Find all files dialog box
Ctrl Key + G	Displays the Go to Folder dialog box
Ctrl Key + N	Displays the New dialog box
Ctrl Key + O	Displays the Open dialog box
Ctrl Key + P	Print dialog box is displayed
Ctrl Key + S	Opens the Save dialog box
Ctrl Key + V	Pastes the object or objects stored in memory after having been copied.
Ctrl Key + X	Cuts selected item or items
Ctrl Key + Z	Undoes last action
Ctrl Key + F4	Closes the active document
Ctrl Key + Esc	Opens the Start menu
Ctrl Key + F6	Displays the next document in an active document window
Ctrl Key while dragging an item	Copies the selected item to new position (Note: You cannot use this method to copy objects to the clipboard.)

Miscellaneous tips and tricks

Here's a list of miscellaneous tips and tricks you might find helpful in working with Windows XP:

- If you have several Internet Explorer windows open and you want to close them all at the same time, right-click the Internet Explorer button on the task bar and choose Close Group.

- Do you have a favorite program you would like kept at the top of the Start menu? There are two ways you can keep an application in the top of the left column: First, if the application name shows anywhere in the left column, drag it up until it is in the top part of the left column. This ensures that the program will not be removed from the Start menu unless you delete it (by right-clicking and choosing Delete from the context menu). Second, if you have an icon on your desktop or you can see it from within an application such as Windows Explorer or My Computer, just drag the program or shortcut onto the Start button and drop it there. That object will now be in the upper-left portion of the Start menu and will remain there until you delete it.

- If you like using the Run command, you can create a shortcut on your desktop by choosing Start and dragging the Run icon onto your desktop. This works for any other application in your list, including the All Programs fly-out menu.

- As long as your Quick Launch bar has not been locked, you can use the previous tip, but instead of dragging it onto the desktop, drag it onto the Quick Launch bar.

A few sample tip Web sites

Here are just a few Web sites that will offer you additional tips. Many of the tips are duplicated on each site, but you can usually find a few different ones that you can use.

www.xpcorner.com/tipsandtricks/tt50.shtml

www.tipsdr.com/windows-xp-tips-2.html

www.rdisruption.com/xp/xpindex4.htm

www.activewin.com/winxp/tips/index.shtml

Done!

REVIEW

- The desktop is the entire working area of the screen.
- Icons are small pictures representing applications, folders, or files.
- The Quick Launch bar is designed to start commonly used applications with a single mouse click.
- Use key combinations to save you from typing extra keystrokes or more mouse clicks.

QUIZ YOURSELF

1. What is the Windows desktop? (See *The Windows XP desktop* section.)

2. What is a dialog box? (See *Populating the desktop with common icons* section.)

3. Why would you use the Quick Launch bar? (See *Displaying the Quick Launch bar* section.)

4. What happens when you press the Windows logo key? (See *Using the Windows logo key* section.)

5. If you press the Ctrl key while dragging an object to a different folder, what is the result? (See *Using the Control key* section.)

Letting Windows Help You

Session Checklist

✔ Starting the Help and Support Center

✔ Using the basic search features of the Help and Support Center

✔ Getting help in dialog boxes

✔ Finding application specific help

✔ Touring Windows XP

✔ Searching for files

**30 Min.
To Go**

Computer users often get frustrated because they can't find the answers to questions about a particular software application, or, in this case, the Windows XP operating system. Using the built-in help system, Windows itself can answer most of your questions. That saves you from having to call your sister-in-law (or 5-year-old grandchild) at 3 o'clock. on a Monday morning, when you have to be at work with a completed project by 7:30 A.M. Since the Help feature works basically the same in nearly all Windows-based programs, what you learn here easily transfers to other applications.

The Help and Support Center

The Windows XP Help and Support Center is displayed by clicking Start ⇨ Help and Support. The Help and Support Center dialog box is shown in Figure 4-1.

Beneath the toolbar is the Search portion of the dialog box. In the space immediately to the right of the word Search, you can type in key words. *Key words* are the important words in a sentence. For example, you might want to ask, "How can I find more information about using a screen saver?" In this case, the key words would be screen and saver. In the following example, we look briefly at using the basic search function of the Help and Support Center.

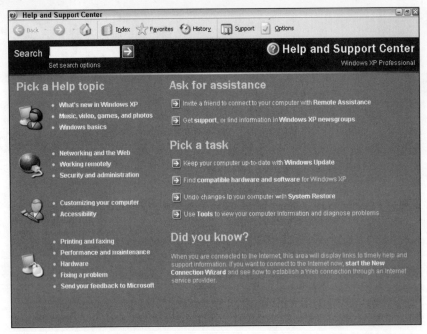

Figure 4-1   *The opening screen for the Help and Support Center offers many options.*

Using the basic search feature in the Help and Support Center

The secret to using the basic search function is to be able to determine the correct key word(s). In this example, we'll take a look at using *screensaver* rather than *screen saver*.

1. Click Start ⇨ Help and Support.
2. In the Search box, type **screensaver.** You can either press Enter or click the arrow to the right of the Search box. Your results should be similar to the ones shown in Figure 4-2.

   There are three main areas in which results can be reviewed: Suggested Topics, Full-text Search Matches, and Microsoft Knowledge Base. In general, there will be more results within the Full-text Search Matches than the other two. In this case, the Search Results area returns eight results, all in the subheading Suggested Topics. The Full-text Search Matches and Microsoft Knowledge Base show no returns. This might be a clue that something is wrong with your key word(s). Looking at the results, notice that there are no references to screensaver, but several to screen saver. This fact, combined with the lack of results in the Full-text Search Matches and the spelling in the Suggested Topics area, means it's a good bet that using screen and saver as the search terms will yield additional results.

The results you see may be different than those seen in the figure, depending on how up-to-date your version of Windows is.

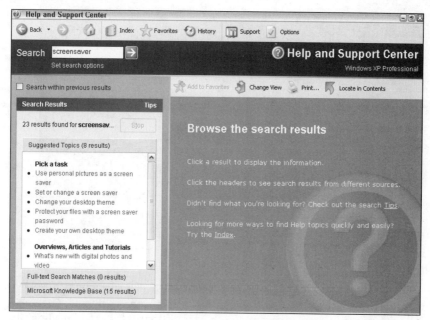

Figure 4-2 *Using screensaver as a search term, the Help screen returns eight results.*

Now try the following search:

1. In the Search box, type **screen saver** and press Enter. This time, notice that 23 results are returned. In this case, the number of Suggested Topics is still more than the Full-text Search Matches, which is unusual but nothing to worry about.

2. If the *Customize a background color* result is available, let your mouse pointer hover over it. As soon as you move the mouse pointer over the topic, it becomes underlined, indicating that it is a hyperlink, and you only need to click once to display the link. The topic results are displayed in the right pane of the Help window, shown in Figure 4-3.

3. Close the Help and Support Center by clicking the X in the upper-right corner of the screen. This should put you back at the main Windows desktop.

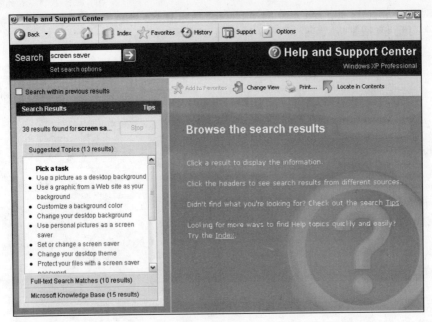

Figure 4-3 *Using screen saver as search terms, the Help screen returns additional results.*

In help screens, words are often underlined in either blue or green. A blue underline (called a hyperlink) means that clicking this link will activate the command. Clicking a word or words underlined in green displays a definition of that word. After reading, just click outside the definition box to close it. At the bottom of each help panel is also an underlined Related Topics area . Clicking this takes you to a screen displaying help topics related to the one currently displayed.

Help screen buttons

Above the displayed help topics are icons for several options. Clicking Add to Favorites adds the topic to the Favorites button on the toolbar. This is particularly helpful if you have trouble finding a topic and want to easily return to it later. Clicking the Favorites button displays the names of all help screens you have added. In the left pane, you see each topic name; double-clicking the topic name displays the topic in the right pane. At the bottom of the left pane, there are three buttons: Rename, Remove, and Display. Click a topic and the Remove button to delete it. Perhaps the most helpful feature is the Rename button. When you add a help screen to Favorites, Windows uses the formal name for the topic. Using the Rename button, you can change the name of the topic to ensure it reflects the information you might want to find later.

The Change View button toggles the left pane and the upper area of the window off, leaving only the Help pane and associated buttons. This is particularly helpful if you want to leave the help instructions visible while completing a task. The Help window can be moved by dragging the Title Bar. It can be resized by dragging any of the window edges (see Session 3 for a review of windows terminology and tasks). Once resized, you can float the Help window over any other window in which you are working.

The Print button opens the Print dialog box. This is the Print button for the Help pane, not for the underlying screen.

 If you have resized the Help pane, when printed, the entire help topic is printed normally. The sizing of the Help pane does not affect the way the topic is printed.

The standard toolbar

Directly beneath the Title Bar is the standard toolbar, shown in Figure 4-4. The buttons, from left, are:

- **Back:** Takes you to the previous screen.
- **Forward:** Takes you to the next screen. (This is only available if you have clicked the Back button.)
- **Home:** Returns to the Help and Support Center home page.
- **Index:** Functions like the index in the back of a paper book.
- **Favorites:** Allows you to store the links to various help screens you might want to use in the future.
- **History:** Presents a list of pages you have viewed during the current and previous sessions.
- **Support:** Takes you to the Support Welcome screen.
- **Options:** Presents links for changing the Help and Support Center options, setting search options, and installing and sharing Windows help.

Figure 4-4   *The standard toolbar offers shortcut buttons for navigating and setting options for the Help and Support Center.*

Using customized search options

When you did a topic search earlier, you used the default search options. You can change these options either by clicking the Options button on the standard toolbar and then clicking Set search options, or by clicking Set search options directly beneath the Search text entry box. The Set search options pane (shown in Figure 4-5) allows you to set the following options:

- **Number of Results Returned per Provider:** The default value is 15. This number can be set as high as 999. A suboption is Turn on search highlight. With this option checked, any word in the search term is automatically boldfaced in the results pane, making the word easier to find (but often making the screen more difficult to read).
- **Suggested Topics:** Leaving this option unchecked removes the Suggested Topics area in the left pane after a search is completed.

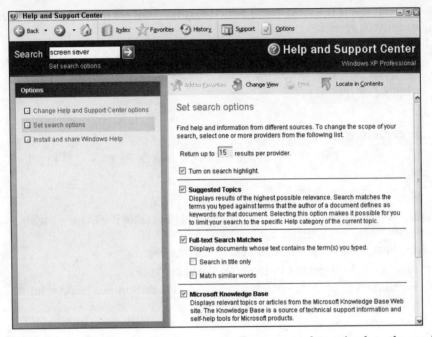

Figure 4-5 *The Set search options pane allows you to determine how the results will be displayed on the screen for any search you conduct.*

- **Full-text Search Matches:** By default, this option is on. Clicking the checkmark turns off the Full-text Search Matches. By default, this option reads every help topic looking for the word(s) you used for your search. Placing a checkmark in the *Search in title only* box forces the search engine to look only at the title of the topic, rather than search the entire topic. Placing a checkmark in *Match similar words* allows Help to look at different word forms (such as hid, hide, or hidden) and return all results.

- **Microsoft Knowledge Base:** In order to access the Microsoft Knowledge Base (MKB), you must have Internet access available. MKB lists reports of specific problems from professional testers or customers, and Microsoft's responses.

Getting Help in Dialog Boxes

In Session 3, you learned that a dialog box is a window with one or more related tabs in which you have the opportunity to change default values. Occasionally, you might not know what one or more of the options are for. As you'll see in this part of the session, there are different ways to get help in dialog boxes.

Although these methods should work in the dialog boxes of any Windows-based application, they don't always. If you have questions you can't find answers to, you might want to check some online sources. Good support sites to visit include www.windows-help.net/WindowsXP/, www.annoyances.org/, www.windowsxpforums.com/, **and** www.labmice.net/windowsxp/default.htm.

Opening a sample dialog box

In this example you will learn to open a sample dialog box from WordPad, which you'll have a chance to use in Session 6.

1. Click Start ⇨ All Programs ⇨ Accessories ⇨ WordPad. If WordPad doesn't fill the entire screen, click the maximize button (the center button in the row of three) in the upper-right corner of the WordPad Title Bar. Your screen should be similar to the one shown in Figure 4-6.

A shortcut for maximizing any window is to double-click any empty area of the Title Bar. This tip works with any window.

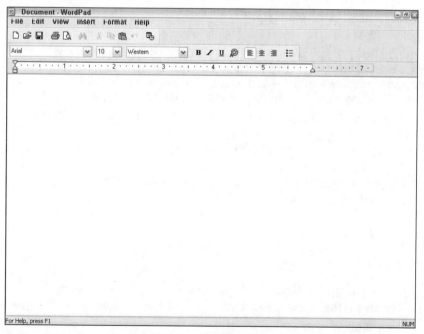

Figure 4-6 *The maximized screen for WordPad takes up the entire screen.*

2. To open a sample dialog box, click View ⇨ Options. The default Options dialog box for WordPad is displayed in Figure 4-7.

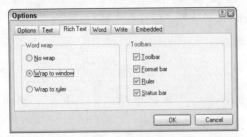

Figure 4-7 *The WordPad Options dialog box allows you to change the default settings.*

Displaying the help information boxes

Once a dialog box is displayed, you can press F1 to get general help, or click the question mark button to get specific help. General help gives you information about the entire dialog box, while specific help offers additional information related to the specific option you click next. In some applications, pressing Shift-F1 also changes the cursor to one used for specific help. This exercise offers the opportunity to look at both general and specific help in a WordPad dialog box.

1. With the Options dialog box open, press F1. A small box is displayed giving an overview of what the selected tab is responsible for doing. This information is very general, and probably won't give you enough information to answer a specific question. Click anywhere to turn off the information box.

2. Click the Help button (the question mark) on the Options dialog box title bar. The cursor changes from an arrow to an arrow with a question mark. This means you can access specific help information on each option.

Instead of clicking the Help button, you can also right-click any option and left-click What's This.

3. Check the Format bar option. An information box is displayed telling you exactly what that option does.

Clicking an option turns off the question mark cursor. To check the information on another option, you must press the Help button to get the question mark again.

4. Click the Cancel button to close the dialog box. Leave WordPad open, and we'll take a look at getting application-specific help.

**20 Min.
To Go**

Application-Specific Help

Getting help in specific applications varies between applications, but most XP applications have similar help structures. WordPad offers an excellent example of standard application help. As you will see, the help screens in applications are quite different from those in dialog boxes, and even very different from the help available in Windows. Clicking Help in any application may result in several options. However, nearly all applications have at least two common help options: Help Topics and About *Application Name* (substitute the name of the application you are using).

Getting About WordPad help

If you need to find information about the version of the application you are working with, the best place to do that is in the About menu. This gives you not only the version but also the licensee and, if applicable, the organization the application is registered to. Most applications also display the amount of free memory. Some applications may have a System Information button, which gives you access to more complete information about your computer. To display the About WordPad dialog box:

1. WordPad should still be open from the previous exercise. Click Help ⇨ About WordPad. The About WordPad dialog box, shown in Figure 4-8, is displayed.

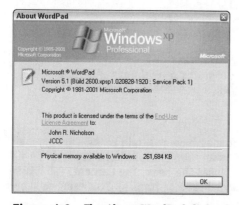

Figure 4-8 *The About WordPad dialog box offers basic information about the version of WordPad you are using.*

Your version may be different. The one displayed is based on the installation of Service Pack 1. Also, available memory will almost certainly be different.

2. Click OK to close the dialog box.

Viewing WordPad help topics

The WordPad Help Topics dialog box (shown in Figure 4-9) is displayed by clicking Help ➪ Help Topics. It looks similar to Help screens seen earlier in this session. The toolbar contains four buttons: Hide, Back, Forward, and Options. The Hide button compresses the screen, hiding the left pane, while leaving the right pane, generally containing instructions, available for reference while you are working on a document. The Back and Forward buttons go back or forward one help screen. (Remember, until you have used the Back button, the Forward button is unavailable.) The Options menu allows you to hide tabs (the same as pressing the Hide button), move forward or back one screen, return to the Help start page, stop searches in progress, refresh the screen (redraw it in case it doesn't look right), set Internet options, and, most importantly, print the current help topic. You can also turn the Search Highlight off, so the search terms are not highlighted.

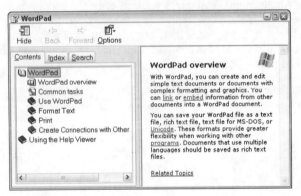

Figure 4-9   *The WordPad Help dialog box contains several ways of getting help.*

Using the Contents tab

Depending on the application, the Contents tab may have multiple *books*. Clicking each book opens it to display multiple topics. Clicking any topic displays the topic in the right-hand column. Clicking the book a second time closes the book. The Contents tab is similar to a table of contents in a book. It lists the major headings (topics). This exercise shows you how to use the Contents tab in WordPad.

1. Click Help ➪ Help Topics.
2. Click the WordPad book in the left pane. You should see two topics and four additional books.

In many applications, books will have a plus sign (+) or a minus sign (−) next to their name. A plus means there are hidden books and topics beneath that book. Clicking the plus expands the book to show all books and topics beneath it. Books beneath may have a plus sign, and clicking it will expand to the next level. Once you have clicked a plus sign, that level is expanded and the symbol changes to a minus sign. Clicking the minus sign collapses that level and hides all sublevels.

3. Click the Format Text book.

4. Click the Create a bulleted list topic. In the right pane, you will see instructions for creating a bulleted list.

Notice that when using the Contents tab, items are grouped by subject area. This is different on the Index tab.

Using the Index tab

On the Index tab, topic headings are also listed, but they are arranged alphabetically. These topics are broken down into much finer categories than on the Contents tab. The Index tab is nearly identical to an index at the back of a book, except that the index points you to a page in the book. In WordPad help, the index actually displays the topic of interest.

1. Click the Index tab. Your screen should appear similar to the one shown in Figure 4-10. Notice that the results of your last topic (Creating a bulleted list) are still displayed in the right pane.

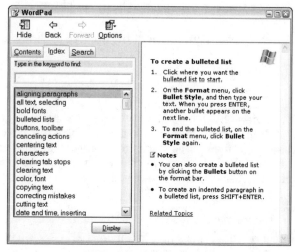

Figure 4-10   *The Index tab arranges topics alphabetically.*

2. Type **Pr** in the Keyword text box. Notice as you type the first letter, the topics beginning with *P* are displayed. Pressing **r** moves to the top of the list of topics beginning with *Pr*.

3. Click the second topic, *printing*. The instructions for creating a bulleted list are still displayed in the right pane.

4. Click Display at the bottom of the left pane. Two relevant topics are listed (as shown in Figure 4-11).

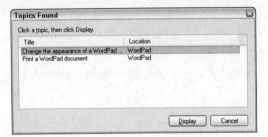

Figure 4-11 *The Topics Found window displays the relevant topics.*

5. Click Print a WordPad document and then click Display. Instructions for printing a WordPad document appear in the right pane.

 Rather than single-clicking a topic and clicking the Display button, you can also double-click the topic to immediately display the results.

6. Close the Help dialog box by clicking the X in the upper-right corner of the WordPad Help dialog box.

7. Close WordPad by clicking the X in the upper-right corner of the WordPad application.

Touring Windows

10 Min. To Go

One of the best ways to get a quick overview of Windows XP is by taking a tour. There are actually several tours available, but we'll just take a look at one, and then you can explore the rest of them as time permits. The tours can either be static (text only) or multimedia (graphics, music, voice). In order to take multimedia tours, you should have speakers (otherwise, the purpose is pretty much defeated). This exercise shows you the basics of displaying tours.

1. Click Start ⇨ Help and Support. The Help and Support Center screen is displayed.

2. Under the Pick a Help topic category, click What's new in Windows XP. Click What's new topics in the left pane. This opens the screen shown in Figure 4-12.

3. Click Taking a tour or tutorial. Two tasks are listed: Take the Windows XP Tour and Take the Windows Media Player Tour. For now, we'll take a quick look at the Windows XP tour, but you might want to follow up later and tour the Windows Media Player. It is a very powerful tool if you will be using your computer for any type of multimedia.

4. By default, the multimedia tour is selected. Click Take the Windows XP Tour.

5. Click Next to begin the tour. The introduction takes about 2 minutes. To bypass the introduction, you can click the Skip Intro button in the lower-left corner of the screen during step 4.

6. Take a few minutes to explore the tour. You might want to start with the Basics options.

7. Close the tour by clicking the large red X in the lower-right portion of the screen.

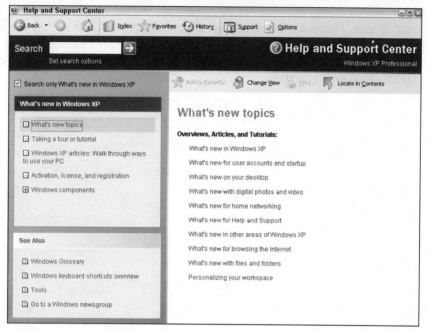

Figure 4-12 *The What's new in Windows XP panel of the Help and Support Center leads you to static or multimedia tutorials.*

Using the Windows XP Search Feature

In this final section, you take a brief look at the Windows Search feature. The Search feature can be used to find all files that fit a specified criterion, such as only music files or only files or folders that reside on a specific drive or in a specific folder. This section gives you an overview of using the Windows XP Search feature. If you have time to view additional material in the Help and Support Center, click Windows Basics ⇨ Searching for Information, and view the appropriate headings in the Overviews, Articles, and Tutorials section.

If you don't see this option, you aren't at the Help and Support Center home page. To return to the home page, click the Home button (the icon of a house, third button from the left on the toolbar).

Searching for specific file types

In this exercise, you take a look at searching for particular file types, rather than for filenames, by having Windows XP search for video files.

1. From the main desktop, click Start ⇨ Search. The Search dialog box, shown in Figure 4-13, is displayed.

Your Search dialog box may not be completely visible unless the window is maximized. Figure 4-13 is displayed in a maximized window so that you can see all of the search options listed in the left pane at the same time. You can either maximize your window or use the scroll arrows in the left pane to scroll through the options.

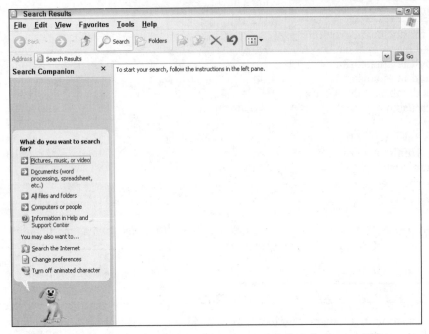

Figure 4-13 *The Search box is ready for you to define the type of file you are looking for.*

2. Click the Pictures, music, or video option. Make sure there is a checkmark by Video only. By not inserting the filename, we will find only video files on our hard drive.

3. Click Use advanced search options. The options expand to let you look for a word or phrase in a file. You can also specify where to look for the file. There are drop-down boxes for last modified date and file size. Finally, there is an option for even more advanced options. The additional advanced options allow you to search:

   - Within system folders
   - For hidden files and folders
   - Subfolders
   - For case-sensitive information
   - A backup tape

4. For now, leave all search information empty (except the checkmark in the video type box). Click Search to begin the search. You should come back with at least three video files (when you installed Windows XP, three video files were installed by default).

5. Click the Back button until you arrive back at the desktop.

Searching for documents

Searching for documents is nearly identical to searching for media types. Documents are any files created by an application (with the exception of specific media file types and files installed by the application that are required for the application to run). This could include a file created in Microsoft Word, as well as Excel spreadsheets, PowerPoint presentations, and Access database tables, and many other file types. In this exercise, you create a file and then search using a partial filename.

1. Click Start ➪ All Programs ➪ Accessories ➪ WordPad.

2. Type **This is a sample WordPad document from Windows XP Weekend Crash Course, Session 4.**

3. Click File ➪ Save As. Notice in the Save as Type box, the default file type is RTF. This stands for Rich Text Format and saves all of the formatting along with the text.

4. In the File Name box, type **winxpwcc session 4**. Click the Save button.

 If you don't add a period to the end of the filename, WordPad automatically saves the file as RTF. If you put a period with no extension and save the file, no extension is added to the file. Windows will not know which application is associated with the file.

5. Close WordPad by clicking the X (Close box) at the top-right corner of the window.

6. Click Start ➪ Search to open the Search Results dialog box.

7. Click Documents (word processing, spreadsheet, and so on).

8. When asked when the last time the file was modified, leave the default as Don't Remember. In the left pane, scroll down until you can see the All or part of the document name text box. Your screen should be similar to the one shown in Figure 4-14. Type **session 4** in the text box.

9. Click the Search button. After several seconds, the winxpwcc session 4.rtf document should appear in the right pane. Right-clicking the file will give you a context menu of things you can do, including opening the file, deleting it, and renaming it.

Figure 4-14 *Once you have specified a search for documents, the left pane includes (from top): the ability to search for a file based on the date last modified, all or part of the document name, and a link to advanced options.*

In the following exercise, you search for a specific text *string*. A string is simply a group of characters.

1. In the left pane of the Search Results dialog box, delete the partial filename you typed, session 4. Scroll down, if necessary, and click Use Advanced Search Options. Scroll down again until you see A Word or a Phrase in the Document. Type **Weekend Crash Course**.

2. Click Search to begin the search. You might have more than one document returned. Notice the three-letter extension on each filename indicating the application that created it.

 If you don't see the three-letter file extension, click Tools ⇨ Folder Options. Then click the View tab. Remove the checkmark from the Hide Extensions of Known File Types option box. Click Apply. Finally, click Apply to All Folders near the top of the window. In the Folders View dialog box, click Yes. Close the Folder Options dialog box.

3. Close the Search Results dialog box.

Done!

REVIEW

- The Help and Support Center is the best place for starting to get help using Windows XP.
- Help is available in dialog boxes by clicking the Help button on the toolbar, by pressing F1, or by pressing Shift-F1.
- Windows XP offers static (text only) or multimedia tours of many Windows XP features.
- The Window XP Search feature can be used to easily find files on any drive.

QUIZ YOURSELF

---

1. How do you open the Windows Help and Support Center? (See *The Help and Support Center* section.)

2. In the Windows Help and Support Center, when is the Forward button available? (See *The standard toolbar* section.)

3. What does the Microsoft Knowledge Base list? (See *Using customized search options* section.)

4. How can you find out what version of an application you are using? (See *Getting About WordPad help* section.)

5. In the WordPad help screen, what is the difference between the Contents and Index tabs? (See *Using the index tab* section.)

6. What steps would you take to begin a multimedia presentation on the basics of Windows XP? (See *Touring Windows* section.)

PART

I

Friday Evening Part Review

1. Is Windows XP a client or server operating system?
2. Which dialog box is used to select which of the four most common icons displayed on the desktop?
3. Which two types of fast Internet connections are commonly found in home offices?
4. What feature of Windows XP allows multiple computers to connect to the Internet using a single Internet connection?
5. How many CPUs and Video Display Terminals (monitors) is the Home Edition of Windows XP capable of handling?
6. What single hardware component would be your best investment to make your computer run faster?
7. What Microsoft file tells you whether your hardware should work with Windows XP or not?
8. What is the legal agreement called that outlines your legal responsibilities in regard to Windows XP?
9. What is the recommended installation type for Windows XP if another operating system is already installed?
10. Does the original Product Key that comes with Windows XP consist of letters, numbers, or both?
11. What is the result of pressing the Windows Logo key?
12. What is the area of the Taskbar called that is used to launch an application with a single click?
13. In Windows XP, on the desktop you will find one or more small pictures representing applications, folders, or files. What are these small pictures called?
14. Between "Windows" and "windows," which one is the operating system?
15. Which dialog box is displayed if you right-click any empty area of the desktop and choose Properties?

16. When doing a search in the Windows XP Help and Support Center, you can use keywords. What are keywords?

17. When saving a topic to the Favorites button, why would you use the Rename option?

18. When doing a search, what is the maximum number of results that can be returned per provider?

19. When a dialog box is displayed, how can you get general and specific help?

20. What are three general components included in the term multimedia?

☑ Friday

☑ **Saturday**

☐ Sunday

Part II — Saturday Morning

Part III — Saturday Afternoon

Part IV — Saturday Evening

PART

II

Saturday Morning

Using the XP Control Panel

Session Checklist

✔ Accessing the Control Panel

✔ Understanding the Control Panel icons

✔ Choosing a Control Panel view

I n this session, you learn how the Control Panel can help you manage hardware, software, and applications that make your computer function. Think of the Control Panel in terms of the dashboard in your car. Your car's dashboard gives you access to controls that enhance your driving experience. For instance, environmental controls (like air-conditioning or heating) allow you to drive in comfort, audio controls provide you with music or news, and mechanical controls allow you to operate safety features such as your windshield wipers, headlights, or hazard lamps.

The Windows XP Control Panel allows you to change the look, feel, and functionality of your computer. From within the Control Panel, you can adjust nearly every aspect of the Windows XP environment, attached hardware, and installed software. Understanding the elements of the Control Panel can help you personalize your computer's look and feel, enhance the functionality of your hardware, and even speed up your computer applications.

Accessing the Control Panel

**30 Min.
To Go**

Fortunately, accessing the Windows XP Control Panel is as simple as a few clicks of your mouse. If you are using the standard Windows XP Start menu, you can access the Control Panel by choosing Start ⇨ Control Panel. If you are using the classic Windows Start menu, access the Control Panel by choosing Start ⇨ Settings ⇨ Control Panel. You can also access the Control Panel by double-clicking the My Computer icon on your desktop and clicking the link to the Control Panel in the left pane.

Understanding the Control Panel Icons

Once you have accessed the Control Panel, you can choose from nine categories, shown in Figure 5-1, that are available for configuring and maintaining Windows XP.

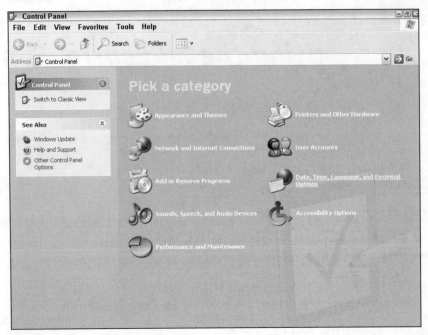

Figure 5-1 *The Control Panel allows you to manipulate the hardware and software installed on your computer.*

In addition to the main categories, the left pane of the Control Panel's main page offers links to five additional services. These services allow you to change the view of the Control Panel (see the *Choosing a Control Panel View* section later in this session), access the Microsoft Windows Update home page, seek help and support through the Windows XP troubleshooters, and access additional Control Panel options.

Appearance and Themes

The Appearance and Themes section of the Control Panel, shown in Figure 5-2, allows you to easily change the look and feel of your Windows XP environment. Just click any of the links and Windows XP opens the appropriate dialog box for changing that element.

For additional information about visual element control in Windows XP, such as themes, backgrounds, and screen savers, see Session 9.

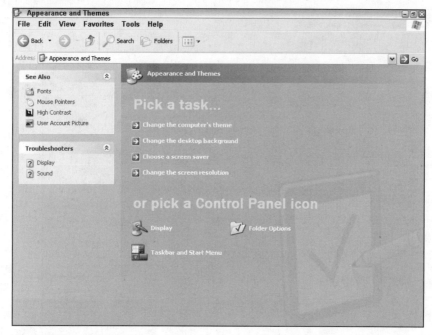

Figure 5-2   *The Appearance and Themes section allows you to change the look and feel of Windows XP.*

Using the Appearance and Themes tasks, you can adjust the individual visual elements of Windows XP including the desktop background, the screen saver, and the screen resolution. If you want to really spice up your Windows environment, use one of the built-in Windows XP themes. You can even create your own Windows theme or download themes that other users have created and loaded onto the Web.

To find tons of Windows XP themes, just point your Web browser to www.google.com **and search for the term** *Windows XP Themes.*

Printers and Other Hardware

The Printers and Other Hardware section of the Control Panel, shown in Figure 5-3, allows you to install, configure, and troubleshoot common hardware peripherals. Using the available options, you can quickly install a printer or view the printers currently installed on your machine.

To configure a hardware peripheral that is currently attached to your system, simply click the icon that represents the hardware category of that peripheral and follow the prompts. In addition, you can use the quick links in the left pane of the Printers and Other Hardware page to add a new device, adjust the display settings of your video card and monitor, configure the audio devices installed in your computer, adjust your computer's power features (such as when your computer goes into standby mode), and view the system properties of your computer.

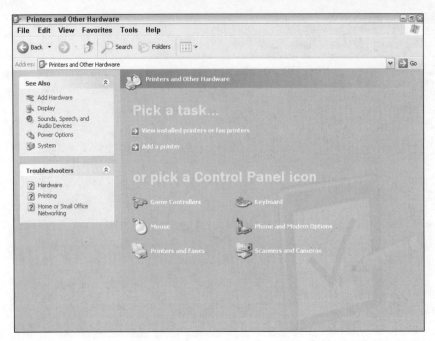

Figure 5-3 *The Printers and Other Hardware section allows you to add, remove, or configure printers and hardware peripherals installed on your computer.*

Network and Internet Connections

Connecting your computer to a network or to the Internet allows you to access shared resources such as network printers or servers and also provides you with access to e-mail and the World Wide Web (also known as the Web). The Network and Internet Connections section of the Control Panel, shown in Figure 5-4, now makes it easier than ever to connect your computer to a network.

In order to connect your computer to a home network, local area network (LAN), or to the Internet, you still need to have the appropriate hardware installed. To connect to a home network or LAN you will need a network interface card (NIC) and to connect to the Internet you will need either a NIC that is connected to your network and/or a cable or DSL modem or a dial-up modem.

Connecting a computer to a corporate network usually requires skills beyond those of the average computer user. If the terms CAT-5, proxy server, router, or TCP/IP make your eyes glaze and your head hurt, give your company's help desk a call and they should be able to get you connected.

For complete details on connecting your computer to a network, check out Session 14.

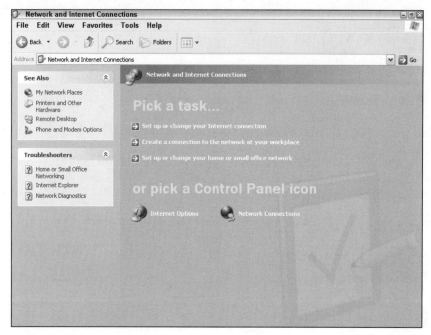

Figure 5-4 *The Network and Internet Connections section provides access to tools to connect your computer to a LAN or the Internet.*

User Accounts

Whenever you sit down to use a computer, it's a natural tendency to customize the environment so that it suits your needs. This might mean changing the background, adjusting the font size, or moving icons into a different arrangement. The problem occurs, however, when another user comes along and changes things to fit *his* needs. Luckily, Windows XP provides you with the ability to establish user accounts that remember how you like your Windows environment set up.

The User Accounts section of the Control Panel, shown in Figure 5-5, allows you to create new accounts, modify existing accounts, and modify how users are able to log in and log out. Using the tasks in this section, you can reset passwords, change the picture associated with the user, and even change the security permissions that allow the user to access certain elements of Windows XP.

In order to be able to do things like change user passwords, create and delete accounts, or change user pictures, you must be set up as an administrator on your machine . All accounts fall into one of two categories: Administrator and Limited. Administrators can do virtually anything to any account on the shared computer, including changing another user's password. A Limited account user can only change his or her own password, change desktop settings, view files you created, and view documents in the Shared Files folder.

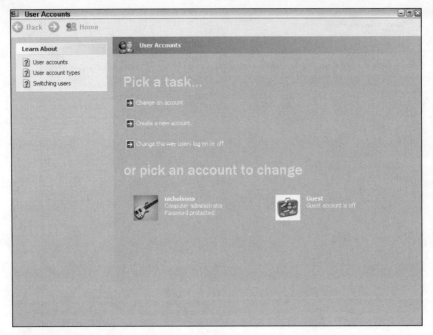

Figure 5-5 *The User Accounts section allows you to control who has access to your computer and what privileges they are allowed.*

For additional information on user accounts see Session 27.

Add or Remove Programs

The Add or Remove Programs section of the Control Panel, shown in Figure 5-6, allows you to control what software applications are installed on your system. The left side of the window allows you to see what applications are installed, change their configuration, and remove the program when it is no longer necessary. When you click a program, Windows XP tells you how much hard drive space the application is using, how frequently you have accessed the program, and the date it was last used.

You will only have the Set Program Access and Defaults icon (the bottom icon in the left pane) if you have changed anything from the complete Windows default.

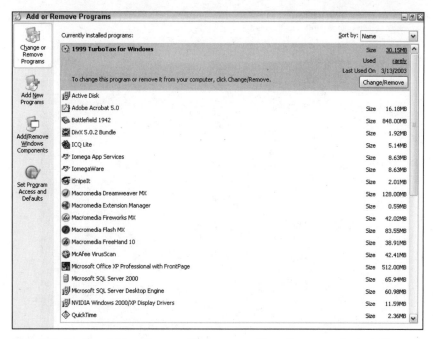

Figure 5-6   The Add or Remove Programs section allows you to install or remove applications from your computer.

The left side of the screen provides you with links that allow you to change or remove currently installed programs, add a new application to your system, add or remove components of the Windows XP operating system, and determine what programs are used for activities such as browsing the Web or sending an e-mail.

Date, Time, Language, and Regional Options

The Date, Time, Language, and Regional Options section of the Control Panel, shown in Figure 5-7, allows you to customize your computer based on your geographic location. For instance, suppose you live in Kansas City (which is in the Central Standard Time Zone), but are getting ready to move to Denver (which is in the Mountain Time Zone). Once you make the move, you can simply unpack your computer, click the Control Panel, and change the time zone by clicking the Change the date and time link.

You can use the Add other languages link to install a language pack. You then have the option of working in any of the languages installed on your computer.

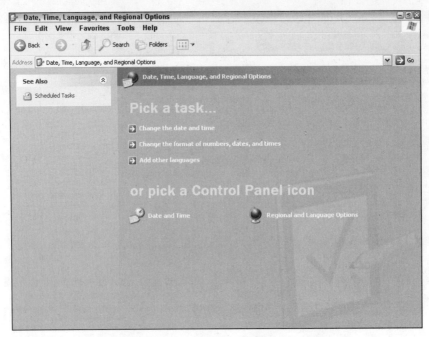

Figure 5-7 *The Date, Time, Language, and Regional Options section allows you to customize your computer according to your geographic location.*

Sound, Speech, and Audio Devices

20 Min. To Go

As the multimedia capabilities of our computers have grown, customizing the way you *hear* your computer has become almost as important as how you *see* it. Audio prompts are used throughout Windows XP to alert us to a wide range of events ranging from the completion of a task to the arrival of new e-mail. More important, without sound, you wouldn't be able to listen to your favorite CD, MP3, or DVD. The Sounds, Speech, and Audio Devices section of the Control Panel, shown in Figure 5-8, allows you to control not only the volume of sound but also to choose a sound scheme, troubleshoot audio devices, and even set your computer up for voice recognition and handicap accessibility.

If you want more control over the specific volume controls of your computer, you can also use the Advanced Volume Controls in the left-hand pane to specify individual volume levels for the master volume, music CDs, and other audio devices.

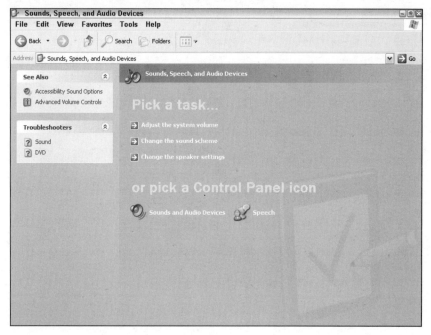

Figure 5-8 *The Sounds, Speech, and Audio Devices section allows you to adjust the multimedia capabilities of Windows XP.*

Accessibility Options

Windows XP provides a wide range of tools that enable physically challenged users to use their computers more easily. Features such as voice recognition and synthesis, screen magnifiers, and keyboard filters all work to make the computing experience enjoyable for everyone.

The Accessibility Options section of the Control Panel, shown in Figure 5-9, provides access to all visual, audio, and tactile tools used to modify the Windows XP environment for use by an individual with a hearing, visual, or mobility impairment. In addition, this section provides easy access to the Screen Magnifier and the On-Screen Keyboard.

For complete details on the accessibility features available in Windows XP, check out www.microsoft.com/enable/ .

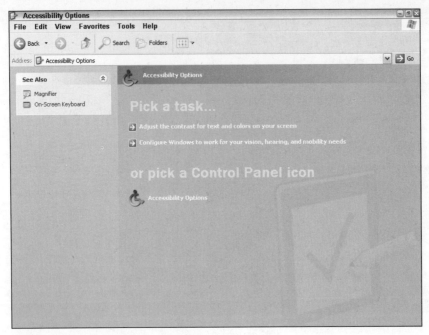

Figure 5-9   *The Accessibility Options section allows you to configure your computer's visual, audio, and tactile features in order to provide access to users with disabilities.*

Performance and Maintenance

We all want our computers to run in peak condition. With the Performance and Maintenance section of the Control Panel, shown in Figure 5-10, you can perform tasks that will ensure that your computer continues to run smoothly.

The tasks within this section allow you to find out information about your computer ranging from the computer name, the hardware you are using, and the updates that have been performed on the operating system. Armed with this information, you can then make adjustments to enhance your computer's performance. For instance, from within the Performance and Maintenance section, you can clean up your hard drive, back up valuable data, and run the Windows Defragmenter to arrange the data on your hard drive in a manner that speeds up your computer.

In addition to the quick tasks, you can also access additional sections of the Control Panel that allow you to automate tasks, administer elements of Windows XP like Internet Information Services (available only in the Professional version), and access detailed information about your system.

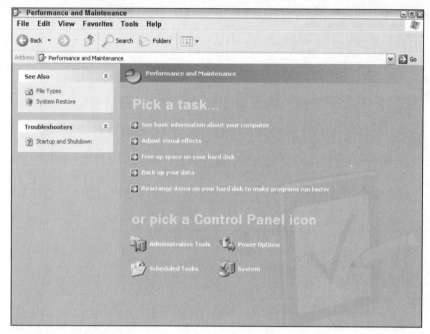

Figure 5-10   *The Performance and Maintenance section helps you keep your computer running smoothly.*

Choosing a Control Panel View

**10 Min.
To Go**

If you have used previous versions of Windows, the Control Panel in Windows XP, shown in Figure 5-11, might seem a little lackluster. Rest assured that those nine streamlined icons provide access to the same options that earlier versions of the Control Panel did.

Microsoft recognizes that some users just won't want to use the new Control Panel and provides access to the Classic look with just the click of a mouse. By clicking the Switch to Classic View link in the left pane of the Control Panel, you can easily switch to the Classic View, shown in Figure 5-12.

> **Tip**
>
> **If you switch to the Classic view, you will still see the common tasks pane on the left side of the control panel. If you truly want your Control Panel to look like it did in Windows 95 and 98, select Tools ⇨ Folder Options from the menu. In the Folder Options dialog box, select the General tab and choose Use Windows classic folders and click OK. Click Apply, then Apply To All Folders. Click Yes. After this is completed, the left pane is removed and the single-window classic look is displayed.**

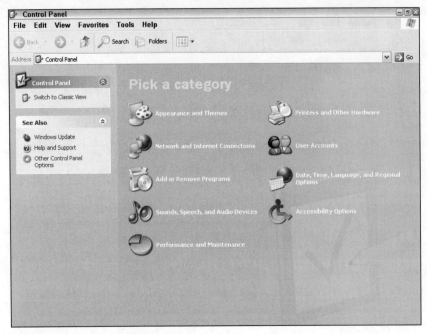

Figure 5-11   *The Windows XP View provides a streamlined set of icons that represent the most commonly used tasks.*

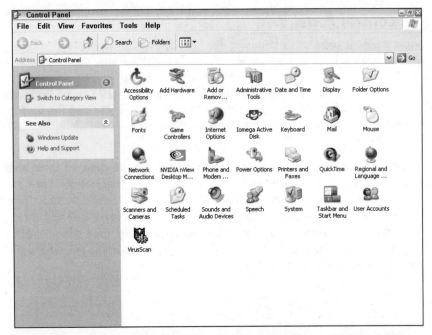

Figure 5-12   *The display has been set to show the classic Windows icons.*

Done!

REVIEW

- The Windows XP Control Panel allows you to customize your Windows environment and manage your computer's hardware and software.
- You can completely customize both the visual and audio aspects of Windows XP from within the Control Panel.
- By managing your user accounts properly, you can customize the look and feel of Windows XP for individual users.
- Windows XP offers a wide range of accessibility options for physically challenged users.
- If you are more comfortable with the look and feel of the Control Panel from previous versions of Windows, you can easily revert to that Classic view.

QUIZ YOURSELF

1. What are the two ways of accessing the Control Panel? (See *Accessing the Control Panel* section.)
2. Which section of the Control Panel is used to manage the desktop background? (See *Appearance and Themes* section.)
3. What Control Panel icon would you click to change the sound card's volume? (See *Sounds, Speech, and Audio Devices* section.)
4. How can you set the Control Panel to the Classic view? (See *Choosing a Control Panel View* section.)
5. How would you change the time zone recognized by your computer? (See *Date, Time, Language, and Regional Options* section.)
6. What features does Windows XP include for individuals with physical impairments? (See *Accessibility Options* section.)

SESSION

6

Windows XP Accessories: The Basics

Session Checklist

✔ Accessing the Accessories

✔ Using the Windows XP Calculator

✔ Using Microsoft Paint for basic graphics

✔ Comparing Notepad and WordPad

✔ Using Windows Explorer

I n this session, you will get a beginning glimpse into the accessories offered with Windows XP. Using these accessories, you'll find that you have access to a variety of tools that can enhance your computer's productivity.

For instance, suppose you have been charged with the task of creating a sales report documenting the activities of your department for the last year. Suppose, however, that at this time, you don't have access to fancy statistical programs, productivity suites, or graphic design software. Never fear — you have Windows XP! Using the accessories that are included with Windows XP, this session shows you how to build a report that will knock everybody's socks off!

Accessing the Accessories

30 Min.
To Go

Accessing the Windows XP accessories is as easy as clicking Start ➪ All Programs ➪ Accessories. The accessories displayed will depend on which installation you have chosen during the setup of Windows XP.

If you are using the classic Start menu, you can access the accessories by clicking Start ➾ Programs ➾ Accessories.

Using the Windows XP Calculator

The first step in building your report would be to crunch the numbers. It may seem kind of silly to showcase the Windows Calculator as one of the exciting accessories offered in Windows XP, but you'd be surprised how many people really love having a calculator that is easy to access and easy to use. Think about it: No more dead batteries or solar cells that don't work under fluorescent lamps. The Windows Calculator is available any time you need it, and it functions exactly like a traditional calculator. And you don't have to go searching in your desk drawer! Follow these instructions to practice using the calculator.

1. To access the calculator, shown in Figure 6-1, click Start ➾ All Programs ➾ Accessories ➾ Calculator.

2. When using the calculator, you have three options for inputting your data. You can either click the buttons on the screen with your mouse, use the numeric keys along the top of your keyboard, or (if you have one) use the numeric keypad on the right side of your keyboard. Try out a few calculations to get familiar with using the calculator.

Figure 6-1 *The Windows Calculator looks and functions like a regular calculator.*

3. To clear the value, you can click the CE key with your mouse or press the Delete key on the keyboard. Clear the calculator and close it.

If you need access to functions beyond the basic adding, subtracting, multiplying, and dividing from the basic Calculator, click View ➾ Scientific from the menu bar and, as shown in Figure 6-2, you have access to a wide variety of scientific functions.

Figure 6-2 *The Windows Calculator also offers a scientific mode for more complex calculations.*

Creating Graphics with XP Paint

Once you have your numbers crunched, you will probably want to present them in a visual manner and Windows XP's Paint can help you do just that. Paint is a limited graphics program with one major advantage over other programs. It's free. It comes with Windows XP, and everyone with a Windows OS will have it unless they have uninstalled it, or chose not to install it during the original Windows XP setup.

Suppose that one of the graphics you would like to include in your report shows the increase in sales over the last 5 years. To create this graphic, follow these steps:

1. Open Paint by choosing Start ⇨ All Programs ⇨ Accessories ⇨ Paint. By default, the Pencil tool is active.

2. From the Paint toolbar, shown in Figure 6-3, select the rectangle icon on the tool palette (see Figure 6-3) and draw a rectangle a little smaller than the size of your canvas. To create a rectangle, position your cursor where you want one corner of the rectangle and, holding down the mouse button, drag it diagonally until the rectangle is the size and shape you want before releasing the button. Figure 6-3 is shown with a rectangle already drawn, nearly to the size of the canvas.

If you make an error, there are three ways to erase it: (1) Immediately after making the error, choose Edit ⇨ Undo; (2) choose either the Select tool or Free-Form Select tool and drag a selection box around the object you want to delete, then press the delete key; or (3) select the Eraser/Color Eraser tool, and wipe over anything while depressing the main mouse button. It is usually easier to erase a mistake and begin again than to try and fix it.

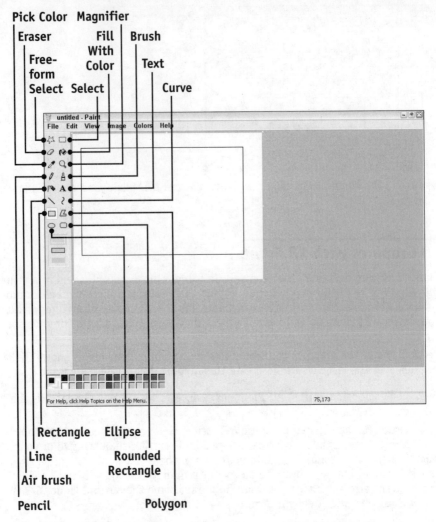

Figure 6-3   *With Paint you can create your own custom images.*

3. Next, choose the Line tool (the sixth from the top, in the left column) and draw three horizontal and three vertical lines to make a grid, as shown in Figure 6-4.

When using the Line tool in Paint, you can hold down the Shift key while drawing your lines and the Line tool draws in a straight line. Additionally, holding Shift while using the Rectangle or Ellipse tool results in a square or circle, respectively.

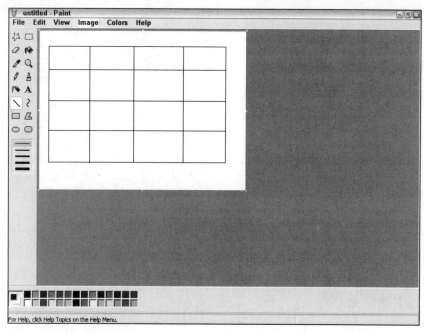

Figure 6-4   *Using the Line tool, create the beginnings of your graph.*

4. Add a title above the table by selecting the Text tool and dragging a box along the
    top of the graphic area. Type **Five Year Sales Chart**. Draw text boxes for each of
    the years at the bottom of each vertical line along the bottom of the chart. These
    will contain the labels for each year. Mark the left-most edge as **1998**, the second
    vertical line as **1999**, and the third through fifth as **2000**, **2001**, and **2002**.

5. Create text boxes for each of the horizontal lines. Type, **4000**, **3000**, **2000**, and
    1000, moving from the top line to the bottom.

> **If you don't like the way one of your text boxes turns out after you have
> entered text into it, choose the Select tool, drag a selection box a little
> larger than the text box, and press Delete. Reselect the Text tool and give it
> another try.**

6. To draw the sales amount lines, click the Line tool. You can change the line width
    by clicking the appropriate selection in the box below the Ellipse and Rounded
    Rectangle tool. You can select a color by clicking the appropriate color in the color
    box along the bottom of the screen. In 1998, the company was just opening, so it
    had no sales. In 1999, the company sales were 600. Draw a line starting at the left-
    bottom corner of the chart (0), and ending at approximately 600 on the 1999 line.
    In 2000, the sales increased to 2500. Draw the corresponding line. In 2001, sales
    dipped slightly, so draw the line to end between 2500 and 2300 along the year 2001
    line. Sales again skyrocketed in 2002, rising to 3500. Draw the appropriate line. The
    final chart is shown in Figure 6-5.

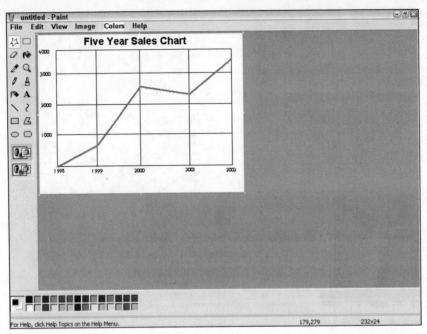

Figure 6-5 *Finish your graph by adding text and data using the Text tool and Line tool.*

7. Once you have completed your chart, save it to your My Documents folder so you can insert it into your report later in this session. To save the picture, choose File ⇨ Save As from the menu bar and name the file **5yearchart.bmp**.

Paint is capable of saving files in a wide variety of formats including bitmaps (BMPs), JPEGs, GIFs, TIFs, and PNGs. All of these formats, with the exception of BMPs, are compressed graphic file formats, meaning they take up less space and are commonly found on Internet Web sites.

Paint is a very basic graphics design program and you should realize that it really isn't meant to create complex charts and graphs. If you find yourself needing a program that can create graphical representations of your data, you might consider using a program like Microsoft Works or Microsoft Excel.

8. Close Paint.

Comparing Notepad and WordPad

20 Min. To Go

Once you have your mathematical work completed, the next step is to write the text portions of the report. With Windows XP, you have two options when it comes to word processors — Notepad and WordPad. Notepad, shown in Figure 6-6, is Windows XP's most basic word processor. You can access Notepad by clicking Start ⇨ All Programs ⇨ Accessories ⇨ Notepad.

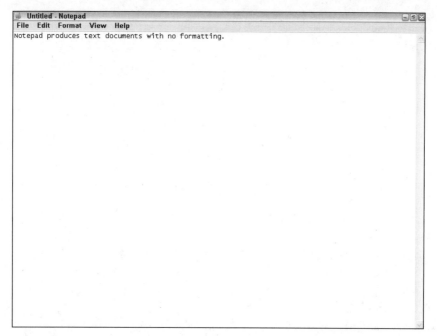

Figure 6-6   *Notepad is Windows XP's most basic word processor.*

With Notepad, you can create simple text documents that don't require any formatting. Features such as bolding or italicizing text, centering paragraphs, or inserting tab stops just don't exist in Notepad. However, even without these features, Notepad remains a favorite among some *because* of its simplicity, especially when it comes to writing HTML code for the Web.

By default, word wrap in Notepad is turned off. *Word wrap* **is the feature that automatically moves the text insertion point to the next line when there is too much text to fit on the current line. When the feature is off, the result is that each paragraph appears on a single line. To turn on word wrap in Notepad, choose Format ⇨ Word Wrap. This is a toggle. If there is a checkmark next to Word Wrap, it is enabled. If no checkmark is present, clicking the Word Wrap option enables it and places a checkmark to the left of the option.**

For your report, however, it would probably be helpful to be able to format your paragraphs and text, so WordPad would be a better choice for your word processor. Shown in Figure 6-7, WordPad provides you with a broader range of tools, ranging from text and paragraph formatting to the ability to insert charts, graphs, and photographs.

To insert the chart you created in the previous section:

1. Open WordPad by choosing Start ⇨ All Programs ⇨ Accessories ⇨ WordPad. Press Enter three times to leave some blank space at the top of the document.
2. From the menu bar, choose Insert ⇨ Object. In the Insert Object dialog box choose the Create from File radio button and browse to the 5yearchart.bmp file you created earlier.

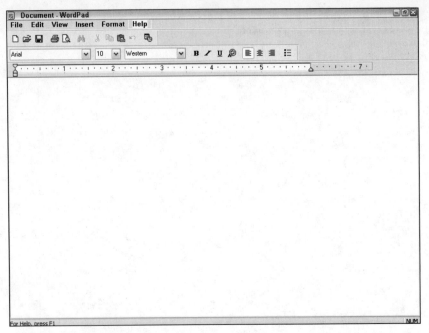

Figure 6-7 *WordPad provides a wider range of features than Notepad.*

3. Click OK and the chart is inserted into your document, as shown in Figure 6-8. If necessary, click the graphic to select it, and drag the bottom right corner up and to the left until the graphic is about 4" in width.

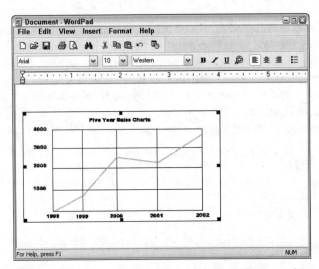

Figure 6-8 *The chart you created in Paint has now been inserted into a WordPad document.*

4. Click in the blank space at the top of the document. Type **This is an estimated sales chart for the years between 1998 and 2002. The last half of 2002 has been projected based on the first 6 months of sales in 2002. The values on the left side of the graph are in thousands of dollars.**

5. Save the document to your My Documents folder as 5yearreport.rtf.

While WordPad is a functional word processor, you may find that it lacks some important features such as mail merge, spell checker, and outlining features. For a more robust word processor application take a look at **Microsoft Works or Microsoft Word.**

Using Windows Explorer

**10 Min.
To Go**

Once you have created all the documents for your report, you can use one of Windows XP's most valuable accessories, Windows Explorer, to put the files together into a single location. Windows Explorer, shown in Figure 6-9, shows you the structure of the drives, folders, and files located on your computer and allows you to set up your files in the most effective way for your use.

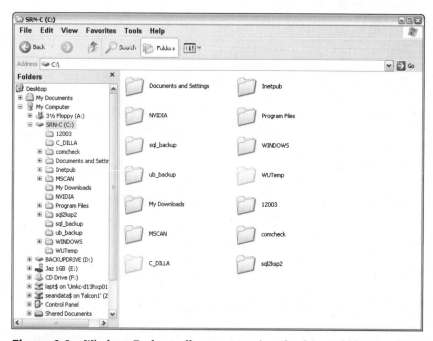

Figure 6-9 *Windows Explorer allows you to view the drives, folders, and files located on your computer.*

From within Windows Explorer you can create new folders and then copy or cut files and paste them to alternative locations. For instance, if you want to create a new folder in your My Documents folder specifically for your report files, do the following:

1. Open Windows Explorer by clicking Start ⇨ All Programs ⇨ Accessories ⇨ Windows Explorer.

2. Within Windows Explorer, click the My Documents icon in the left pane of the window. Windows Explorer displays the contents of the My Documents folder in the right pane.

3. On the menu bar, choose File ⇨ New ⇨ Folder. Windows Explorer places a new folder in the right pane. Name this folder **5YearFiles**.

4. In the right pane, right-click the 5yearreport.rtf file and choose Cut from the context menu. Right-click the 5YearFiles folder and choose Paste from the context menu.

5. Locate the 5yearchart.bmp file and cut and paste it into the 5YearFiles folder.

You can accomplish the same file and folder manipulation using the My Computer icon on your desktop. However, My Computer does not have the split right and left panes available in Windows Explorer. For this reason, Windows Explorer is a more useful tool when copying and pasting files to multiple locations.

Done!

REVIEW

-   The Windows XP Calculator provides access to both simple arithmetic functions and complex scientific functions.

-   Paint allows you to create simple graphics in a variety of formats.

-   Notepad and WordPad are word processor programs built into Windows XP.

-   Using Windows Explorer, you can alter the location of the files and folders located on your computer.

QUIZ YOURSELF

1. How can you access the scientific functions of the calculator? (See *Using the Windows XP Calculator* section.)

2. How would you draw a straight line using Paint? (See *Creating Graphics with XP Paint* section.)

3. What file formats is Paint capable of creating graphics in? (See *Creating Graphics with XP Paint* section.)

4. What are the differences between Notepad and WordPad? (See *Comparing Notepad and WordPad* section.)

5. What accessory would you use to move a file from one folder to another? (See *Using Windows Explorer* section.)

Windows XP Accessories: Advanced

Session Checklist

✔ Accessing the accessory categories

✔ Understanding the programs within the accessory categories

✔ Capturing audio and video

✔ Organizing your accessories

I n this session, you will learn about the advanced accessories that are included with Windows XP. These programs and utilities provide a broad range of functions that include enhancing your computer's accessibility to physically challenged users, keeping your operating system running at peak performance, and even capturing and editing audio and video clips.

In addition to introducing these advanced features, this session shows you how to organize your accessories to better suit your individual needs.

Accessing the Accessory Categories

**30 Min.
To Go**

By default, Windows XP has four categories of accessories. You can access each of them by clicking Start ⇨ All Programs ⇨ Accessories. The accessory categories are the Accessibility, Communications, Entertainment, and System Tools folders. Each of the four categories is in its own folder. When you hover your cursor over any of the four folders, the accessories within are shown from a fly-out menu. To start an accessory, simply click it.

Accessibility accessories

By including the Accessibility accessories in Windows XP, Microsoft has recognized the fact that many physically challenged individuals are using computers. These tools enhance the computing experience for those with visual, hearing, and physical impairments by creating an interface that is tailored for their needs.

For instance, the Screen Magnifier, shown in Figure 7-1, allows users with visual disabilities to zoom in on a section of the screen in order to see it more clearly.

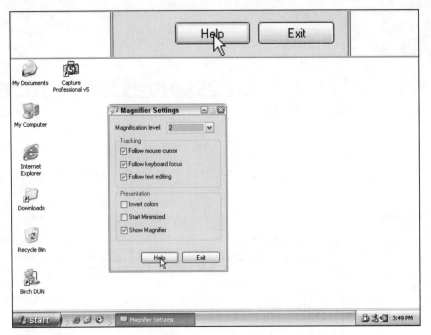

Figure 7-1 *The Screen Magnifier zooms in on the section of the screen where your mouse is located.*

 Microsoft has devoted a section of its Web site at www.microsoft.com/ enable **to showcase and support the accessibility features in Windows XP and some of their other products.**

Other Accessibility accessories include the Accessibility Wizard, which helps to clarify which of the accessories need to be set up; Narrator, which reads the screen to you; an onscreen keyboard, which allows you to use a mouse to press the keys, rather than an actual keyboard; and the Utility Manager, which allows you to set options for the various accessories and allows you to start and stop them, too.

Communication accessories

The Communication accessories are used to assist you in connecting your computer to a Local Area Network (LAN), home network, or even directly to another computer. While hovering your mouse over the Communications menu, a fly-out menu offers the following accessories: HyperTerminal, Network Connections, Network Setup Wizard, New Connection Wizard, and Remote Desktop Connection. HyperTerminal acts as a dialing program for your modem, or if you have a phone hooked to your modem, you can also use HyperTerminal to dial your phone. When connecting your computer to a network, the Network Connections panel, shown in Figure 7-2, can help you determine whether the connection has been made and the properties of that connection.

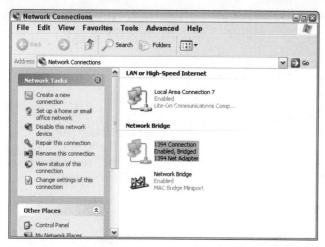

Figure 7-2 *The Network Connections panel allows you to see your computer's connections to a LAN or home network.*

In addition to the Network Connections panel, you can also use the Communications accessories to connect your computer to the Internet or take control over another computer using the Remote Desktop tool (in XP Professional only). For instance, imagine being able to sit in front of your home computer and have complete access to your computer at work. As shown in Figure 7-3, with the Remote Desktop interface, you are able to interact with a second computer using only your Web browser.

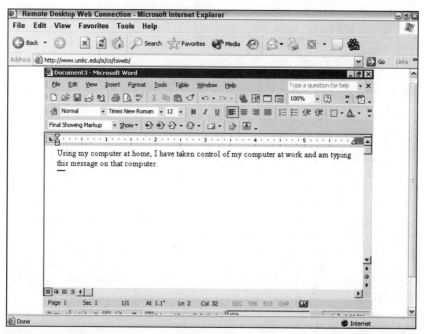

Figure 7-3 *Using the Remote Desktop tool, you can remotely access other computers.*

For details on how to set up and use the Remote Desktop feature, visit www.microsoft.com/WindowsXP/pro/using/howto/gomobile/remotedesktop/default.asp.

20 Min.
To Go

Entertainment accessories

What fun would a computer be without some music and video? Luckily, Windows XP includes some audio and visual accessories that will allow you to listen to your favorite music or watch a video clip on your computer. The Windows Media Player, shown in Figure 7-4, allows you to play audio and video clips using the same program. The Windows Media Player is available from the Entertainment fly-out menu.

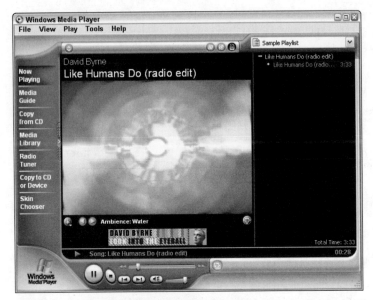

Figure 7-4 *The Windows Media Player takes care of all your audio and video computer needs.*

To play a music CD in your computer, simply place the CD in your CD-ROM drive. Windows XP should detect the CD and begin playing it. If the CD is not detected, click File ⇨ Open on the menu bar and browse to your CD-ROM drive (most often the D: drive). Point to any of the audio tracks on the CD and click OK.

You can use the Media Guide button to access online media. In the default mode, this button accesses www.windowsmedia.com/mg/home.asp?, a site dedicated to multimedia news, entertainment, and other constantly changing topics. The Radio Tuner button accesses the same Web site, but offers a list of radio stations. You must be connected to the Internet for either of these buttons to work. A fast connection (such as cable or ISDN) is preferable for streaming media.

You can use the Copy from CD to copy music tracks to your hard drive. Versions of Media Player previous to 9 could only save files in the Windows Media Audio (WMA) format. Most players do not support this format. With the introduction of Version 9, Media Player is now able to copy to the MP3 file format, a much more widely accepted format.

In addition to the Windows Media Player, the Entertainment accessories also include a sound recorder, which lets you record audio from a microphone or other input and a volume control for your audio settings.

System Tools

Of all the advanced accessories, the System Tools are the ones that you should become most familiar with. The System Tools category includes tools that allow you to view detailed information about your computer, back up your data, and perform routine system mainte- nance. The Disk Defragmenter, shown in Figure 7-5, rearranges the data on your hard disk in a manner that allows your computer to access it more quickly. This, in turn, makes your computer run faster.

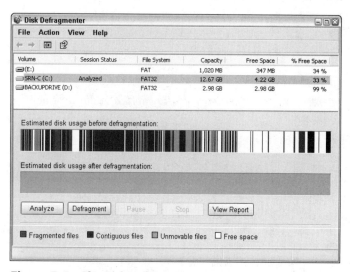

Figure 7-5 *The Disk Defragmenter helps you keep your hard disk organized in a manner that makes your computer run faster.*

Be sure to run the Disk Cleanup wizard periodically to reduce the number of unnecessary files taking up space on your hard disk. You can even use the Task Scheduler (another util- ity in the System Tools category) to automate the task.

The Backup and Restore tools are covered in Session 18. Other tools are dis- cussed in Session 17.

**10 Min.
To Go**

Audio and Video Capture Accessories

Have you ever wanted to edit your own home movies? Well, now's your chance! Using your digital camcorder, the Windows XP Sound Recorder, and Windows Movie Maker, you have all the tools you need to make great cinematic works of art (or at least really cool movies that will impress your friends and relatives).

Windows XP Sound Recorder

Capturing sound and video editing are activities that go hand-in-hand and since Microsoft has added basic video editing capabilities into Windows XP, it's only logical that it retain the Sound Recorder application that has been present in most of the previous versions of Windows. The Windows Sound Recorder, shown in Figure 7-6, is a very easy to use application once you have your hardware set up properly .

Figure 7-6 *The Sound Recorder program allows you to capture audio clips using a microphone or other audio device.*

Once you have your microphone connected to your sound card, you can record an audio clip by following these steps:

1. Open the Sound Recorder by choosing Start ⇨ All Programs ⇨ Accessories ⇨ Entertainment ⇨ Sound Recorder.
2. Click the Record button (the round circle) and speak into your microphone. While speaking, you should see the green line move up and down with the changes in inflection in your voice.
3. To stop recording, click the Stop button (the black rectangle).
4. Save your file by choosing File ⇨ Save on the menu bar.

If you begin recording and the green line doesn't move, it usually means that either your microphone is switched off or the input volume for your microphone is muted. If the microphone is switched on, choose Start ⇨ Control Panel and choose the Sounds, Speech, and Audio Devices category. In the Sound, Speech, and Audio Devices panel, click the Sounds and Audio Devices icon and select the Voice tab. In the Voice Recording panel, click the Volume button and be sure that the Mute checkbox is not checked under Mic Volume.

Windows Movie Maker

The Windows Movie Maker utility, shown in Figure 7-7, is a handy tool for transferring video footage from your digital camcorder to your computer. Once the video has been captured, you can then use the program to edit the video, add sound, and even add a music soundtrack.

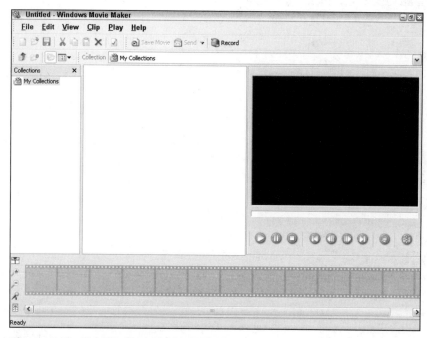

Figure 7-7   *The Windows Movie Maker lets you capture video clips from your digital camcorder and then edit them right on your PC.*

In order to capture video to your Windows XP computer, you need to have a digital camcorder, a 1394 video capture port (sometimes called a "FireWire" port) installed on your computer, and a 1394 cable to connect the two.

Even though the Windows Movie Maker may not be as fancy as some of the more expensive applications on the market, it does a great job doing the basics. If you plan to get into more advanced video editing, you might consider looking into programs like ULead Video Studio or Adobe Premier.

For additional information on how to use the Movie Maker, go to www. microsoft.com/windowsxp/moviemaker/default.asp. **This Microsoft site offers samples and tutorials on using Movie Maker. Another option is to go to** www.google.com/advanced_search/ **and in the With the Exact Phrase text box, type windows movie maker tutorial. You should find several options there.**

Organizing Your Accessories

Suppose you want to create a new category of accessories, say, to hold your favorite games, or just reorganize the setup a little bit. Windows XP allows you complete control over how your accessories are listed on the Start menu, and Windows Explorer, shown in Figure 7-8, makes it a snap to organize them. Following the instructions below, you will be able to create new folders and rearrange current ones.

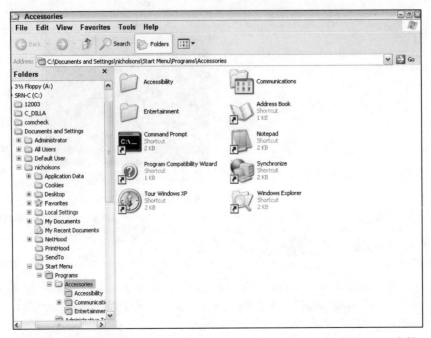

Figure 7-8   *Windows Explorer allows you to view the drives, folders, and files located on your computer.*

To reorganize your accessories, simply follow these steps:

1. Click Start ➪ All Programs and right-click on Accessories. In the context menu, choose Windows Explorer. Windows Explorer opens.

2. In Windows Explorer, you can create new folders by choosing File ➪ New ➪ Folder. Rename the folder to reflect its contents.

3. You can copy and paste or cut and paste programs from one folder to another by right-clicking on the icon and choosing Copy (or Cut) from the context menu. Then, right-click the destination folder and choose Paste.

Done!

REVIEW

- The Advanced accessories are organized into different categories.
- The Accessibility accessories provide extended computer access to physically challenged users.
- The Communication accessories help you to connect your computer to a network or to the Internet.
- The Entertainment accessories let you play audio and video files on your computer.
- The System Tools accessories help you keep your computer running at peak performance.
- The Sound Recorder and Windows Movie Maker programs allow you to capture sound and video.
- Using Windows Explorer, you can organize the Accessories folder to your tastes.

QUIZ YOURSELF

1. What accessory might you use to zoom in on the screen in order to assist a user with a visual disability ? (See *Accessibility accessories* section.)

2. What accessory might you use to view the network connections used by your computer? (See *Communication accessories* section.)

3. What accessory allows you to play music or video on your computer? (See *Entertainment accessories* section.)

4. What accessory might you use to capture and edit video clips from your camcorder? (See *Windows Movie Maker* section.)

5. What accessory would you use to reorganize the Accessories folder? (See *Organizing Your Accessories* section.)

Basic Desktop Customization

Session Checklist

✔ Understanding how to access your desktop

✔ Using Auto Arrange to organize your desktop

✔ Manually moving the icons on your desktop

✔ Choosing a Start menu view

✔ Sorting the programs in your Start menu

In this session, you learn to customize your desktop in Windows XP. With a few clicks of your mouse, you can create a desktop environment that provides access to your commonly used programs and you can organize the way they are displayed.

   In addition, this Session guides you through the process of customizing your Start menu and reorganizing the programs and folders by name.

 Experienced users may want to just skim this session, to make sure they are familiar with the topics covered. These are very basic topics, and you might want to skip ahead to Session 9.

Accessing Your Desktop

**30 Min.
To Go**

When your computer first starts up, you have a clear view of the desktop and all its icons. Once you begin opening applications, however, your desktop becomes hidden behind the open programs. You can return to your Windows XP desktop in either of two ways. The easiest, most common method of viewing the desktop is simply to close or minimize all programs, one at a time. As shown in Figure 8-1, when no programs are visible or active, the desktop is visible.

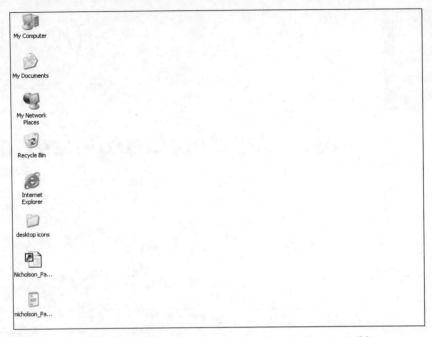

Figure 8-1 *With no programs open or active, the desktop is visible.*

The second method of accessing your desktop is via the shortcut in your Windows XP Quick Launch bar. The icon noted in Figure 8-2 automatically minimizes all programs and makes the desktop visible.

Quick Launch bar

Show Desktop icon

Figure 8-2 *The Show Desktop icon minimizes all programs so the desktop is visible.*

If the Quick Launch bar is not available as part of your Windows Taskbar, simply right-click an empty area of the Windows Taskbar, and choose Properties from the context menu. In the Properties dialog box, check the box that says Show Quick Launch and click OK. The Quick Launch bar is now visible.

Arranging Your Desktop

As you install more applications and save more data on your computer, it is likely that your desktop will become cluttered with shortcuts to applications, folders, and files. It's a good idea to get into the habit of managing your desktop icons, deleting those that are unnecessary, and arranging those that are necessary in a manner that makes them easier to use.

For instance, take a look at the desktop in Figure 8-3.

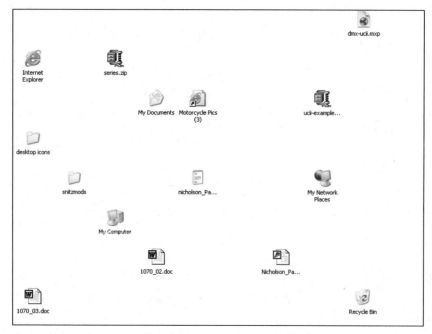

Figure 8-3   *With a cluttered desktop, icons are difficult to locate.*

This is a perfect example of how confusing a cluttered desktop can be. Suppose you wanted to access the Recycle Bin to restore a file. The time wasted hunting for the icon could be avoided by simply reorganizing the icons in a more useful manner.

 For information about using the Desktop Cleanup Wizard, see Session 9.

Using Auto Arrange

The first step in cleaning up your desktop is to turn on the Auto Arrange feature. With Auto Arrange enabled, your desktop will automatically line up all icons on the left side of your desktop and place them in an orderly position. To enable Auto Arrange, follow these steps:

1. Make your desktop visible by either minimizing all active programs or clicking the Show Desktop icon in the Quick Launch bar.

2. Right-click any empty part of the desktop and choose Arrange Icons By ⇨ Auto Arrange from the context menu.

    As shown in Figure 8-4, the icons are now lined up on the left side of your desktop.

Figure 8-4   *The desktop icons can be automatically arranged by Windows XP, making them easier to locate.*

   The Auto Arrange feature can be turned off just as easily as it was turned on. To turn it off, just follow the steps outlined above and it should reverse the process.

Sorting your desktop icons

Even with the icons all arranged in a more orderly fashion, it still might be difficult to locate the Recycle Bin. To resolve this, you can further enhance the usability of your desktop by ordering the icons in a manner that allows you to more quickly locate a folder, file, or shortcut. The most logical way to organize your desktop items is by their type. For instance, you might group all folders together, all system icons together, and so on. To accomplish this, simply right-click any empty part of the desktop and choose Arrange Icons By ⇨ Type. Once the icons are arranged by type, as shown in Figure 8-5, you can see that the system icons (My Documents, My Computer, My Network Places, Recycle Bin, and Internet Explorer) are all placed first in order. After the system icons come the folders, followed by the various document and file types.

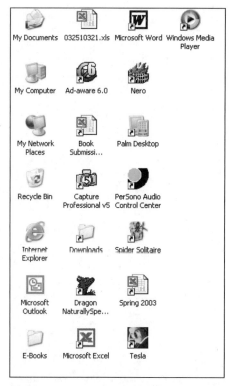

Figure 8-5　*Arranging your desktop icons by type allows you to easily group system icons, applications, folders, data files, and any shortcuts located on the desktop.*

20 Min. To Go

Manually arranging your desktop icons

Another way you can personalize your desktop is to manually arrange the icons in an order that better suits your needs. For example, you might find it easier to group commonly used icons on the left side of the desktop and keep the seldom used ones on the right side. Or you could line up your applications on the left side and data files on the right.

To manually move an icon, follow these steps:

1. Make your desktop visible by either minimizing all active programs or clicking the Show Desktop icon in the Quick Launch bar.

2. Click any icon, drag it to a new position, and release the mouse button. For instance, as shown in Figure 8-6, by dragging the My Documents icon between the My Computer and My Network Places icons and releasing the mouse button, you can manually relocate the My Documents folder to be the second icon in the list.

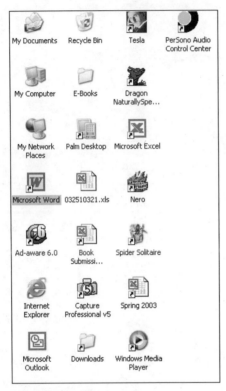

Figure 8-6 *You can manually rearrange your icons by dragging and dropping them into the correct location.*

You can only manually position your desktop icons anywhere on the desktop if the Auto Arrange feature is disabled. If it is enabled, you can still change the order of the icons within the boundaries of the automatically arranged icons.

Changing the View of Your Start Menu

The next step in changing your Windows XP desktop to suit your needs is to choose the way your Start menu is displayed. Windows XP offers two different views for the Start menu: the Windows XP view and the Windows Classic view.

Displaying the Windows XP view

The default Start menu view with Windows XP displays the Start menu in a very different way from previous versions of Windows. As shown in Figure 8-7, the Windows XP view displays the most commonly used programs on the left and a variety of useful system icons on the right. In addition, you can view all the programs available on your computer by choosing the All Programs submenu.

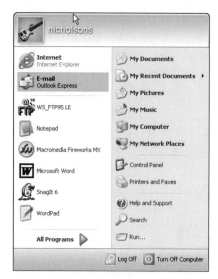

Figure 8-7   *The Windows XP view of the Start menu provides a different look and feel than previous versions of Windows.*

If your Start menu does not look like the one shown in Figure 8-7 and you would like to switch to the Windows XP view, follow these steps:

1. Make your desktop visible by either minimizing all active programs or clicking the Show Desktop icon in the Quick Launch bar.
2. Right-click an empty area of the Taskbar and choose Properties from the context menu.
3. In the Taskbar and Start Menu Properties dialog box, click the Start Menu tab.
4. Select the Start menu radio button and click OK.

Throughout this book, the Windows XP menu style is used.

Classic view

If the Windows XP view of the Start menu doesn't meet your needs, rest assured that you can always switch back to the same Start menu that was used in Windows 95 and 98. The Classic View, shown in Figure 8-8, provides a more categorized list of programs, documents, and system tools.

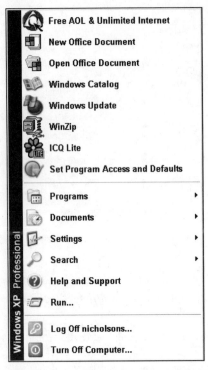

Figure 8-8 *The Classic View of the Start menu allows you to switch back to the way the Start menu was displayed in previous versions of Windows.*

If you are currently using the Windows XP Start menu and would like to use the Classic View, follow the steps for using the Windows XP view in the previous section, but select the Classic Start option instead.

10 Min. To Go

Sorting the programs in your Start menu

Whenever you install a new program on your computer, Windows usually places a new short-cut to that program in your Start menu. Unfortunately, Windows often adds the new icon to the bottom of the list, so your Start menu can quickly become disorganized. However, in the same way you organized the icons on your desktop, you can also organize the icons on your Start menu, although Windows only allows you to sort the folders and program short-cuts by their names.

To sort your Start menu:

1. Click the Start button.
2. If you are running in the Windows XP view, click All Programs. If you are running in the Windows Classic view, click Programs.
3. Right-click any icon in the programs list and choose Sort by Name from the context menu. Windows reorganizes the programs in your Start menu alphabetically.

If you auto-arrange by type and then add a new system, application, folder, file, or shortcut, the icon is added as the last member of that particular group. To correctly arrange them again, just right-click any empty area of the desktop, and select Arrange Icons by ⇨ Type and all icons will again be arranged. This holds true for arranging them by any criteria you select.

Done!

REVIEW

- The Desktop can be accessed by minimizing all programs or clicking the Show Desktop icon on the Quick Launch bar.
- Auto Arrange automatically arranges your icons into columns on the left side of your desktop.
- You can automatically sort icons on your desktop by a variety of properties.
- You can manually move icons on your desktop to custom locations.
- Windows XP offers two different views for the Windows Start menu.
- You can easily sort the programs on your Start menu.

QUIZ YOURSELF

1. How would you rearrange your icons so that Windows automatically lines them up? (See *Using Auto Arrange* section.)
2. How would you enable or disable Auto Arrange? (See *Using Auto Arrange* section.)
3. How many ways are there to view the Start menu in Windows XP? (See *Changing the View of Your Start Menu* section.)
4. How would you rearrange the program icons in your Start menu? (See *Sorting the programs in your Start menu* section.)

Advanced Desktop Customization

Session Checklist

✔ Understanding how to select a theme

✔ Changing your desktop background image

✔ Selecting a screen saver

✔ Adding and removing shortcuts to the desktop

✔ Using the Desktop Cleanup Wizard

✔ Understanding customization and administration rights

I n this session, you learn how to use Windows XP's display settings to further customize your Windows XP environment. By adjusting settings such as your desktop background, screen saver, and theme, you can personalize your computer in a variety of ways. This session also introduces you to the Desktop Cleanup Wizard and explains why an administrator might restrict access to customization options.

**30 Min.
To Go**

Changing the Display Options

Changing your display options is a relatively easy task in Windows XP and can provide you with a whole new way of looking at your computer. To make these changes, you can access the Display Properties dialog box in one of three ways:

1. Right-click any empty area of your desktop and select Properties from the context menu.

2. If you are in the Windows XP view, choose Start ⇨ Control Panel ⇨ Appearance and Themes, and click the Display icon.

In the Appearance and Themes dialog box, you will see four options in the Pick a Task area. Each of these options takes you to the Themes tab in the Display Properties dialog box. From there, you need to choose the appropriate tab to complete your task.

3. If you are in the Windows Classic view, choose Start ➪ Control Panel ➪ Display icon.

Picking a theme

The Display Properties dialog box, shown in Figure 9-1, consists of five different tabs. The Themes tab allows you to choose from one of Microsoft's preinstalled Windows XP themes, or even create a theme of your own. A _desktop theme_ determines the overall appearance of your desktop by providing a predefined set of icons, fonts, colors, mouse pointers, sounds, background pictures, screen savers, and other window elements. If you modify a predefined theme by changing any individual feature of the theme, it automatically becomes a custom theme.

For complete instructions of modifying all aspects of your desktop, see the Microsoft article at www.microsoft.com/windowsxp/pro/using/howto/customize/overview/default.asp. Make certain you read all eight pages to get the most out of desktop customization.

Figure 9-1 _The Display Properties dialog box allows you to customize the way Windows XP looks._

To choose a different Windows XP theme:

1. Open the Display Properties dialog box.
2. If it is not already selected, click the Themes tab.

3. From the Themes drop-down menu, select any theme.

4. Click OK to apply the changes and close the Display Properties dialog box.

 If you don't see a theme that you like, you can select the More Themes Online option and Windows XP will direct you to the Microsoft Plus! Themes site where you can choose from a wide variety of desktop themes.

Changing your background image

One of the simplest changes you can make to a computer to make it more "yours" is to change the desktop background image (sometimes referred to as your *wallpaper*). Because Windows XP supports a broad range of graphic formats, the image you use for your background image can be virtually any type of graphics file and can be located anywhere on your computer. If you don't have a particular picture or photo you would like to use, you can select from the many preinstalled images that come with Windows XP.

To change your desktop background image:

1. Open the Display Properties dialog box.

2. Click on the Desktop tab. As shown in Figure 9-2, you are provided with the option to select a new background image. If you have stored a digital photo or a favorite graphic on your computer, browse to its location.

Figure 9-2 *The Desktop tab allows you to change your desktop background image.*

 You can use any graphic with a .bmp, .gif, .jpg, .peg, .dib, or .png extension as a background.

3. In the Background: panel, choose a different background image.

4. Click OK to apply the changes and close the Display Properties dialog box.

Changing your screen saver

A *screen saver* is a mini-application that allows you to show one or more pictures on your computer monitor after a specified time has elapsed without any input from the mouse or keyboard. Windows XP comes with its own set of screen savers, or you can download screen savers (generally for about $20) from the Internet or purchase them from a computer store. Screen savers are a useful way to avoid monitor burn-in, a problem that occurs when a computer monitor sits unused for a length of time with the same image on the screen. Essentially, what happens is that whatever image was left on the screen eventually etches itself permanently into the screen, causing irreparable damage to the monitor. Screen savers, however, change the image on the screen constantly, which helps to avoid the possibility of burn-in.

To choose a screen saver and adjust its settings, follow these steps:

1. Open the Display Properties dialog box.

2. Click the Screen Saver tab. As shown in Figure 9-3, you are provided with the option to select a new screen saver.

Figure 9-3 *The Screen Saver tab allows you to select a screen saver and adjust its settings.*

3. In the Screen Saver drop-down menu, choose a screen saver.

4. In the Wait box, type the number of minutes you would like the computer to wait without input before displaying the screen saver.

Does Screen Burn-In Still Happen?

We have consistently been told that since the advent of VGA and higher monitors, screens will not burn in. In most cases, that is true. However, I have Dell 19" and Dell 17" monitors with Sony Trinitron tubes. These are not cheap monitors, but top of the line. The larger monitor was used by police to monitor security cameras, and the camera windows and boxes for the time and camera number burned into the screen after a long period of use without turning off the computer. The second monitor was in a college setting, and the log-in screen was left on for over 2 months during summer vacation. The monitor was ruined. So take a tip: Either use a standard screen saver, buy one you like, create a slide show of your own, or simply set the monitor to blank after a specified length of time. This is not nearly the problem it used to be, but better safe than sorry.

By checking the On resume, password protect box on the Screen Saver tab, you can have Windows XP lock your computer when the screen saver activates. The computer can then only be unlocked by using a password to unlock it.

5. Click OK to apply the changes and close the Display Properties dialog box.

Creating a personalized screen saver

You can create your own screen saver using pictures that have a .jpg, .tif, .wmf, .gif, .bmp, or .dib extension. Here are the steps to create your own personalized screen saver.

To complete the following exercise, you will need to have at least two graphics in the My Pictures folder, located within the My Documents folder. See Session 12 to learn more about these folders.

1. Double-click the My Documents icon. Double-click the My Pictures icon. Right-click any empty area of the right panel and choose New ⇨ Folder. An icon for the new folder appears, and is named New Folder. Type **Screen Saver Pix** and press Enter to change the folder name.
2. Move any graphics you want to use in your screen saver by dragging them from the My Pictures folder to the Screen Saver Pix folder.
3. Close the windows until you are back at the desktop.
4. Right-click an empty area of your desktop and click Properties. The Display Properties dialog box is shown.
5. Click the Screen Saver tab.
6. The Screen Saver panel is in the center-left panel. Click the down arrow next to the Screen Saver name and choose My Pictures Slideshow.
7. Click the Settings button. The My Pictures Screen Saver Options dialog box, shown in Figure 9-4, is displayed.

Figure 9-4 *The My Pictures Screen Saver Options dialog box allows you to adjust the configuration of your slide show.*

8. The pictures can be rotated at intervals ranging from 6 seconds to 3 minutes. The time increases as you slide the Changing bar to the right. You can also change the size of the picture to be between 20 and 100 percent of the screen. Make sure you use the Browse button to change the picture location to include the Screen Saver Pix folder. Change any settings you want and click OK to return to the Display Properties dialog box.

 Setting the picture screen size doesn't always work. If the picture is a small graphic, the graphic is presented at its original size, but moved around 90 percent (the default) of the screen.

9. To see what your screen saver looks like, click the Preview button. Do not move the mouse or touch the keyboard. When you are satisfied, move the mouse or press a key and you are returned to the Display Properties dialog box.

10. In the Wait box, use the scroll buttons to increase or decrease the default 30-minute value. This is the time that no input has been made to the computer before the screen saver starts. If you have a checkmark in the On resume, display Windows welcome screen, instead of the desktop being displayed, you see the Welcome screen. If your computer is password protected, you need to reenter the password before you can return to the desktop. Click OK to return to the desktop.

Adding and Removing Shortcuts

20 Min. To Go

In Session 8, you learned how to organize the shortcuts that are located on your desktop and arrange them in an order that makes them easier to use. But what if you need to add a shortcut to your desktop or remove one? Windows XP has made it very easy to accomplish both tasks.

Adding a shortcut to your desktop

Adding a shortcut to your desktop can be done in a variety of ways. The simplest, however, is to:

1. Right-click on an empty area of your desktop.
2. From the context menu, choose New ⇨ Shortcut.
3. In the Create Shortcut dialog box, shown in Figure 9-5, click the Browse button.

Figure 9-5 *You can add a shortcut to your desktop using the Create Shortcut dialog box.*

4. Using the Browse button, find the program or file you would like your shortcut to open and click OK.

Nearly all executable files have an extension of .exe. A few will have a .bat extension. If you can't see the extensions, from any open window, click Tools ⇨ Folder Options. Click the View tab in the Folder Options dialog box. Remove the checkmark from the Hide extensions for known file types check box. Click Apply in the bottom-right corner, and then click Apply to All Folders button at the top of the dialog box. Click OK to close the dialog box.

5. Click Next in the Create Shortcut dialog box.
6. In the Select a Title for the Program dialog box, type the name for your shortcut. This name is what will be displayed on your desktop.
7. Click the Finish button. You should now see a new shortcut on your desktop.

Suppose you are browsing the Web with Internet Explorer and you come across a site that is so useful, you want to have a shortcut to it on your desktop. To do this, simply browse to the site and choose File ⇨ Send ⇨ Shortcut to Desktop from the file menu and a shortcut to that site will automatically be placed on your desktop.

If a portion of the desktop is visible behind the browser window, you can drag the icon immediately to the left of the URL onto the desktop. This creates a shortcut to the page.

Also, if a filename is displayed in any window, and you want to create a shortcut on your desktop, right-click the filename, and from the context menu, choose Send To ⇨ Desktop (as a shortcut).

Removing a shortcut from your desktop

Removing a shortcut from your desktop is much easier than creating one. To remove a shortcut from your desktop:

1. Right-click on the application icon that you wish to remove.
2. From the context menu, choose Delete.
3. In the Confirm Shortcut Delete dialog box, shown in Figure 9-6, click the Delete Shortcut button.

Figure 9-6   *The Confirm Shortcut Delete dialog box reminds you that deleting the application shortcut does not delete the program itself.*

If you are deleting a file shortcut, rather than an application shortcut, you will see the warning box shown in Figure 9-7.

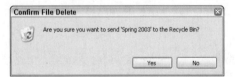

Figure 9-7   *The Confirm File Delete dialog box appears as if the data file is going to be sent to the Recycle Bin. Be assured that only the shortcut will be deleted. The original file is left intact.*

Using the Desktop Cleanup Wizard

**10 Min.
To Go**

Cleaning up old or unused icons from your desktop should be part of your regular computer maintenance. To assist you in performing this task, Microsoft has included the Desktop

Cleanup Wizard in both the Professional and Home editions of Windows XP. Earlier versions of Windows do not include this tool. To use the Desktop Cleanup Wizard:

1. Right-click any empty spot on your desktop and choose Properties from the context menu.

2. Click the Desktop tab and click the Customize Desktop button.

3. In the Desktop Items dialog box, click the Clean Up Desktop Now button. The Desktop Cleanup Wizard dialog box opens. Click Next.

4. In the dialog box shown in Figure 9-8, confirm that the icons the wizard has selected to remove from your desktop are the ones you want to have removed. Uncheck the box next to any shortcuts that you wish to remain on your desktop. Click Next.

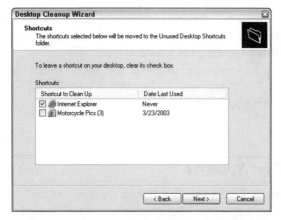

Figure 9-8   *Choose which programs you want the wizard to remove from your desktop.*

5. Click Finish to complete the process and you will notice that the unused shortcuts have now been placed in a folder on your desktop named Unused Desktop Shortcuts. If you are sure you will no longer need the deleted shortcuts, delete them from this folder. You can easily recreate a shortcut using the steps described above.

Why Won't My Administrator Let Me Customize?

If you work in a corporate environment, it's possible that you are not able to customize your desktop background image or your screen saver. Instead, when you attempt to access the Display Properties dialog box, you receive a notice that your administrator has disabled access to this function. Because the Display Properties dialog box also provides access to elements that are vital to the functionality of your computer such as your video adapter settings and drivers, some network administrators choose to lock the computer down completely rather than risk the performance of the computer in order to allow users to change their wallpaper.

Although network administrators everywhere are probably groaning right now, here is one way that you can adjust your computer's desktop background image to something a little more personal without having to ever access the Display Properties dialog box:

1. Open Internet Explorer.
2. From the menu bar, choose File ⇨ Open and browse to the graphic file you would like to set as your desktop background. Click the OK button and the graphic should open in Internet Explorer.
3. Right-click on the graphic and choose Set as Background from the context menu. The picture should now be set as your desktop background image.

Done!

REVIEW

- You can easily change your theme, desktop background image, and screen saver from within the Display Properties dialog box.
- You can add a shortcut to your desktop by using the Create Shortcut Wizard.
- Removing a desktop shortcut is easy, but remember that this does not uninstall the program.
- The Desktop Cleanup Wizard can assist you in removing unused icons from your desktop.

QUIZ YOURSELF

1. How would you change your Windows XP theme? (See *Picking a theme* section.)
2. How would you change your background image? (See *Changing your background image* section.)
3. Can you delete a program from your machine by deleting its desktop icon? (See *Removing a shortcut from your desktop* section.)
4. What tool is used to help you periodically clean up unused icons from your desktop? (See *Using the Desktop Cleanup Wizard* section.)

File and Folder Basics

Session Checklist

✔ Understanding how to create a new folder

✔ Creating folders within folders

✔ Finding the path to a folder

✔ Moving, copying, and deleting folders

✔ Renaming folders

For anyone experienced with Windows 95 or later, a vast majority of this session should be very familiar to you. You might want to skim through it, to see if there are any new tips you might pick up. Once you have skimmed this session, moving directly to Session 11 will save you time and frustration with rehashing familiar material.

One of the most common ways to organize information is using a filing cabinet. Look around your home or work office and you're bound to find at least one filing cabinet. Take a moment and think about the way filing cabinets are used to categorize information. You start with the drawer, which often allows you to break the information down by subject or by alphabetical indicator. Inside that drawer are folders that contain individual files. A single folder might contain an individual file or it could hold hundreds of files. This system of organization, however, allows you to find a specific file much more easily than if it were just stuffed in a drawer with thousands of other files.

Your computer is organized in a manner very similar to a filing cabinet. Each physical drive (that is, a hard drive, floppy drive, Zip drive, and so on) represents a filing cabinet drawer. That drive is then further divided into directories, which are now commonly referred to as folders. Inside each of these directories are files that operate the software applications on your computer or simply store data. Just as the organization of a filing cabinet allows you to locate information quickly, the structure of your computer's drives ensures that your computer can find the necessary information and operate at peak performance.

In this session, you'll begin to understand your computer's file structure and manipulate it by creating, moving, copying, and deleting folders located on your hard drive. In addition, you learn to identify the location of a folder and rename it.

The term *directory* was more common when computers were using operating systems that relied upon the command prompt. As graphical operating systems, like Windows, became more commonplace, the term folder gradually replaced directory. Don't get confused, however, if you hear someone ask you to look in a certain directory — it's the same as a folder.

Creating New Folders

30 Min. To Go

When you double-click the My Computer icon on your desktop, you are presented with a list of available drives and commonly used folders that are present on your computer. As shown in Figure 10-1, these resources might include your personal documents, hard disks, removable storage, and even network drives.

If the My Computer icon doesn't show on your desktop, refer to the *Populating the desktop with common icons* section of Session 3.

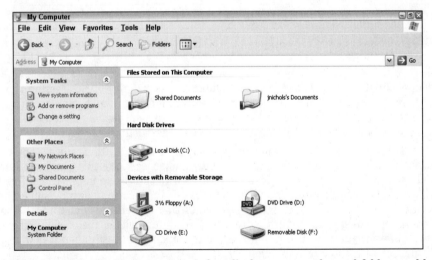

Figure 10-1 *The My Computer window displays commonly used folders and hardware resources available on your computer.*

Just as you might add a new folder to your filing cabinet drawer, you can easily create a new folder on your computer's hard drive where you can store data. To create a new folder on your local hard drive, follow these steps:

1. Double-click the My Computer icon on your desktop.

2. In the My Computer window, double-click the C: drive. As shown in Figure 10-2, the folders and files located on your C: drive are displayed.

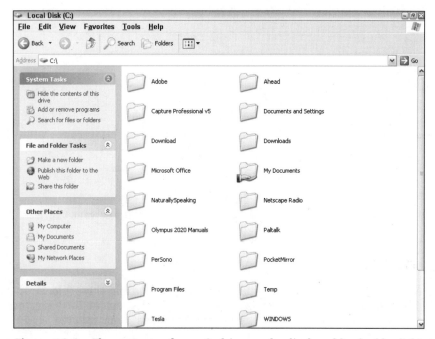

Figure 10-2 *The contents of your C: drive can be displayed by double-clicking the Local Disk (C:) icon.*

3. With the contents of your C: drive displayed, click File ➪ New ➪ Folder from the menu bar. As shown in Figure 10-3, a new folder is created.

4. Type the name **Test Folder** to give the new folder a name.

To avoid confusion, Windows XP does not allow duplicate filenames. If, for some reason, you already have a folder named Test Folder, Windows would display an error and ask you to provide a unique name.

5. Close the My Computer window for now.

Windows XP provides a variety of ways for you to display the contents of your folders, called *views*. To learn more about folder views, refer to Session 12.

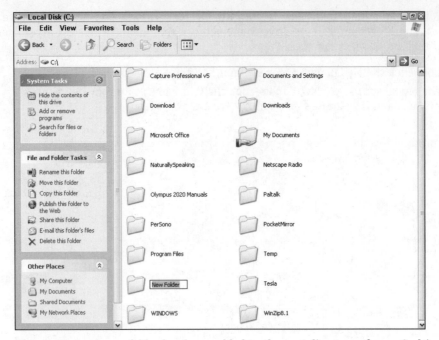

Figure 10-3   *A new folder has been added to the root directory of your C: drive.*

Creating Folders within Folders

Once you have created top-level folders, you can create folders within these folders. These folders are often referred to as subfolders. By creating subfolders, you can further categorize your data by subject, month, name, or just about any other identifying criteria.

To create a subfolder within your Test Folder, follow these steps:

1. Double-click the My Computer icon on your desktop.
2. In the My Computer window, double-click the C: drive and then double-click the Test Folder icon.
3. Click File ⇨ New ⇨ Folder from the menu bar and name the new folder **January**.

> You can also create a new folder by right-clicking any empty space in the window (not a folder or file icon) and choosing New ⇨ Folder from the context menu.

4. Right-click any empty space in the window and choose New ⇨ Folder from the context menu. Name the new folder **February**. As shown in Figure 10-4, you now have two subfolders within your Test Folder.

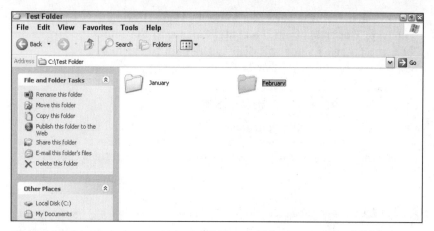

Figure 10-4 *There are now two subfolders within your top-level folder.*

Finding the Path to a Folder

Once you have created a system of folders and subfolders to organize your data, it's likely that you'll want to remember how to access those subfolders again. The location of a sub-folder located on your hard drive is often referred to as its *path*. For instance, the January folder you created in the last section has a path of C:\Test Folder\January. This means that it is located on your computer's C: drive in the folder named Test Folder. A folder's path can easily be determined by navigating to the folder and looking at the Address bar in the Window. For instance, to determine the path of the February folder you recently created, follow these steps:

1. Double-click the My Computer icon on your desktop.

2. In the My Computer window, double-click the C: drive and then double-click the Test Folder icon.

3. Double-click the February folder icon. As shown in Figure 10-5, the path to this folder is C:\Test Folder\February.

Folder path

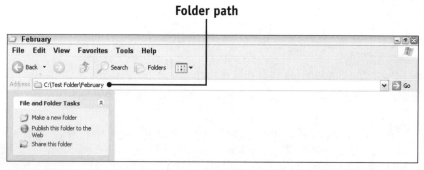

Figure 10-5 *You can easily determine the path to a folder by looking in the address bar.*

You can also find the path to a folder by right-clicking on the folder and choosing Properties from the context menu. In the Folder Properties dialog box, the Location value will display the path to the folder.

Moving, Copying, and Deleting Folders

Once you have created and organized your folders and subfolders, you may find that you need to move, copy, or even delete a folder. Luckily, Windows XP makes it extremely easy for you to manage your folders, and with the click of a mouse you can relocate or further categorize your data.

Moving a folder to a new location

In the previous sections, you created January and February folders to hold data for those months. But what if you have data for January 2002 and January 2003? The ideal way to organize this data would be to create separate folders for both 2002 and 2003, with each containing a January and February subfolder. To accomplish this, follow these steps:

1. Open the Test Folder.
2. Create a new folder by choosing File ⇨ New ⇨ Folder from the menu bar and name it **2002**.
3. Right-click the January folder and choose Cut from the context menu.
4. Right-click the 2002 folder and choose Paste from the context menu. As shown in Figure 10-6, the January folder is no longer visible because it is located within the 2002 folder.
5. Open the 2002 folder to see the January folder. To return to the 2002 folder, click the Up arrow button on the toolbar.

Figure 10-6   *The January folder is now a subfolder of the 2002 folder.*

6. Repeat steps 3 and 4 to move the February folder into the 2002 folder.

 You can also relocate a folder by left-clicking its icon and dragging the icon onto another folder. This method is referred to as drag-and-drop.

If you want to select multiple folders (or files), click the first one, hold down the Ctrl key and click any other folders (or files) you want to select. Also a quick way to select all folders (or files) on the screen is to press Ctrl + A.

Copying a folder

10 Min. To Go

Now that you have created the 2002 folder with the appropriate January and February sub-folders, you need to create an identical folder for 2003. Because Windows XP has an easy-to-use copy feature, you can accomplish this task with a couple of clicks of your mouse.

When you copy a folder within Windows XP, the entire structure of the folder (including all subfolders and files) is included. For this reason, be careful about what folders you copy because you don't want to end up storing duplicate copies of the same data all over your hard drive.

To create an identical folder:

1. Navigate to the Test Folder and open it. (Remember the Up arrow button if you need to move to a higher-level folder.) Right-click the 2002 folder and choose Copy from the context menu.

2. Right-click any white space in the window and choose Paste from the context menu. As shown in Figure 10-7, Windows XP places a copy of the folder in the directory named Copy of 2002.

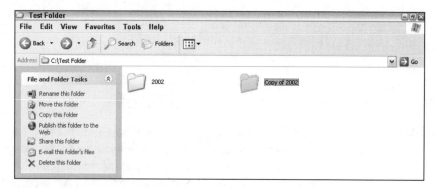

Figure 10-7   *A duplicate folder has been created.*

3. Double-click the Copy of 2002 folder and notice that it contains the January and February subfolders just as the original 2002 folder does.

Renaming a Folder

Now that you have two folders with the appropriate subfolders, you need to rename the copied folder to appropriately reflect the 2003 data. To rename the folder:

1. Navigate to the Test Folder and open it.
2. Right-click the Copy of 2002 folder and choose Rename from the context menu. The filename is highlighted, and you can now type a different name. Type **2003** for the new folder name. The result is shown in Figure 10-8.

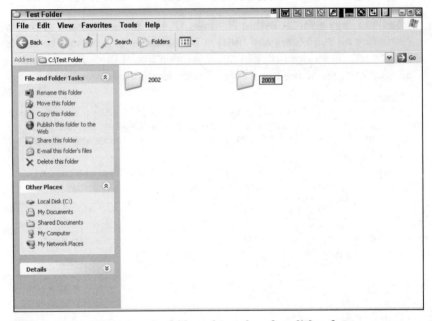

Figure 10-8   *Renaming the folder takes only a few clicks of your mouse.*

You can also rename a folder by highlighting the folder and choosing File ⇨ Rename from the menu bar. An additional way to rename the folder would be to single-click twice on the folder's name. While a standard double-click opens the folder, two single clicks with a brief pause in between highlights the folder name and allows you to rename it.

Deleting a folder

Now that you have a duplicate folder, suppose that there is no information to be stored in the January folder for 2003. Rather than just keeping the folder, you could easily delete it. To delete the January folder, follow these steps:

1. Navigate to the 2003 folder and right-click the January folder.

2. Click Delete from the context menu and click OK to confirm that you want to move the folder to the Recycle Bin. As shown in Figure 10-9, the only subfolder that now remains is the February folder.

Figure 10-9 *Once the January folder is deleted, the only one that remains is the February folder.*

You can also delete a folder by selecting the folder and choosing File ⇨ Delete from the menu bar. You can also select the folder and press the Delete key.

Done!

REVIEW

- You can create new folders and subfolders by navigating to a folder or disk drive and choosing File ⇨ New ⇨ Folder.
- The path of a folder designates its location on a hard drive, floppy disk, or network drive.
- You can determine the path to a folder by navigating to the folder and looking in the address bar.
- Once folders have been created, you can copy, paste, rename, and delete them using the File menu.
- A folder can be renamed in a variety of ways.

QUIZ YOURSELF

1. How would you create a new folder on your local hard disk? (See *Creating New Folders* section.)
2. How would you determine the path to a folder? (See *Finding the Path to a Folder* section.)
3. How would you move a folder from one location to another? (See *Moving a folder to a new location* section.)
4. Is there more than one way to rename a folder? How would you go about it? (See *Renaming a Folder* section.)

PART

II

Saturday Morning
Part Review

1. What does the Windows XP Control Panel help you manage?
2. Which Control Panel category would you use to assist in troubleshooting problems with common hardware peripherals?
3. To connect your computer to a home network or Local Area Network, what piece of hardware must you first have installed in your computer?
4. Name two built-in accessories that Windows XP provides for physically impaired users.
5. If you want to clean up your hard drive, back up valuable data, and run the Windows Defragmenter to arrange the data on your hard drive in a manner that speeds up your computer, which link would you choose in the Categories view of the Control Panel?
6. How do you display the list of installed Windows XP accessories?
7. What are the three ways of inputting data into the Calculator accessory?
8. If you need to add paragraph or character formatting, such as changing the font or adjusting the alignment of paragraphs, would you use Notepad or WordPad?
9. To insert an object, such as a graphic, into WordPad, what choices would you make from the menu?
10. What are two reasons you might use Windows Explorer?
11. What are the four categories (subfolders) of accessories in a standard Windows XP installation?
12. What Web site address would be a good place to find out more about the accessibility accessories available in Windows XP?
13. Which accessory category would you use to set up Remote Desktop?
14. To change the volume control for your audio accessories, which accessory category would you use?
15. To defragment your disk (put all of the files in order), which accessory category would you use?

16. What are the two ways to see all of your desktop?

17. Why might you want to rearrange your desktop?

18. If you want to arrange your desktop into groupings of similar types of files, what command would you use?

19. How can you manually rearrange your desktop icons?

20. When you install a new program, where does Windows XP generally place the shortcut icon on the Start menu?

21. What does a desktop theme do?

22. What built-in feature of Windows XP can help reduce the chance of monitor burn-in?

23. How can you add a password to your screensaver?

24. Nearly all executable files have what three-letter extension?

25. If you are browsing the Internet and find a site so useful you want to add a short-cut icon to your desktop, how would you do so?

26. In Windows, we often hear the term *folder*. In earlier operating systems, what were folders called?

27. What are the two ways you can determine the path to a particular folder?

28. What happens if you try to name a folder or file the same name as an existing folder or file?

29. You can move a folder from one folder to another by clicking the folder to be moved and dragging the icon to the new folder where it is to be located. What is this movement called?

30. What happens to subfolders when you copy a folder from one place to another?

PART

III

Saturday Afternoon

Advanced File and Folder Operations

Session Checklist

✔ Encrypting a file or folder

✔ Moving files and folders to other computers

✔ Copying your files and folders to other media

✔ Changing the attributes of a file or folder

✔ Sharing a folder

Now that you understand the basics of creating folders and relocating them, I'll move on to some advanced folder functionality included in Windows XP. Using these features, you can perform tasks such as protecting your data by encrypting it, setting it as read-only, or even hiding the file or folder from other users. In addition, this session shows you how to move data from one computer to another using removable media.

**30 Min.
To Go**

Encrypting Files and Folders

Imagine a situation where your laptop or desktop computer has been stolen and your hard disk contained important personal or corporate information. If you took advantage of Windows XP's security feature that allows you to encrypt your data, you won't have to worry about the thief gaining access to it. The new Encrypting File System (EFS) encrypts each individual file and uses a file encryption key to prevent unauthorized access to the data. Unlike other types of encryption, EFS doesn't require a specific password for you to open encrypted files. If you are the user who created the file, your "credentials" assigned when you log on to the computer show that you own that file. Also, unlike other methods of encryption, you cannot assign other users the ability to open that file.

EFS doesn't actually encrypt *folders*. Rather, an attribute is set on the folder telling it that all files placed in that folder are to be encrypted using EFS. If the folder itself were encrypted, you couldn't open it and see the contents (unless you personally had created the folder). Remember, only the files themselves are actually encrypted, not the folders.

Keep in mind, however, that your computer must be using the NTFS file system in order to use this feature. If your computer uses the FAT32 file system, you need to convert your disk drive to NTFS before encrypting the data.

Windows XP uses one of two ways to store the files and folder on your computer, depending on how you or the manufacturer first set it up. The first file system, called FAT32, uses a *file allocation table* (FAT) to keep track of all the pieces of data stored on your hard drive. When your computer wants to access a file, it checks the file allocation table to determine the location of the file, much in the same way you might use a phone book to look up a friend's address. The downside to the FAT32 file system comes from the fact that your computer breaks up data files and places the pieces in different locations on your hard drive. When it needs to access the data, not only does the computer need to look up the location of all of the pieces, it has to gather and reassemble them.

The second file system, called *New Technology File System* (NTFS), doesn't fragment files by spreading them out across the hard drive nearly as much as the FAT system does. Instead, NTFS breaks the data up and stores it in contiguous sectors, making the data much easier (and quicker) for the computer to locate and reassemble. An additional benefit of running the NTFS file system comes from the fact that you can specify file and folder permissions that determine which users are able to access particular data.

Checking your computer's file system type

Before you can use the encryption features in Windows XP, you first have to determine whether your computer is running the NTFS file system. To do this, follow these steps:

1. Double-click the My Computer icon on your desktop.

2. In the My Computer window, right-click the C: drive and choose Properties from the context menu. As shown in Figure 11-1, you can determine your drive's file system type by looking at the File system entry. In the Professional version of Windows XP, there will be a fifth tab, titled Quota. This is turned off by default, but it can be used to assign a maximum amount of drive space to nonadministrative accounts.

If you determine that your computer's file system is FAT32 and you want to use encryption, you can convert your drive to NTFS by choosing Start ⇨ All Programs ⇨ Accessories ⇨ Command Prompt. At the command prompt, type convert [drive letter] : /fs:ntfs. **For instance, if you wanted to convert your C: drive, you would type** convert c: /fs:ntfs.

File system type

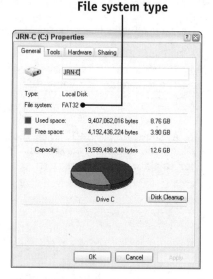

Figure 11-1 *The Local Disk box allows you to determine your file system type.*

You can convert a drive from FAT32 to NTFS without loss of data. However, once converted, it cannot be returned without reformatting the drive and requiring you to back up your data in order to prevent loss. Also, all applications will have to be reinstalled.

Additional Disk Management

Although we have talked about some basic disk management techniques, there is another feature you might want to take a brief look at: the Computer Management console. You can see it by clicking Start ⇨ Control Panel ⇨ Performance and Maintenance ⇨ Administrative Tools ⇨ Computer Management. In the left pane, under Storage, click Disk Management. In the right pane, you see each of your drives. You can right-click any of the drive letters and choose Properties from the context menu. This also brings up the Properties dialog box for each disk. From here, you can also change the drive letter assigned to each drive. This dialog box is actually a Microsoft Management Console (MMC) and is used consistently to administer Windows XP. Throughout the sessions I'll be referring to sample MMCs, but Session 26 takes a deeper look into monitoring a system using an MMC.

Encrypting a folder

Once you have the appropriate file system (NTFS), encrypting a folder is a very easy task. To encrypt a folder, follow these steps:

1. From the My Computer window, open the C: drive. With the contents of the C: drive visible, choose File ⇨ New ⇨ Folder and name the new folder My Encrypted Data.

2. Right-click the new folder and choose Properties from the context menu.

3. In the folder properties, click the Advanced button. As shown in Figure 11-2, the bottom panel of the Advanced Properties dialog box allows you to control encryption. Click the Encrypt contents to secure data option box to place a checkmark in it.

Figure 11-2 *The Advanced Attributes dialog box allows you to enable encryption.*

4. Click OK in the Advanced Attributes dialog box.

That's all there is to encrypting a folder. Any files or subfolders that were located in that folder are now encrypted and any files or subfolders that are added in the future will be encrypted as well.

Moving Files and Folders to Other Computers

**20 Min.
To Go**

Now that you have your files and folders organized on your computer, it's time to figure out how to share data with other users. Whether it's a company report, hardware driver file, or any other type of data, it's likely that at some time you will need to move data from your computer to a different computer.

The instructions in the following sections assume that the computers are *not* networked.

Copying data to other media

One of the most common ways to move data from one computer to another is called a *sneaker-net*. A sneaker-net works by you copying your data files to a floppy disk or CD-ROM and walking (in your sneakers) to the other computer where you want the data located. Whereas floppy disks have traditionally been the preferred method of transferring data via a sneaker-net, the need for larger capacity media has fueled the development of alternative media such as Zip disks, Jaz disks, and CD-ROM.

Copying data to a removable disk

Nearly every computer on the market comes equipped with a floppy disk drive (although that is changing as manufacturers look for ways to save money), which makes transferring small amounts of data between computers relatively easy. To transfer a folder using a floppy disk, follow these instructions:

1. Insert a floppy disk into your floppy drive and double-click the My Computer icon on your desktop.
2. In the My Computer window, double-click the C: drive.
3. Right-click the My Encrypted Data folder and choose Copy from the context menu.
4. Click the Back button on the menu bar and right-click the A: drive (floppy disk).
5. From the context menu choose Paste. When the copy process is complete, double-click the A: drive and, as shown in Figure 11-3, the folder has been copied to your local floppy disk.

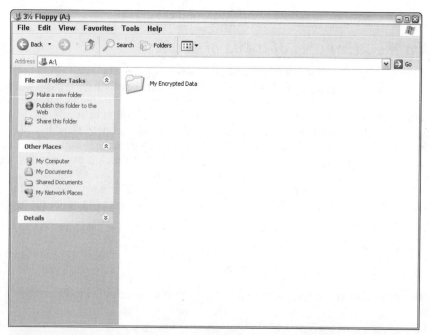

Figure 11-3   *The folder has been successfully copied to the floppy disk.*

A typical high-density floppy disk is limited in capacity to 1.44 MB of data. Files that are larger than 1.44 MB will need to be either compressed to fit on a floppy or copied to media with a larger capacity such as a Zip drive or CD-ROM.

As file sizes continue to grow, removable data drives such as Zip and Jaz drives are becoming more and more popular among computer users. Similar in functionality to a floppy disk, a Zip disk is capable of holding 250 MB and a Jaz drive has a capacity of 2 GB, huge in comparison to the paltry 1.44 MB of a floppy disk. The only downside of placing data on a removable disk is you must be sure that the computer to which you want to transfer the data has the same type of removable drive as well. To transfer a folder using a Zip disk or Jaz cartridge, follow the steps for copying data to a floppy disk, but choose the drive letter for the desired removable drive.

Copying data to a CD-ROM

Transferring data to a blank CD-ROM is a little more difficult than just copying and pasting or dragging and dropping onto a floppy or Zip disk. Before data can be written to a CD-ROM, the media has to be formatted using the software that came with your CD-ROM drive. Once formatted, data can usually be transferred in a manner very similar to that of a floppy. The final step in transferring data to a CD-ROM entails "burning" the CD, where the data is transferred onto the CD and the burning session is closed. Once the data is burned, the CD is no longer able to be written to again.

Because the method of burning a CD varies among applications and CD recording drives, you need to consult your documentation on the specific steps for transferring data via a CD-ROM.

Modifying the Attributes of a File or Folder

10 Min.
To Go

Once you have your files and folders organized and understand how to move them between computers, you will probably want to take a look at the attributes that determine when a file or folder is visible and when another person can make changes to them. The two basic attributes that you should be familiar with are the *hidden* and *read-only* attributes. Designating a file or folder as hidden means that users with the standard Windows XP settings will not be able to view the files, even though they exist on the computer. The benefit to this is keeping users from editing or deleting files that they shouldn't be tinkering with. Another way to keep users from editing important files is to mark them as read-only. Doing so allows other users to open the file and view its contents, but in order to make changes, the user has to save the file with a different filename, thus leaving the original file intact.

Making a folder read-only

To set a folder as read-only, follow these steps:

1. Right-click the My Encrypted Data folder and choose Properties from the context menu.
2. In the Properties dialog box, check the Read-only box as shown in Figure 11-4.

Figure 11-4 *Checking the Read-only attribute keeps others from editing any files in the folder.*

3. Click OK to close the dialog box and apply the change.

If the option box already has a check in it and is grayed out, it means that while the entire folder is not read-only, one or more files or subfolders located within it are set as read-only. To change the entire folder to read-only, click the option box once to clear the checkmark and click it again to place a check in the box.

Making a folder hidden

To set a folder as hidden, follow the same steps outlined for making a folder read-only. Instead of placing a checkmark in the Read-only option box, place it in the Hidden option box.

Done!

REVIEW

- If you are using the NTFS file system, you can encrypt your data so that it is inaccessible by other users.
- If you are currently using the FAT32 file system, you can convert your file system to NTFS in order to take advantage of heightened security features.
- Using Windows XP, you can share your data via a variety of methods, including floppy disks, Zip or Jaz cartridges, and CD-ROM.
- You can change the attributes of a file or folder and set it as hidden or read-only.

QUIZ YOURSELF

1. In order to encrypt a file or folder, what file system must you be using? (See *Encrypting Files and Folders* section.)

2. What command converts a FAT32 drive to the NTFS file system? (See *Checking your computer's file system type* section.)

3. What is a sneaker-net? (See *Moving Files and Folders to Other Computers* section.)

4. Why would you want to make a folder read-only? (See *Modifying the Attributes of a File or Folder* section.)

5. Name two types of removable media. (See *Copying data to a removable disk* section.)

The My Documents Folder and Folder Views

Session Checklist

✔ Locating the My Documents folder

✔ Understanding the default subfolders

✔ Explaining folder views

Saving and organizing documents is an important element of operating your computer. A good habit to develop is to understand where your documents are being saved and to organize them by topic so that you can easily find the information at a later date. To help you in this endeavor, Windows XP creates a My Documents folder that is linked with your user account to serve as a starting point for organizing your documents.

In this session, you learn how to locate your My Documents folder, identify the default subfolders, and organize the content within the folder. In addition, you learn about the pros and cons of moving the My Documents folder from its original location.

Locating the My Documents Folder

**30 Min.
To Go**

In previous versions of Windows, the My Documents folder was very easy to locate. By default, it had a path of C:\My Documents. The problem with this was that (unless specifically set up otherwise) the same My Documents folder was used for all user accounts. This meant that coworkers who shared the same computer often shared the same My Documents folder. This doesn't sound like much of a problem until one worker accidentally deletes the important presentation created by another worker.

Windows XP, however, now sets up a unique My Documents folder for each user account. While this secures and separates the user data, it also makes it a little more difficult to find the path to the My Documents folder. Rest assured, Windows XP still places a shortcut to your My Documents folder on the desktop, so unless you delete it you can always access the folder by clicking the desktop shortcut.

If the My Documents icon is not on the desktop, right-click any empty area of the desktop, click Properties, click the Desktop tab, click Customize Desktop, put a checkmark in the My Documents option box, and click OK twice to return to the desktop.

The easiest way for you to find the path to your My Documents folder is to follow these steps:

1. Double-click the My Computer icon on your desktop.
2. In the My Computer window, double-click the C: drive.
3. In the C: drive window, double-click the Documents and Settings folder.
4. In the Documents and Settings folder, find your username and double-click the folder associated with it.
5. In your user folder, double-click the My Documents folder. If you look in the address bar, the path to your My Documents folder should be something like C:\Documents and Settings*yourusername*\My Documents.

If you try to move the My Documents folder to a different location, you may experience problems. Some applications such as those in the Microsoft Office suite rely on the default location of your My Documents folder in order to properly save documents. If you move the folder, you will experience errors as these applications try to perform tasks such as autosaves.

If you feel that you must relocate your My Documents folder, it is a good idea to refer to each of those applications and adjust the path to your My Documents folder so that the applications can function properly.

Understanding the My Documents Subfolders

**20 Min.
To Go**

Microsoft has already taken a few steps to help you organize the content of your My Documents folder by creating some default subfolders. You can either use these folders to further organize your files or delete them (or rename them) and create new folders of your own.

My Pictures

The My Pictures folder, shown in Figure 12-1, is a good place to store images downloaded from the Web, scanned in from your scanner, or captured using your digital camera.

if you have a CD-RW drive, an additional item shows up at the top on the left underneath Print pictures, called Copy all items to CD. As long as you have a formatted CD in the drive, this copies the entire folder to your CD.

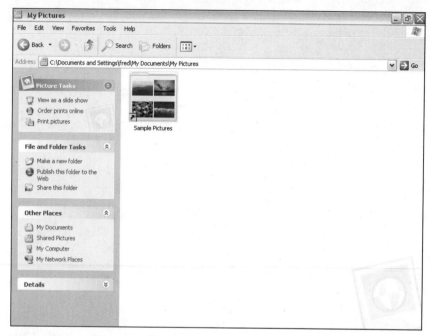

Figure 12-1   *The My Pictures folder is a great place to store your images.*

By default, the folder view displays files and folders in the thumbnail view (see the *Thumbnails* section later in this session), which means that you see a small version of the image rather than just the file icon and the name. Windows XP also includes a sample image and sample folder to help you see how valuable the thumbnail view can be when working with images.

 Because the My Pictures folder is set to the thumbnail view by default, it may take a little while to open and display all the files. This is because prior to displaying the files, Windows has to process each graphic or image and create a thumbnail of it. This extra step may slow down the process slightly, but the value in being able to see the images is well worth the extra wait.

My Music

The My Music folder, shown in Figure 12-2, can be used to store audio files such as MP3s, MIDI, and WAV files. It can actually be used to store any file type, but its real purpose is to organize your music files.

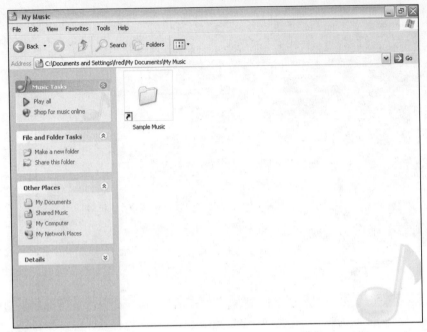

Figure 12-2 *Store audio files such as MP3s in your My Music folder.*

Like the My Pictures folder, the My Music folder contains sample files that demonstrate Windows XP's multimedia capabilities. If you are a collector of digital music, keep a careful eye on your My Music folder as audio files are often very large in size and this folder can eat up hard drive space quickly.

 As you install other Microsoft products, additional folders will be added to your My Documents folder. For instance, if you install FrontPage 2002, a folder called My Webs is added to your My Documents folder. Other applications might install folders such as My Videos, My Downloads, and so on.

Choosing a Folder's View

**10 Min.
To Go**

Windows XP provides a variety of ways for you to display the contents of your folders. By using the views effectively, you can personalize your new folders and help yourself identify files without having to open them and view the contents. In addition, using some of the views, you can view valuable information such as when the file was created and when it was last modified.

To change a folder's view, follow these steps:

1. Click the Views button drop-down menu and choose from one of the five options

   or

2. On the Menu bar, click View and choose from one of the five View options (these are found in the second set of options).

Thumbnails

For folders that contain primarily graphics, the Thumbnails view provides a quick and easy way for you to see your images without having to open each one in a graphic editor. The downside to viewing images in the Thumbnails view comes from the fact that it takes longer for this view to load than any other view and because the thumbnails have to be large enough to see, fewer are displayed on the screen, requiring you to scroll down to see all the files in the folder. Figure 12-3 shows a folder set to display files in the Thumbnails view.

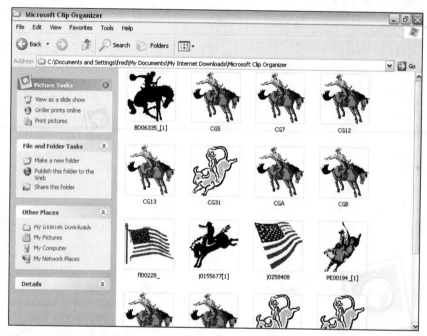

Figure 12-3 *A folder that contains graphics is best viewed using the Thumbnails view.*

Tiles

If you like the larger icons but don't need to see graphics of thumbnails, the Tiles view allows you to maintain the larger look and view the document type and size. The Tiles view also loads faster than the Thumbnails view because the generic application icons are displayed. As with the Thumbnails view, the downside is that due to the larger icon size, fewer of the files and folders are displayed on the screen, requiring you to scroll to view all your files. Figure 12-4 shows a folder in the Tiles view.

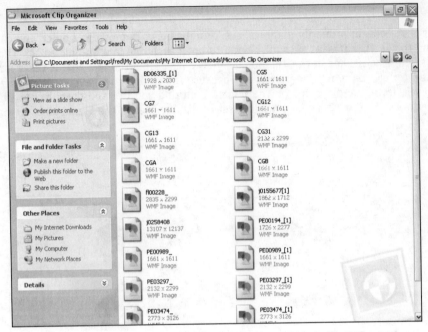

Figure 12-4 *The Tiles view displays large icons and basic file information.*

Icons

If you want to keep the standard application icons, but want to fit more on the page, the Icons view is probably your style. Because no application type or file size is displayed, the Icons view is capable of displaying substantially more icons on the screen than the Tiles view. Without this information, however, it is a bit more difficult to identify exactly what the contents of the file are without opening it. Figure 12-5 shows a folder in the Icons view.

List

The List view displays the largest number of icons on the screen at any time. If you have a folder that contains a large number of files, the List view is often the easiest to scroll through in order to find your file. Similar to the Icons view, however, no file data is displayed, so you have to identify the file from its name. Figure 12-6 displays a folder in List view.

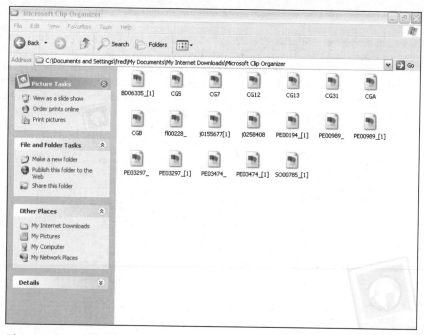

Figure 12-5 *The Icons view displays only the application or file icon and its name.*

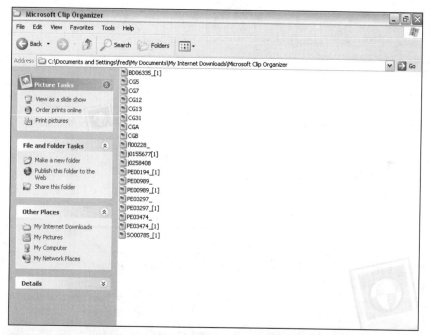

Figure 12-6 *The List view displays only the application or file icon and the associated name.*

Details

The final way of viewing your folder is the Details view. Using the Details view, you can see information such as the filename, file size, application type, and date the file was last modified. This view provides an easy way to sort your files by clicking on the column title. For instance, if you want to see all files that have been modified most recently, just click the Date Modified title and the files are sorted according to the date they were last modified. The files can be sorted by any of the visible column names. Figure 12-7 shows a folder sorted alphabetically by name in the Details view.

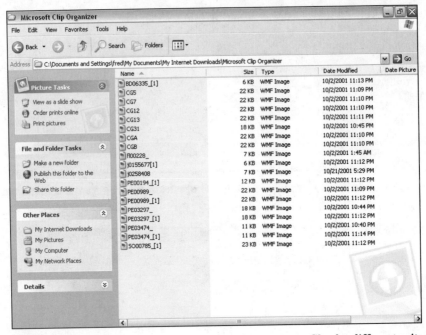

Figure 12-7   *Using the Details view, you can sort your files by different criteria.*

 To sort the file in the reverse order from which they are currently sorted, simply click the column heading a second time.

Done!

REVIEW

- The default path to your My Documents file is C:\Documents and Settings\ *yourusername*\My Documents.

- If you move your My Documents folder, you run the risk of interrupting the way your applications function.

- The typical installation of Windows XP includes a My Documents folder for each user account and two subfolders — My Pictures and My Music.

- Just like any other folder, you can easily create subfolders within your My Documents folder to further organize your documents.
- There are five views from which you can view folder information: Thumbnails, Tiles, Icons, List, and Details.

QUIZ YOURSELF

1. How would you navigate to your My Documents folder? (See *Locating the My Documents Folder* section.)

2. What two subfolders are automatically included in each My Documents folder? (See *Understanding the My Documents Subfolders* section.)

3. Which folder view allows you to view small images associated with each file? (See *Choosing a Folder's View* section.)

4. Which folder view shows you the most files on the screen at one time? (See *Choosing a Folder's View* section.)

Printing with Windows XP

Session Checklist

✔ Installing or removing a local printer

✔ Setting your printer preferences

✔ Selecting a default printer

✔ Printing a Windows XP printer test page

I f you own a computer, it's likely that you also own a printer. Although printers are generally not that difficult to set up and configure, connecting the cable from the computer to the printer usually isn't quite enough to get you up and running. In this session, you learn to properly add and configure the printer from within Windows XP and, if necessary, remove the printer from your system.

In addition, this session shows you how to set up your printer preferences, assign a default printer, and print a test page for troubleshooting purposes.

Installing a Local Printer

30 Min. To Go

In most cases installing a printer using Windows XP is a relatively easy process. Windows XP has an easy-to-use Printer Installation Wizard that walks you through the entire process. To activate the Wizard and install a printer follow these steps:

1. From the Start Menu, choose Start ⇨ Printers and Faxes.
2. In the Printers and Faxes window, shown in Figure 13-1, double-click the Add a Printer icon to start the Add Printer Wizard.

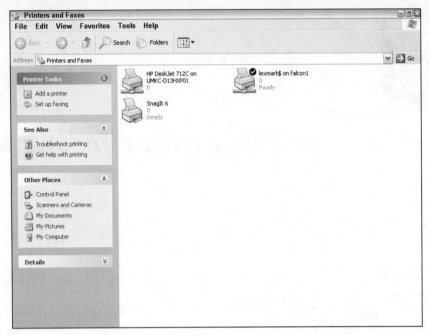

Figure 13-1   *The Printers and Faxes window shows you what printers are installed on your machine.*

3. In the Add Printer Wizard, click the Next button to begin the process.

4. If the printer is connected directly to your workstation, click the Local printer attached to this computer radio button in the Wizard, which is shown in Figure 13-2. If you think your printer is a Plug and Play printer, check the box that allows your computer to detect the printer.

Plug and Play, called PnP for short, is the ability of an operating system to detect and automatically configure various hardware devices. When it works correctly (which is nearly all of the time in Windows XP), you do not need to make any configuration or manual switch settings on the device. You simply plug in the device and reboot your system. In Windows XP, you can hot-swap PnP devices. Hot-swapping is the ability to safely add and remove devices without turning the power off first. A PnP device must be rated for the operating system on which it is being installed. This compatibility is stated on the outside of the device box. For help troubleshooting PnP devices, see Session 29.

If you are installing a computer on a business network, you will probably need to contact your network administrator about installing and configuring your network printer. On a small home network, you install the printer as a local printer on any of the computers, and then share it with others.

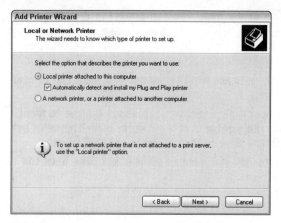

Figure 13-2 *The Add Printer Wizard allows you to install both local and network printers.*

5. After you have chosen whether you are installing a local or network printer, click the Next button to proceed.

6. In most cases, if you are installing a printer that is attached to your computer it is attached to LPT1, so select the radio button to use that port. If you need to choose a different port, you'll need to consult your printer documentation. (LPT stands for Line Printer Terminal. LPT1 is often called the Parallel port.)

7. Once you have chosen your printer port, select the manufacturer and model of the printer you are installing. As shown in Figure 13-3, the left pane contains the list of manufacturers and the right pane contains the printer models. Once you have selected the printer, click Next.

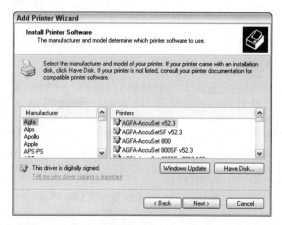

Figure 13-3 *The Add Printer Wizard allows you to choose the manufacturer of the printer as well as the specific model number.*

If your printer came with a driver disk, you can place the disk in your floppy drive (or CD drive) and click the Have Disk button and browse to the driver location on the appropriate disk.

8. Choose a name for your printer and indicate whether or not you want the printer to be your default printer. Click Next.

9. If you plan to share your printer over a network, you can select a name to identify the printer. If you are not sharing the printer over a network, leave the radio button selected for not sharing. Click the Next button to move to the final step.

10. In the final step, choose whether or not you want to print a test page once the installation is completed.

Removing a Local Printer

Removing a printer from your computer is even easier than adding a printer. To remove a printer from your computer, follow these steps:

1. On the Start menu, choose Start ⇨ Printers and Faxes.

2. In the Printers and Faxes window, right-click the printer you would like to remove and click Delete.

3. When asked to confirm the delete, click Yes.

When you remove a printer from your computer that uses software drivers other than those that typically come with Windows XP, you might be prompted to decide whether you want Windows XP to remove the software that was previously used. If you do not ever intend to reinstall this printer, it's okay to let Windows XP delete the files.

20 Min. To Go

Setting Your Printer Preferences

Once you have installed your printer, you should take a look at your printer preferences and adjust them to your needs. Keep in mind that the settings in the printer preferences indicate the default settings for each print job. You are able, however, to modify those settings on a job-by-job basis using the print controls located within Word, Excel, or other programs.

To adjust your default printer preferences, follow these steps:

1. On the Start menu, choose Start ⇨ Printers and Faxes.

2. In the Printers and Faxes window, right-click the printer you would like to adjust the preferences for and choose Properties from the context menu.

3. In the Properties dialog box, shown in Figure 13-4, select the General tab and click the Printing Preferences button.

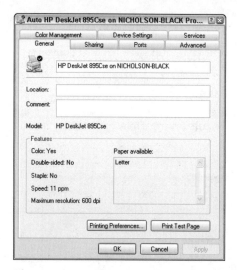

Figure 13-4   *The Printer Properties dialog box allows you to adjust your printing preferences.*

4. In the Printing Preferences dialog box, shown in Figure 13-5, choose the options that you would like to set for your default print jobs.

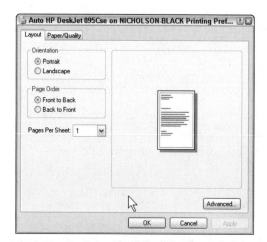

Figure 13-5   *The Printing Preferences dialog box allows you to adjust your printing preferences.*

5. Click OK to apply the changes and then click OK to close the Printer Properties dialog box.

**10 Min.
To Go**

Selecting a Default Printer

If you have more than one printer installed on your computer, you need to choose which printer is set as the default for print jobs. To choose a default printer:

1. On the Start menu, choose Start ➪ Printers and Faxes.

2. In the Printers and Faxes window, right-click on the printer you would like to use as your default printer and choose Set as Default Printer from the context menu. This process is shown in Figure 13-6.

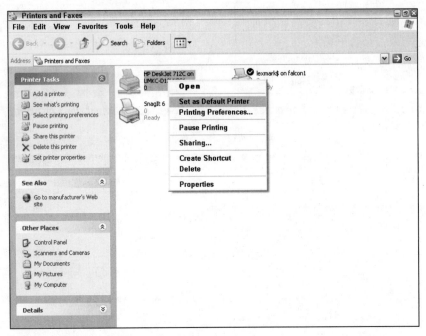

Figure 13-6 *From the context menu, you can choose your default printer.*

Printing a Windows XP Test Page

At times, you might find yourself with a printer that is not functioning correctly (or maybe not at all). The first step in troubleshooting a malfunctioning printer (other than ensuring that it is plugged in and turned on) is to print a Windows XP test page. By doing this, you can usually rule out the possibility that the operating system or the software drivers are the source of the problem. To print a Windows XP test page:

1. On the Start menu, choose Start ➪ Printers and Faxes.

2. In the Printers and Faxes window, right-click the printer you would like to use to print your test page and choose Properties from the context menu.

3. In the Properties dialog box, choose the General tab and click the Print Test Page button.

4. When the print job is sent from the computer, you receive the dialog box shown in Figure 13-7, asking you to confirm whether the print job was completed. If the print job was successful, click OK.

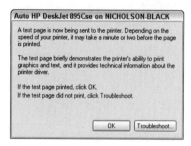

Figure 13-7 *Once the page is sent to the printer, Windows XP asks you to confirm whether it actually printed or not.*

If you are able to successfully print a Windows XP test page and you are still unable to print from an application, it is possible that the application is using its own printer driver. In this case, check with the manufacturer of the software to see if there is an updated printer driver for Windows XP.

Done!

REVIEW

- The Install Printer Wizard assists you in the process of adding a printer to your computer.
- Removing a printer is as easy as right-clicking the printer icon and choosing delete from the context menu.
- Using the printer preferences, you choose default settings for your print jobs.
- You can choose a default printer by right-clicking the printer and choosing Set as Default from the context menu.
- Printing a Windows XP test page can assist you in troubleshooting printer problems.

QUIZ YOURSELF

1. How do you add a printer in Windows XP? (See *Installing a Local Printer* section.)
2. How would you remove a printer from Windows XP? (See *Removing a Local Printer* section.)
3. If your default print jobs are set to portrait, how would you change it to landscape? (See *Setting Your Printer Preferences* section.)
4. Why would you want to print a Windows XP test page? (See *Printing a Windows XP Test Page* section.)

Networking with Windows XP

Session Checklist

✔ Developing a basic understanding of networking

✔ Differentiating between LANs and workgroups

✔ Understanding basic protocols of communication

✔ Setting up your home network (workgroup)

✔ Sharing your Internet connection

When listing the differences between Windows XP Home Edition and Professional, Microsoft notes that Home Edition can't be used for networking. This is not really the full truth. In this session, you'll get an overview of networking, learn some of the associated terminology, and learn which parts of networking Home Edition can handle and which require the Professional version.

An Overview of Networking

**30 Min.
To Go**

The purpose of a network is to share resources. Networking comes with other advantages, also. For example, you can have additional security, automatic installation of applications, and automatic backup of all data from computers stored on a central computer. In reality, there are two ways to connect computers to enable them to share resources: the domain model and the peer-to-peer workgroup model (usually just called a workgroup).

The domain model of networking

A minimum domain model network consists of one or more desktop computers, a hub acting as a connection point for each of the desktop computers, a server running an operating system, such as Windows 2000 Server or Windows 2003 Server, and, optionally, shared resources such as printers, drives, applications, mail servers, or scanners. Figure 14-1 illustrates a very basic model of a domain network.

You learn more about sharing resources in Session 23.

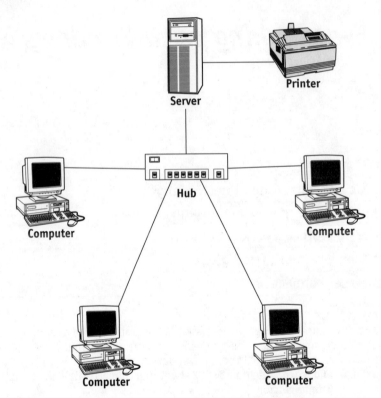

Figure 14-1 *A basic domain network consists of desktop computers, a hub to connect everything, and a server, and it may include shared resources such as printers, shared drives, and even applications.*

A domain controller (often referred to as a server) is responsible for routing traffic on the network, for enhancing security, and for the sharing of network resources.

For purposes of this book, a domain controller and a server are considered to be the same thing. In reality, you can have a stand-alone server that doesn't participate in the control of the network.

When you log on from any client, your request goes directly to the domain controller, and you are granted or denied access to resources based upon your username, password, and group membership. The domain controller's security features grant you access to specific resources.

The hub acts as the connecting point between the desktop computers (clients) and the server. Any request for services goes through the server. Shared resources, such as the printer, may be connected to the server, to a desktop computer, or to a standalone server (a server that is not responsible for controlling the network but may have a specific job, such as a print server).

Windows XP Professional is a client operating system and can be part of any domain but cannot function as a server (controller of the domain). Windows XP Home Edition cannot function as a member of a domain.

The peer-to-peer workgroup model of networking

In a peer-to-peer workgroup, computers can also be connected together and share resources. Unlike a domain, however, a workgroup has no server. In a domain network, a single computer is responsible for all security. In a workgroup no one computer is any more important than any other. Each individual computer keeps track of its own security and allows or denies access to its resources. Figure 14-2 shows a simplistic workgroup.

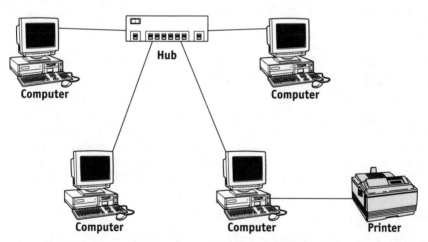

Figure 14-2   *A basic workgroup network consists of desktop computers, a hub to connect them, and a shared resource (usually connected to one of the computers), such as a printer.*

In a workgroup either Windows XP Professional or Home Edition can be used as the operating system on any of the computers. This means that with either version you can buy Network Interface Cards (NICs, pronounced "Nicks"), an inexpensive hub, and cabling and set up a simple home network to share resources for well under $100.

You can buy inexpensive wireless networks, but the overall cost will be higher in the long run. You may find that by comparison to a 100-MB cabled system, an 11-MB wireless system may seem very slow. Note that this affects speeds only over the local network and doesn't have an effect on connection speed to the Internet.

**20 Min.
To Go**

Protocols

In order for computers to communicate with each other, they must be speaking the same language. A *protocol* is a set of rules for communication. In our world, if I use a Spanish protocol for speaking to you and you are using a French protocol, we would be unable to communicate clearly. So it is with computers. In Windows XP, communication between computers in a domain or a workgroup most often relies on Transmission Control Protocol/Internet Protocol (TCP/IP), the standard protocol used for communication on the Internet. If your computer doesn't have these protocols, or if they are incorrectly installed, the computers will not be able to communicate with one another.

You should realize that there are many additional protocols for communications between computers, some more secure than others, some doing specialized jobs. For now, you don't need to know their names, or what each one of them does. If you decide to expand your knowledge of networking, expect an understanding of protocols to be an important part of your training.

An excellent free online tutorial of network protocols can be found at www.networkmagazine.com/article/NMG20000720S0002.

Setting Up Your Home Network (Workgroup)

As a user of Windows XP Professional or Home Edition, you cannot set up what is typically called a domain-based Local Area Network (LAN), because you would also require server software (either Windows 2000 or 2003 Server). Instead, you will be setting up a workgroup. The instructions here are for setting up a very basic workgroup, with the only purpose being to share resources. Shared resources can be nearly anything: printers, faxes, hard drives, folders containing files, or anything else that can be attached to one of your computers.

The hardware

If you want to set up a workgroup at home or in your small business, you first need the essential hardware. The following items are only basic suggestions, and you may want to enhance your workgroup by adding additional components, particularly a router, as discussed in the section *Sharing Your Internet Connection* later in this session.

If you really want to set up a client/server network rather than a workgroup, you will need to purchase software other than Windows XP. It is only a client operating system and not capable of controlling a network. You will also need to purchase hardware to be used as a server (although for a small network, say, under 25 workstations, a high-end workstation will do nicely, rather than spending the extra few thousand dollars to buy a server.

You will need to purchase the following hardware:

- An Ethernet Network Interface Card (NIC) for each computer to be connected
- A combination 56.6K modem/Ethernet card (if you are going to use a laptop)

- A hub with enough connections to add all of your computers, plus any you might want to add in the near future
- CAT 5 cables with ends already attached, cut to predetermined lengths to reach from each computer to the hub

You might want to buy a kit from a single company if one is available for the number of computers you want in your workgroup. As far as hardware is concerned, there is no difference between whether it will be used in a domain network or a workgroup. Buying from the same company might cost a little more up front, but it ensures that technical support will not say any problems are the fault of the other manufacturer.

In addition, you may want to purchase a *Keyboard, Video, and Mouse (KVM) switch*. A KVM switch allows you to control all computers hooked to it through a single keyboard, video display, and mouse (hence the acronym, KVM). You can buy one to control two or four computers. Having four computers in your workgroup means you must have a keyboard, video display, and mouse for each, unless you have a KVM switch.

10 Min. To Go

Wireless networking

If your computers are located throughout the house, you might want to look at the possibility of a wireless network. These tend to be more expensive than the cabled networks, but if your computers aren't clustered, this is an option for you. Wireless networks tend to be slower and can often be difficult to set up (unless you buy all the hardware from the same manufacturer). Keep in mind that using wireless networks only gets rid of the cable. You still need to buy the wireless NICs and a hub. They must also be wireless.

How fast do you want to go?

As we rely more and more on computers in our work and daily life, computer speed becomes more vital. What used to take 30 seconds to do now aggravates you unmercifully if it takes longer than 10 seconds. If it took 10, then 5 is too long. You'll want to know how fast your computer is. Although the answer to this depends on many things, how fast your computers operate in a workgroup is a function of the hardware described in the preceding sections. Computer processing speed is measured in terms of megabytes (MB) (one million) or gigabytes (one thousand million characters), each character (such as a letter) being exactly one byte.

NICs

Inexpensive NICs are generally available in three speeds: 10 MB, 100 MB, or a combination of 10/100. I recommend the latter: 10/100 cards from 3 COM and Linksys are both good buys. You can also purchase the newly released GB network cards, considerably pricier, but certainly the wave of the future. Gigabyte network cards are certainly overkill for a home network.

The term NIC card is redundant. NIC stands for Network Interface Card, so to refer to a NIC card means you are talking about a Network Interface Card card. Although this is grammatically incorrect, you will generally hear technicians speaking about NIC cards.

Hubs

Linksys and DLink offer inexpensive home hubs. Again, they are rated the same speeds as NICs.

Cable

For a long time, technicians used standard telephone wire to connect small networks. In three words, don't do it! Use Cat 5–rated cable with preinstalled RJ45 connectors. These are rated at speeds up to 100 MHz, but you can also purchase a higher-quality cable. Cat 5E offers connection speeds up to 350 MHz. Cat 6 cable is capable of transfer speeds up to 500 MHz. Each costs more than the previous, but connection speed is faster.

Regardless of the speed of the hardware components being used, the actual speed will only be as fast as the slowest-rated component on the system.

If you are considering running any wires through the walls or ceilings, keep in mind that these may be gnawed on by mice, squirrels, or small children playing in your attic. Be very careful with this solution, as it can be difficult to both troubleshoot and fix. If you find that you have to run a lot of wires through walls and difficult points of access, you may want to consider a wireless network.

Connecting the hardware

The first thing you need to do, *before* buying anything, is to find out if your computer(s) came with NICs already installed on the motherboard. If so, you need to find out what kind, that is, make, model, and speed.

Match your hub and cables with the cards in your computer. If a NIC wasn't included, you need to turn off the power to the computer, take the cover off, and decide what type of slot you need (this will normally be a PCI slot). Make sure all power remains turned off until after you have installed the hardware in each of the computers. Run the cable from the NIC to the hub. Repeat the process for each computer. Plug in each of the computers and restart them. Turn on the hub. There won't be anything to see on other computers until at least one thing is shared on each computer.

Sharing resources

The actual sharing of resources is covered in Session 23. Although not an overly complex topic, it is one that will take a full 30-minute session to describe. If you want to share resources right now, you might want to skip ahead to that session.

Sharing Your Internet Connection

When you connect to the Internet, you generally do so by means of a cable modem or DSL connection. Your Internet Service Provider (ISP) normally allows you to connect a single computer to the Internet at one time. In theory, then, you would have to have a separate high-speed connection (cable or DSL) for each computer you want connected to the Internet. With the introduction of Windows XP, you can now have that single connection and have other computers within the workgroup share that connection. This feature is called Internet Connection Sharing (ICS).

Windows Internet Connection Sharing (ICS) is a weak software program and may cause you more problems than benefits. Your best bet is to buy another piece of hardware called a *router*. A router's purpose is actually to control the traffic (data) flow between separate networks. Using a router on your home or small business workgroup is easy. You run a Cat 5 cable from each NIC to the router, and then plug in a cable between the router's output and your Cable or DSL connection. Most hardware routers today have a built-in firewall. A *firewall* is used to block unwanted traffic to and from the Internet. Software firewalls are generally free or cheap (in fact, Windows XP includes the Internet Connection Firewall in an attempt to offer more security). Since a quality router can cost less than $100 today, your best bet is to invest in one if you are going to have a permanent connection to the Internet. This helps decrease the chances of outsiders invading your network. A hardware router makes sharing a single Internet connection a matter of a few minutes' work, plus provides you with considerable security against hackers breaking into your system.

Done!

REVIEW

- There are two basic models of networking: domain and workgroup.
- Although Windows XP Professional can be used as a client operating system on a domain network, it cannot be used as network controller software. Windows XP Home Edition cannot be used as a client operating system on a domain network.
- A workgroup does not require a server.
- Protocols are sets of rules for communicating between computers.
- To set up a home network, you will need Ethernet cards, a hub, and Cat 5 cables or higher.
- If you want to share an Internet connection, a router is the best piece of hardware for this job.

QUIZ YOURSELF

1. What is the purpose of a network? (See *An Overview of Networking* section.)

2. Can Windows XP be used as the Server software on a network? (See *The domain model of networking* section.)

3. What is a protocol? (See *Protocols* section.)

4. What three or four pieces of hardware do you need to set up a small home workgroup? (See *The hardware* section.)

5. What piece of hardware makes Internet connection sharing easier and affords additional protection against hackers? (See *Sharing Your Internet Connection* section.)

Internet Explorer Basics

Session Checklist

✔ Opening Internet Explorer

✔ Accessing a Web site

✔ Setting a home page

✔ Adding shortcuts to your Favorites

✔ Deleting a shortcut from your Favorites

✔ Organizing your Favorites

O ver the last decade, the Internet has grown to become one of the most valuable (not to mention entertaining) computer-based resources out there. Whether it's sending and receiving e-mail, doing research for work, or maybe just surfing the World Wide Web (WWW or the Web), it's likely you will be using your computer to connect to the Internet. To assist you in navigating the Web, Windows XP includes an application called Internet Explorer (IE). As you will see in this session, IE is an easy-to-use, highly configurable application that allows you to easily access Web sites, track where you have been, and revisit pages that are of interest to you.

If you are already familiar with the Internet, you might just want to quickly scan this session and move on to Session 16. This is a very basic session, designed for those who have no experience with Internet Explorer or with the World Wide Web.

Accessing Internet Explorer

**30 Min.
To Go**

New to Windows XP Professional and Home Edition is the inclusion of Internet Explorer 6 (IE6). At Windows XP release time, this was the most current version of Internet Explorer. By summer of 2003, the first service pack (group of previous small upgrades) had been issued. Many of the updates involved increased security. Some of the features new to IE6 include:

- Inclusion of 128-Bit Cipher Strength (encryption), rather than previous 64-Bit encryption. This strength is needed to access many secure Web sites. (This is only included in the U.S. version of IE6.)
- Media Playback
- Automatic picture resizing
- Increased security over previous versions

There are a variety of ways for you to open IE, but by default Windows XP places a shortcut to Internet Explorer on your desktop. So, by simply double-clicking the icon shown in Figure 15-1, you can easily access the Web.

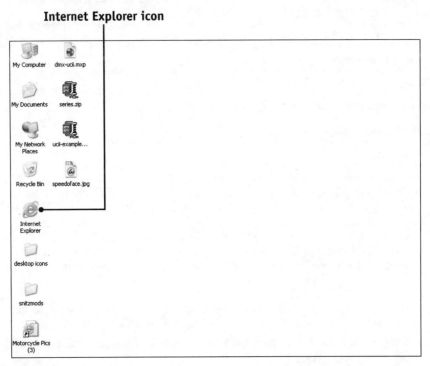

Figure 15-1 *The desktop shortcut to Internet Explorer allows you to easily access the Web.*

If you like to keep your desktop as uncluttered as possible and have deleted the shortcut to Internet Explorer, you can also access Internet Explorer in a few alternative ways. To open IE using the Start menu, click Start ⇨ All Programs ⇨ Internet Explorer. You can also open IE using the Run command by clicking Start ⇨ Run and typing **Iexplore** in the Open field and clicking OK, as shown in Figure 15-2.

If you still don't have the IE icon on your desktop, refer to the *Populating the desktop with common icons* section of Session 3.

Figure 15-2 *Using the Run command, you can also access IE.*

Much of the content in this session and Session 16 assumes that you have access to the Internet via a dial-up connection or a local area network. If you don't have an active connection, you can still walk through the sessions and understand the content, but you might encounter a pop-up that asks you if you want to connect to the Internet or work offline. Just choose to work offline and you should have no problems.

Accessing a Web Site

After you open Internet Explorer, the next step is to start your surfing and navigate to a new site or a new page. The most common way of moving to a different Web site is to type the site's address in the Address bar, shown in Figure 15-3, and either press the Enter key or the Go button.

There are several alternative methods, however, of opening a new Web site. The following sections explain how to use these methods.

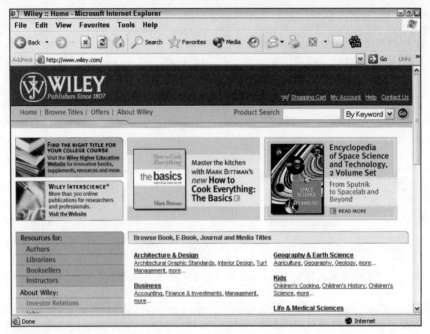

Figure 15-3 *The Address bar allows you to specify what site you would like to visit.*

Accessing a site using the Menu bar

1. Open an active connection to your Internet Service Provider (ISP).
2. Open Internet Explorer.
3. Choose File ⇨ Open from the Menu bar. In the Open dialog box, shown in Figure 15-4, type `www.wiley.com` and click the OK button.

Figure 15-4 *You can also visit a Web site using the Menu bar.*

Although all Web site addresses start with `http://`, it is not necessary to type this in. If it's not there, Windows XP assumes that's what you want and translates the address accordingly.

Finding a site using the Search Companion

From this point on, the instructions assume that you have an active connection to your ISP and have IE6 open.

1. Click the Search button from Internet Explorer's button bar and the Search Companion, shown in Figure 15-5, will appear.

Figure 15-5 *The Search Companion can help you find a site even if you don't know the exact Web address.*

2. Type **Wiley** in the Search Companion and click the Search button. In the main browser window, you will see a list of sites that match the term Wiley. Click the link to www.wiley.com and you'll be taken to the Wiley home page.

3. Click OK to close the dialog box.

Setting a Home Page

**20 Min.
To Go**

When you first open Internet Explorer, a page commonly referred to as your *home page* loads into the browser window. A home page is the first site displayed when you open IE. By default, IE uses MSN.com as the home page, but you can configure this to be just about any page on the Web. You can set your new home page by following these steps:

1. From the Menu bar, choose Tools ⇨ Internet Options.

2. In the Internet Options dialog box, shown in Figure 15-6, type the address of the page you would like as your new home page. For instance, if you want the Wiley home page to be your home page, type `www.wiley.com` into the Address field and click OK.

Figure 15-6   *The General Internet Options allow you to change your home page.*

 Don't confuse the terms "your home page" and "the Wiley home page." *Your* **home page refers to the page that first loads when you open Internet Explorer. The Wiley home page (or any other Web site's home page) refers to the page that loads when you first visit that Web site.**

An alternative way of setting a home page is by browsing to the page you want to use as your home page. From the Menu bar, choose Tools ➪ Internet Options. Under the Home page tab, click the Use Current button. Click OK to close the dialog box.

Shortcuts to Your Favorite Sites

Have you ever been surfing the Web and found a great site, but surfed away from it only to find that you can't seem to locate it again at a later time? With millions of pages of data being served (displayed) on the Web every day, it's no wonder that Web surfers have a tough time remembering what pages they have visited and what search terms were used to find them. To avoid losing pages that you find of interest, Internet Explorer has a feature that allows you to create a shortcut to your favorite Web pages (these are also often referred to as bookmarks). By adding a page to your Favorites list, you can be sure that the page can be accessed at any time in the future. In addition to adding sites to your Favorites list, you can also categorize them and delete them when the site is no longer active or is of no interest to you anymore.

Adding a site to your Favorites

In IE, there are several ways to add a page to your Favorites through the use of menu commands, shortcuts, or context menus. To see how easy it is to create these shortcuts, follow these steps:

1. Browse to the Wiley home page at www.wiley.com.

2. Right-click any part of the page that is not a graphic and choose Add to Favorites from the context menu. In the Add to Favorites dialog box, shown in Figure 15-7, name the shortcut Wiley Home and click OK.

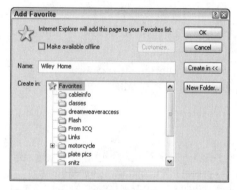

Figure 15-7 The Add to Favorites dialog box allows you to create a shortcut to a site for future reference.

3. You can now access that site at any time by clicking the Favorites button on the button bar and clicking the link to Wiley Home.

 You can also create a shortcut to a site by browsing to the site and choosing Favorites ⇨ Add to Favorites from the Menu bar.

Deleting a shortcut from your Favorites

10 Min. To Go

After you have a list of your favorite sites, you might find that a link no longer works or you just don't need to access the site anymore. You can remove the shortcut from your favorites just as easily as you created it. To delete a shortcut from your Favorites:

1. Choose Favorites ⇨ Organize Favorites from the Menu bar.

2. In the Organize Favorites dialog box, shown in Figure 15-8, right-click the shortcut you would like to delete and choose Delete from the context menu.

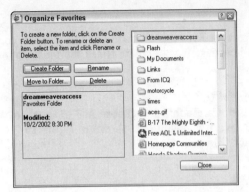

Figure 15-8 *The Organize Favorites dialog box allows you to remove unwanted shortcuts.*

3. When asked to confirm that you wish to send the shortcut to the Recycle Bin, click Yes and then Click OK to close the Organize Favorites dialog box.

Organizing bookmarks

Another handy feature of the Organize Favorites dialog box is the ability to create subfolders and categorize your favorite sites into logical groups. For instance, by choosing Favorites ⇨ Organize Favorites from the Menu bar, you can use the Create New Folder button to create a folder called Favorite Publishers. Next, click any shortcut in your list of Favorites and click the Move To Folder button and the shortcut is automatically transferred to that folder. In addition, when you are adding a site to your Favorites, you can select a folder from the list and choose the Create In button to automatically add the shortcut to the appropriate folder.

Reviewing Your History

Another way to review where you have been on the Web is to use the History feature included in Internet Explorer. By default, IE will keep a history of your surfing habits for 20 days, which allows you to figure out just where you were when you found that killer site that now you just can't seem to locate. To access your browser history:

1. Click the History button from the button bar.

The History button looks like a small clock with an arrow on the left side.

2. In the History panel, shown in Figure 15-9, click the link to the time frame that you would like to review.

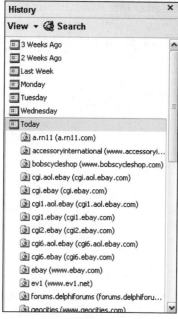

Figure 15-9   *The History panel allows you to track where you have been on the Web.*

3. With the desired time frame expanded, click any link and you are taken to the site. (Don't forget to add the site to your Favorites list now that you've found it again!)

Done!

REVIEW

- Windows XP provides you with numerous ways to access Internet Explorer.
- Using the Internet Options dialog box, you can specify a home page of your choice.
- You can use the Favorites feature in Internet Explorer to track sites that are of interest to you.
- Using the Organize Favorites dialog box, you can edit, arrange, and delete shortcuts to Favorites.
- Use the History feature to show a list of Web sites you have visited within a selected time period.

QUIZ YOURSELF

1. What are two ways to open a Web site? (See *Accessing a Web Site* section.)
2. How would you change your current home page to www.google.com? (See *Setting a Home Page* section.)

3. What are two ways to create a shortcut to a favorite site? (See *Adding a site to your Favorites* section.)

4. How would you delete a site from your Favorites? (See *Deleting a shortcut from your Favorites* section.)

Advanced Internet Tasks

Session Checklist

✔ Adjusting Internet settings

✔ Sharing an Internet connection

✔ Protecting your computer and family from offensive Web sites

A s the Internet grows, users who understand more than just how to browse from site to site will be able to take advantage of all of the resources it has to offer. Creating connections to the Internet, adjusting security settings, restricting access to content, and even developing a basic understanding of HTML code are all skills that can help you access, view, and eventually publish content on the Web.

This session begins by covering some of the basic Internet settings that you should be familiar with when using Windows XP and Internet Explorer. The session continues by demonstrating how to share a single Internet connection among two or more computers on your home or company network. Finally, you learn how to protect your computer and family from Web sites you consider objectionable using Content Advisor.

**30 Min.
To Go**

Adjusting Internet Settings

With the wide variety of file types and platforms currently used on the Web, it's amazing that browsers such as Internet Explorer (IE) are able to keep up and serve us the content we seek. Whether they are basic HTML pages, database-driven product catalogs, graphics, audio/video, or a host of other content types, we expect IE to process the data and display it on our monitor screens with no problems. This, unfortunately, doesn't always happen.

When a problem occurs, however, we have access to a wide variety of settings that can help IE adjust to overcome the problem.

Adjusting your Internet options can cause your browser to function improperly, so be very careful when you make any changes. The purpose of this section is to introduce you to the various options, but just because you *can* make changes, doesn't necessarily mean that you *should*.

To view Internet Explorer's Internet Options, double-click the Internet Explorer icon on your desktop (or open Internet Explorer using one of the alternative methods discussed in Session 15). From the Menu bar, choose Tools ➪ Internet Options and click the tabs to see the various options.

- The *General* tab of the Internet Options dialog box, shown in Figure 16-1, allows you to choose a home page, adjust your temporary Internet files settings, and manage your browser history.

Figure 16-1 *The General tab of the Internet Options dialog box allows you to make basic adjustments to your home page, temporary Internet files, and history.*

- The *Security* tab, shown in Figure 16-2, has four different default levels of security. Any site added to the Restricted sites list disables nearly all features, such as downloading files and the installation of desktop objects by the site. The Trusted sites setting should only be used if you absolutely trust the site (not always a good idea). It has the lowest security level. If you are part of a domain network, your intranet (sites within the company) can be added to this category. Finally, any sites not added to one of the other three categories automatically fall into the Internet category, which places a medium amount of security for each site. To view the security settings for each of these categories, choose one of the four categories and click the Custom Level button.

Figure 16-2 *The Security tab allows you to filter out pages and sites based on their perceived security level.*

- From the *Privacy* tab, shown in Figure 16-3, Internet Explorer's privacy settings allow you to specify whether or not third-party Web sites are able to place cookies on your machine. Cookies are small files that are usually placed on your computer to store information about your browsing activities. For instance, when you visit your favorite online book seller, its Web site may place a cookie on your machine that stores the categories and titles of books you searched for. Because this cookie exists, next time you visit the site, it creates a more customized interface based on the information stored in the cookies.

- On the *Content* tab you find access to features such as the Content Advisor (see the section, *Protecting Your Family from Offensive Material* later in this session), which assists in blocking unwanted content based on criteria such as nudity or violence.

- The *Connections* settings allow you to adjust the way your computer connects to the Internet. If you use a dial-up connection to gain access, you probably see a link to that connection in the Dial-up and Virtual Private Network settings. If, however, you connect using a broadband connection such as cable, DSL, or a LAN connection, the box is probably empty.

- Click the *Programs* tab and you are shown the various programs that are associated with different Internet-related tasks. As shown in Figure 16-4, you are able to specify which program should be used for editing Web pages, reading e-mail, and managing your calendar and contacts.

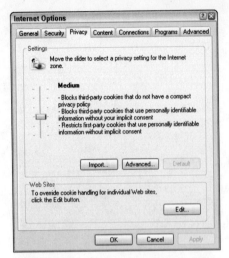

Figure 16-3   *Internet Explorer's privacy settings allow you to choose what types of cookies can be stored on your computer.*

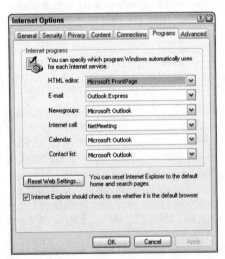

Figure 16-4   *Using the Programs tab, you can specify which programs Windows XP should use to perform Internet-related tasks.*

- The *Advanced* Internet Options, shown in Figure 16-5, allow you to tweak many of Internet Explorer's settings manually by turning them on or off. Keep in mind that adjusting some of these settings may cause your browser to stop displaying pages correctly, so only adjust them if you absolutely need to. If your browser is not working properly, you can always click the Restore Defaults button to bring the settings back to the way they were when Internet Explorer was first installed.

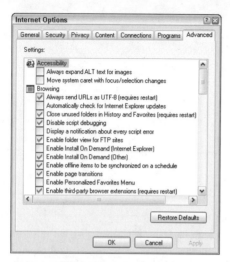

Figure 16-5 *The Advanced tab allows you to fine-tune many of Internet Explorer's features.*

Sharing an Internet Connection

**20 Min.
To Go**

If you have more than one computer in your home or office, it's likely that you'll want to share a single Internet connection between the two computers. To accommodate this, Windows XP includes a handy feature that allows computers that are connected via a LAN to share the same connection.

Before you attempt to share a single Internet connection, you should first be sure that your local area network is functioning properly. Because the Internet connection-sharing utility uses the TCP/IP protocol used by your LAN, it's important that both computers can talk to one another over the network before they can share an Internet connection.

For a review of networking principles, see Session 14.

To set up the Internet Connection Sharing, follow these steps:

1. Click Start ⇨ Control Panel and click the Network and Internet Connections icon.
2. Click the Network Connections link and right-click the connection that you would like to share with other computers. Choose Properties from the context menu.
3. In the Local Area Connection Properties dialog box, shown in Figure 16-6, click the Advanced tab and check the box to allow other computers to use the connection.

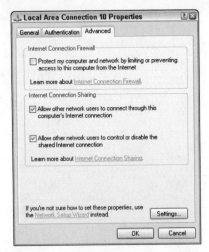

Figure 16-6 *You can share an Internet connection with other computers using the Advanced properties of the connection.*

   In order to use Internet Connection Sharing (ICS), you must be connected as part of a workgroup or domain network. Otherwise, the ICS panel will not be displayed.

4. If you would like other users to be able to enable or disable the shared connection, check the box to allow this.

5. Click the OK button to close the Local Area Connection Properties dialog box.

Protecting Your Family from Offensive Material

If you have used the Internet at all, you are probably aware that there are many sites that contain offensive material. There are many *third-party programs* (programs written by someone other than Microsoft) that can be purchased to protect users of your computer from viewing unsavory sites. However, if your needs are fairly simple, Microsoft has included a feature for protecting viewers from inappropriate Web sites.

   Although Microsoft does a fairly good job of protecting you and your children from inappropriate sites, it doesn't have some of the more advanced features of third-party programs. For example, third-party programs come with a database listing thousands of sites that are inappropriate for family viewing. In Microsoft, you have to add each site you visit. One highly rated third-party application is Net Nanny. You can find additional information on this program at www.netnanny.com.

Microsoft's feature is built into Internet Explorer and is called Content Advisor. To begin using this feature, open IE and choose Tools ⇨ Internet Options. Click the Content tab. Your screen should be similar to the one shown in Figure 16-7.

Figure 16-7 *By default, the Content Advisor is turned off. You must enable it to use the features.*

The Content Advisor is turned off by default, allowing access to any Web site, regardless of content. Click the Enable button to view the Content Advisor dialog box, shown in Figure 16-8.

Figure 16-8 *The Ratings tab of the Content Advisor dialog box allows you to control the level of offensiveness allowed to be viewed.*

**10 Min.
To Go**

The Ratings tab

The top panel on the Ratings tab allows you to first select one of four categories: Language, Nudity, Sex, or Violence. By default, all settings are set at the *most* restrictive level. If you want to allow a more liberal setting, you must adjust the slider beneath the categories panel separately for each of the four categories.

Setting approved sites

Clicking the Approved Sites tab displays the dialog box shown in Figure 16-9. The Approved Sites tab is something of a misnomer. Actually, from this tab you control both the Approved and Disapproved sites. In the Allow this Web site box, type the name of the home page you want approved *or disapproved* and click the Always button (for approved sites) or the Never button (for disapproved sites). After a site has been approved or disapproved, you can highlight it and click the Remove button to remove it from the list.

Figure 16-9 *The Approved Sites tab of the Content Advisor dialog box allows you to control approved and disapproved sites.*

The General tab

If you enable Content Advisor without going to the General tab, any Web site that has not been rated by Internet Content Rating Association (ICRA) will not be displayed unless you type the password to override Content Advisor. The General tab of the Content Advisor dialog box, shown in Figure 16-10, offers a way to beat this problem.

Microsoft decided to leave the Users can see sites that have no rating option turned off by default. What that means in real life is that you won't be able to view every site you are trying to visit. So the first thing you should do is place a checkmark in this option box.

Figure 16-10 *The General tab of the Content Advisor dialog box allows you to set some common options, as well as change the supervisor's password.*

To change the password, you must first type the *old* password (the password hint is displayed above the box for entering the old password). Then enter the new password twice and type a new hint. When you are done, click OK.

Features on the Advanced tab would not generally be used. This tab is used to access ratings by other rating authorities. If you have a need for it, the service to which you subscribe will provide the appropriate instructions.

Enabling the Content Advisor

Once you have completed the configuration, you need to actually enable the Content Advisor. To do so, simply click the OK button. The Create Supervisor Password, shown in Figure 16-11, is displayed.

Figure 16-11   *The Create Supervisor Password dialog box allows you to create a password and save a hint that reminds you of the password.*

Like nearly all passwords, this one is case-sensitive. You must enter it twice in exactly the same way. You can type a hint, which will be shown each time you try to do any task that requires the Supervisor's password (so don't use a hint like *My Birthday*). Click OK to enable the Content Advisor.

Disabling the Content Advisor

To disable the Content Advisor, open IE, choose Tools ⇨ Internet Options and click the Content tab. In the Content Advisor panel, click Disable. You will have to provide the Supervisor's password in order to use this option.

When you disable Content Advisor, none of the settings are lost. You can enable the Content Advisor again by going to the Content tab and clicking Enable. You will still need your Supervisor's password to enable Content Advisor.

Done!

REVIEW

- The Internet Options dialog box allows you to configure Internet Explorer.
- Using the Advanced tab of the Internet Options dialog box, you can restore your browser settings back to the default settings.
- Windows XP allows you to share your computer's Internet connection with other computers.
- The Content Advisor allows you to protect your family from sites containing offensive material. Sites that are added to the Disapproved list cannot be viewed without a Supervisor's password.

Quiz Yourself

1. How do you access the Internet Options? (See *Adjusting Internet Settings* section.)

2. In order to share an Internet connection between computers, what has to be functioning first? (See *Sharing an Internet Connection* section.)

3. What are the four categories in which you can set the ratings level? (See *Protecting Your Family from Offensive Material* section.)

4. By default, is the Content Advisor on or off? (See *Protecting Your Family from Offensive Material* section.)

5. If you set approved sites on the Approved sites tab, where do you set the Disapproved sites? (See *Setting approved sites* section.)

PART III

Saturday Afternoon
Part Review

1. Does the Windows XP Encrypted File System require a password?

2. Which file system fragments your files the most (breaks them up into nonconsecutive sections on the drive): NTFS or FAT32?

3. Can you convert your hard drive from FAT32 to NTFS and back to FAT32 without loss of data?

4. How much data can a typical floppy disk hold?

5. If you are trying to make a folder read-only, and a checkmark is already in the check box but the option is grayed out, what does it mean and how can you fix it?

6. Does Windows XP automatically create the My Documents folder?

7. Where is the best place to store your images?

8. What is the default view in the My Pictures folder?

9. How do other folders get added to the My Documents folder?

10. Which view shows you the most information about files?

11. What is the most common port where a printer is installed?

12. What should you do if your printer came with a floppy disk or CD-ROM driver?

13. If you set the default printer preferences to print in Portrait mode (where the image is printed on paper that is taller than it is wide), can you temporarily change the settings from within an application to set the printer for landscape?

14. When would you choose a default printer?

15. If you are successfully able to print a Windows XP test page, but a specific application won't allow you to print, what is the most likely problem and how would you fix it?

16. What are the two basic models of sharing resources?

17. Whether in a domain or a workgroup, what piece of hardware connects the computers?

18. What are the two major disadvantages between a wired network and a wireless network?

19. In Windows XP, whether in a domain or a workgroup, which protocol is used for communication between computers?

20. If you want to set up a domain network, what piece of hardware and what piece of software will you need to purchase in addition to those required for a workgroup?

21. Web site addresses begin with http://. Is it necessary to type this into the address window of your browser?

22. What does the Search button do?

23. Why would you want to change your Home Page to a site other than the default?

24. What are shortcuts to your favorite Web pages called?

25. What are the four major functions you can perform from the Organize Favorites dialog box?

26. In what language, or code, are Web pages developed?

27. What can happen if you incorrectly set your Internet options?

28. Which feature would you use if you want your browser to control the level of language, nudity, sex, or violence accessible to sensitive users?

29. In order to use ICS, what conditions must be present?

30. In computer terminology, what are cookies?

PART

IV

Saturday Evening

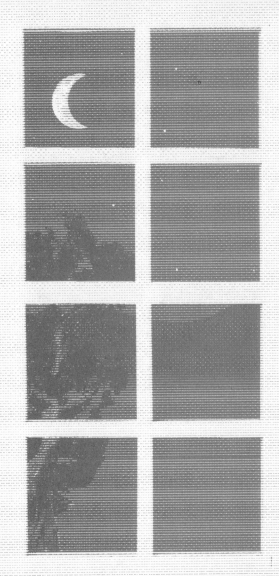

Managing Your Computer

Session Checklist

✔ Accessing the Computer Management console

✔ Understanding the System Tools

✔ Analyzing your Storage options

✔ Introducing Services and Applications

U nderstanding how your computer functions can often help you diagnose errors and avoid potential problems. In Windows XP, one of the most valuable tools for learning about your computer's health is the Computer Management console. Using this utility, you can troubleshoot errors, diagnose your hard drive's health, and even manage the users and groups that are able to access the computer.

In this session, I introduce quite a few features but do not cover them in a lot of detail. You can find much more detail in the Help and Support Center. Also you can search on the Internet for any tutorials or step-by-step help that is available.

This session takes a look at the basic functions of the Computer Management console and introduces many of the features that are available to keep your computer running at peak performance.

Accessing the Computer Management Console

30 Min.
To Go

There are a couple of ways to access the Computer Management console. Using the Start menu, you can access the panel by choosing Start ⇨ Control Panel ⇨ Performance and Maintenance and then clicking Administrative Tools. A much easier way to open the Computer Management panel, however, is to right-click the My Computer icon on your desktop and choose Manage from the context menu. Using this method, you can accomplish in two clicks a task that takes several clicks the "traditional" way.

Understanding the Computer Management Categories

To make managing your computer a little easier, the services offered by the Computer Management console have been divided into three separate categories. These categories, shown in Figure 17-1, break the various services and utilities up into System Tools, Storage, and Services and Applications.

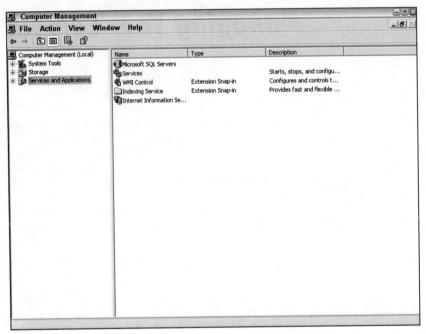

Figure 17-1 *The Computer Management console offers several options for keeping your computer healthy.*

Each of these categories is then broken down further into subcategories and applications that assist you in managing your computer. To see the subcategories, double-click the topic in the left panel.

System Tools

The System Tools category provides you with quick access to information about the performance of your system. Using the system tools, you can perform tasks such as diagnosing application errors, determining what information is available to other users, and managing your computer's hardware configuration.

Event Viewer

While your computer is operating, Windows XP is keeping tabs on all the software and hardware, making sure that it is performing properly. If an application freezes or a hardware component malfunctions, the operating system makes note of it in the event logs. Using the Event Viewer, you can review problems that have occurred and use the information in the event log to troubleshoot the issue. To see how the Event Viewer works and see some of the information that is stored there, follow these steps:

1. Open the Computer Management console by right-clicking the My Computer icon on your desktop and choosing Manage from the context menu.

2. In the Computer Management console, click the plus symbol next to System Tools and then click the plus sign next to the Event Viewer folder. As shown in Figure 17-2, the Application, Security, and System logs are now visible.

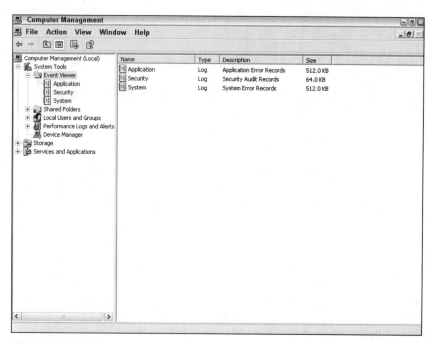

Figure 17-2   *The Event Viewer allows you to view Application, Event, and Security information.*

3. Click the Application log icon and you see a variety of application events. Each event includes the type of event, when it occurred, the application that caused the event, and what user was logged in when the event occurred.

4. Double-click any event. As shown in Figure 17-3, the Event Properties dialog box displays valuable information about the event and why it occurred.

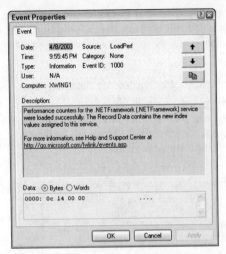

Figure 17-3 *The Event Properties dialog box allows you to view specific information regarding events occurring on your computer.*

5. Click OK to close the Event Properties dialog box.

One of the most valuable pieces of information that you can gather from the Event log is the Event ID. This code assists a support professional in determining what happened and often helps troubleshoot the issue.

Shared Folders

The second category in the System Tools allows you to view which folders are currently being shared with others on your network or in your workgroup. To view the subcategories in the Shared Folders, just click the plus sign next to Shared Folders or double-click the icon. Once expanded, you can click the Shared folder and see the share name, the path to the specific folder, and how many people are currently connected to the folder via the share. In addition, you can use the Sessions and Open Files sections to determine information about users who are accessing information stored on your computer and which files they are accessing.

Local Users and Groups

**20 Min.
To Go**

The Local Users and Groups category allows you to control who has access to the computer by adding, editing, and removing user accounts. In addition, you can combine individual user accounts into groups in order to apply settings and control access based on a group rather than on an account-by-account basis.

You will learn more advanced user and group management techniques in Session 27.

Performance Logs and Alerts

The Performance Logs and Alerts category provides advanced users with a method to monitor how well the system is operating. By default, this service is disabled but if you choose to track how your system is using resources and establish alerts that occur when events such as low memory or poor performance take place, you can start this service manually.

To manually start any service, click Start ⇨ Control Panel ⇨ Performance and Maintenance ⇨ Administrative Tools and double-click Services. Right-click the service, for example, Performance Logs and Alerts, and choose Start. If a service is already running and you want to stop it, repeat the process and choose Stop as the final step.

If you choose to start this service and record your computer's performance in log files, be aware that these log files can get big relatively quickly. Always check to be sure that your log files are not eating up space on your hard drive and either archive them to alternative media or delete them when they are no longer necessary.

Device Manager

The Device Manager allows you to see what hardware is currently installed on your machine, configure and remove peripherals, and build custom hardware profiles. In addition, you can use the Device Manager to troubleshoot hardware problems and update drivers. To familiarize yourself with the Device Manager, follow these steps:

1. Open the Computer Management console.
2. Click the plus symbol next to System Tools and then click the Device Manager icon. As shown in Figure 17-4, various hardware components installed on your computer are now visible.
3. Click the plus sign next to any hardware category you want to check and double-click any device in the list. The Device Properties dialog box, shown in Figure 17-5, allows you to view information about the component and troubleshoot problems.

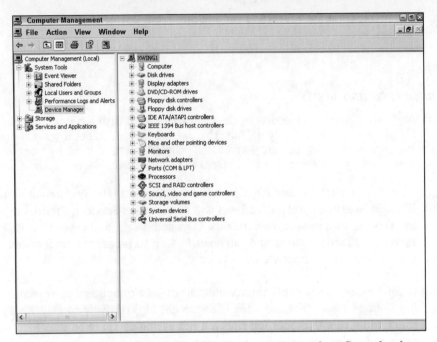

Figure 17-4 *The Device Manager allows you to view and configure hardware installed on your computer.*

Figure 17-5 *The Device Properties dialog box helps you identify and troubleshoot your computer hardware.*

4. Click OK to close the Device Properties dialog box.

Storage

The Storage category of the Computer Management console allows you to view and optimize storage components such as your local hard drive and any removable storage devices that are attached to your system. In addition, you can view and manage the file system used by your computer (and even adjust the size of your disk partition if you are using a dynamic disk).

**10 Min.
To Go**

Disk Defragmenter

One of the most valuable maintenance tasks you can perform on your computer is to defragment your hard drive. Think of your hard drive as a hotel that stores chunks of data rather than guests. Each room (called a sector on a hard drive) can only hold so much data, so files that exceed the sector limit must be broken up and stored over multiple sectors. The problem arises in the fact that Windows does not necessarily store the broken-up data in adjoining sectors. So, it would be like a large family going to a hotel and instead of three adjoining rooms, they get one room on the second floor, another on the fifth floor, and the third on the twenty-first floor. When this separation of files occurs (referred to as file fragmentation), it takes longer for Windows to find the pieces and put them back together.

To avoid this slowdown, you can run the Windows XP Disk Defragmenter, which will search through your hard drive and bring the pieces of data back together. This often results in a substantial increase in speed. To run the disk defragmenter, follow these steps:

1. Open the Computer Management console.
2. Click the plus symbol next to Storage and then click the Disk Defragmenter icon. As shown in Figure 17-6, the Disk Defragmenter allows you to choose a hard drive to defragment.

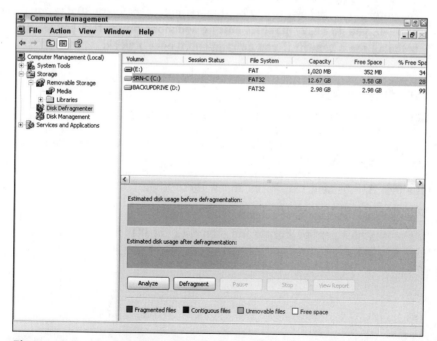

Figure 17-6 *The Disk Defragmenter allows you to choose a hard drive to defragment.*

3. Choose the C: drive and click the Analyze button. Once Windows is finished analyzing your hard disk, it will let you know whether you need to defragment or not, as shown in Figure 17-7.

Figure 17-7 *The Disk Defragmenter will let you know if you need to defragment your hard drive.*

4. Once the Disk Defragmenter dialog box is displayed, you can either view the report (which tells you the number of fragmented files and number of noncontiguous sectors on which they are stored) or click Defragment to begin the defragmentation process.

5. The defragmentation process may take quite a while to complete. When it is finished, close the window. Depending on how bad the file fragmentation was, you may notice little difference in speed or a great deal of difference.

How often you should run the defragmenter depends on how much you use your computer and the kinds of tasks you perform. If you use your computer to check e-mail, create word processor documents, and surf the Web, your computer would benefit if you ran the defragmenter every 30 days or so. If, however, you do heavy graphics editing and video production you would probably see a benefit if you defragmented once a week.

Disk Management

The final utility in the Storage section is the Disk Management tool. Using the Disk Management tool, you can view information about your hard disk(s), including the File System, status of the drive, and capacity. This tool also allows you to create new partitions in unused space and even reformat a partition if necessary. Be careful, however, when using this tool. The last thing you want to do is reformat a drive that contained data you needed. To see how the Disk Management tool works, follow these steps:

1. Open the Computer Management console.

2. Click the plus symbol next to Storage and then click the Disk Management icon. As shown in Figure 17-8, the Disk Manager allows you to choose a hard drive to manage.

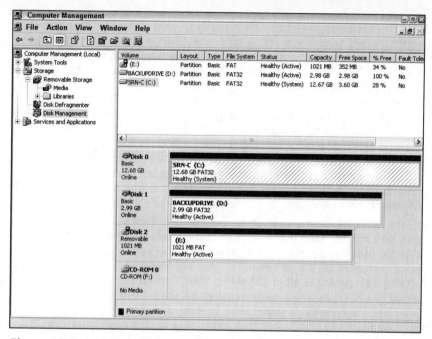

Figure 17-8 *Using the Disk Management tool, you can choose the hard disk you want to manage.*

3. Take a look at your C: drive and determine whether its status is currently healthy and determine what file system you are running.

If your disk does not show a "healthy" status, right-click on the error and Windows will either run an appropriate tool to fix the disk problem, or point you to a third-party tool, such as Symantec Utilities, to help fix the issue. Not all errors are fixable using software. In some cases you will have to reformat the drive, and in others, the drive may require replacement.

Services and applications

The last category in the Computer Management console is the Services and Applications category. The subcategories and tools located in this section allow you to start, stop, and configure several different services including Web services and the Windows XP Indexing Service. The following sections take a look at two services that you might need: the Indexing Service and the Internet Information Services.

Indexing Service

The Windows XP Indexing Service is a utility that looks through your computer's hard disk and analyzes information about your files, such as the filename, size, and the last time each file was used. It then places this information in a catalogue and organizes the information in a manner that is much more search-friendly than the file and/or folder structure of your hard disk. Each time you run a search on your hard drive, the operating system looks at the catalogue, rather than your entire hard drive, with the idea that searching through the database can substantially speed up your searches. Unfortunately, this is only true for computers that meet or exceed the recommended memory and processor requirements of Windows XP. If your computer is older and you installed or upgraded to Windows XP without upgrading your hardware, you might consider leaving the Indexing Service off, as it won't provide any improvement in performance. Remember, the Indexing Service only provides increased performance when you are doing a Search, not while you are using your computer.

By default, the Indexing Service is disabled, but the first time you conduct a search of your hard drive, you will be asked if you want to make future searches faster. By choosing Yes, you enable the Indexing Service, so you can choose No if your computer isn't up to the task. If Indexing is enabled on a slow computer, you will find a decrease in performance as the service attempts to catalogue all of the words. Even though this service can make your drive searches up to 100 times faster, some experienced users feel that since they don't do many drive searches, the computing power used to make additions to the catalog is not worth the slight decrease in performance they experience during application use.

To turn on the indexing service, click Start ⇨ Search ⇨ Change Preferences ⇨ With Indexing Service On.

Internet Information Services (IIS)

The other function controlled by the Computer Management console that you might find a need for is the Internet Information Services. These services allow you to turn your Windows XP Professional computer into a mini-Web server (with substantial limitations) where you can build and test your own Web pages.

Microsoft did not include access to the IIS in the Home Edition. If you are considering doing Web work, it's recommended that you upgrade to the Professional edition. You actually build the Web pages in a program like Front Page, and then display them in IIS. For additional information on using IIS, open the Help and Support Center and search for IIS.

Done!

Review

- The Computer Management console provides you with basic information regarding the performance of software and hardware installed on your computer.
- The System Tools category allows you to track errors that have occurred, manage users, and configure the hardware installed on your computer.

- Using the Storage category of the Computer Management console, you can view information about your hard drive and removable media.

- The Services and Applications category provides you with access to services such as the Indexing Service and Internet Information Services.

QUIZ YOURSELF

1. What element of the Computer Management console allows you to view the health of your hard drive? (See *Disk Management* section.)

2. How would you find out what application caused an error and determine its error code? (See *Event Viewer* section.)

3. What is the easiest way to access the Computer Management console? (See *Accessing the Computer Management Console* section.)

4. What element of the Computer Management console allows you to view the hardware that is currently installed on your computer? (See *Device Manager* section.)

5. How often should you defragment your hard drive? (See *Disk Defragmenter* section.)

Disaster Recovery

Session Checklist

✔ Explaining disaster planning

✔ Backing up your data

✔ Identifying the attributes of a file

✔ Demonstrating how to do a backup of one or more files

✔ Naming the five types of backup, and the advantages and disadvantages of each

✔ Restoring your data

When disaster strikes your system, and it's not a matter of if, but rather when, it could be a catastrophe for your small business and stressful if it happens at home. If you have developed a disaster recovery plan and stuck to it, your loss of data will be minimal, the downtime for your system will be something you can live with, and your stress level will be such that your heart doesn't stop along with your computer(s).

In this session, I define disaster recovery in considerably looser terms than are currently used in the industry. In other words, in a larger business, there will be a fully written disaster recovery plan, covering any possible contingency; more strict backup policies not only of data, but entire drives; and a stronger differentiation of when to use each of the five types of backups described in this session. The focus in this session is on only one element of a disaster recovery plan: preventing data loss.

An Overview of Disaster Planning

In this session, I'm really looking at only one part of the disaster planning question. How can you protect your data from loss? Disaster planning is a type of insurance. You hope that your hard drive waits to fail until you have given the computer to one of your children or grandchildren. But if it can't wait that long, how can you minimize the loss of personal data you have created? You might even want to prioritize data into appropriate categories: I can't live without it, it would be nice to keep, and who cares what happens to the wedding announcement I designed for a friend 5 years ago.

Loss of data from hard drive failure is not the only potential problem. Viruses, discussed in greater depth in Session 28, are also a problem. They can't harm your hardware, but they can destroy everything on the hard drive. What happens if a thief steals your computer, or you have a fire, or a natural disaster occurs? What happens if you make a backup of your data, and the backup won't restore to its original condition? An electrical spike could destroy your hardware unless you take proper precautions.

Backing Up Your Data

The Microsoft backup utility (ntbackup.exe) is automatically installed with Windows XP Professional. It is not installed and cannot be added through the Add/Remove programs utility in the control panel in the Home Edition. It does, however, exist for Home Edition users who know how to get to it. On your original Windows XP CD, it is located in the Valueadd\Msft\Ntbackup folder. The filename is NTbackup.msi. Simply double-click this file and follow the prompts to install the backup program.

 An .msi extension is used with Windows Installer files. Running a file with an .msi extension automatically installs the program in Windows. Many programs today come with an .msi extension, and these files can be used for automatic installation across a network.

You should understand the difference between copying a file to a backup disk and using the backup utility in order to duplicate a file for safekeeping. Copying a file leaves the file in exactly the same state it was in originally. To back up your files, you would have to copy each one individually. By using the backup utility, two major differences occur: You can choose to copy groups of files with a single click, and, most importantly, the copied files are compressed, normally to about half their original size. Both of these are positives. However, there are two downsides to using the backup utility. First, all of the files are stored in a single file, so if that file becomes corrupted, all your backed up files become inaccessible. Second, in order to restore the files to their original state, you must have a working copy of the same version of the backup utility you used to create the backup set running on your hard drive.

In previous home versions of Windows, the backup program was extremely limited, allowing you to back up your data only to floppy disks. The version included with Windows XP has been greatly enhanced. The backup application is now able to back up data to other hard drives, network hard drives (if you are on a network and using Windows XP Professional as your operating system), to tape drives, to removable media drives, including Zip and Jaz as well as floppy drives.

 Windows XP backup application is not capable of making backup copies to your data to CD-ROM drives. However, most CD-ROM drives come with their own software capable of performing this action.

Preparing for Backing Up Your Files

Before you begin to back up your files, there are several steps you should take in order to most efficiently use the program. Following these steps will save you a lot of time and make the actual backup easier and more meaningful.

File Attributes

Before learning about backup types, you need to be familiar with a particular file attribute — the archive attribute. You can see a file's archive attribute by right-clicking the filename and choosing Properties. In the Properties dialog box click the Advanced button. You will see a window similar to the one shown in Figure 18-1.

Figure 18-1   *The Advanced Attributes dialog box for a file shows the backup status in the Archive and Index attributes pane.*

If the file has not been backed up since its creation or since a change has been made to the file, a checkmark is automatically placed in the File is ready for archiving option box. If no flag is in this option box, it will not be backed up on the next backup, unless you do a full backup. You don't control the backup flag. It is set or cleared automatically, depending on the type of backup being conducted.

Formatting a Floppy Disk

If you want to format a floppy disk, you must remember that formatting erases all data on the disk. Here are the steps to formatting a floppy disk:

1. Close any existing documents or applications.
2. Double-click the My Computer icon on the desktop.
3. Put your floppy disk in the A: drive, and right-click. Choose Format. The dialog box shown in Figure 18-2 appears.

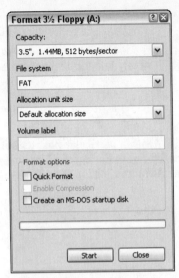

Figure 18-2   *The Format 3 1/2 Floppy (A:) dialog box allows you to format a floppy disk.*

4.   All defaults should be acceptable, unless you want to change or delete the Volume label of the disk. Make sure that there is not a checkmark in the Quick Format option box or the Create an MS-DOS startup disk.

5.   Click Start.

6.   You see a reminder that all data will be destroyed if you continue. Click OK to continue. It may take a few minutes, so wait. When formatting is complete, a Completed dialog box is displayed.

 If you have already formatted the disk, you can do a Quick Format. This simply erases the data index, and only takes a few seconds. However, it doesn't check all the sectors on the disk, which is done if the Quick Format option is not enabled.

7.   Click OK to close the dialog box, and click Close in the Format dialog box.

 Before rebooting your computer, make certain that the floppy disk is removed from the drive. Otherwise, you may get a "System not found" error. If that happens, remove the floppy and press CTRL + ALT + DEL to reboot.

Understanding backup types

**20 Min.
To Go**

According to Microsoft, there are five types of backups. These five backup types will determine which files are archived. The five backup types are Normal (commonly called full), Copy, Daily, Incremental, and Differential.

When your computer is set up exactly as you want it (applications customized when desired, all configurations set), do a normal backup of your entire hard drive. That resets (turns off) the archive flags on all the files. After that, once a day, week, month, whatever, perform either an incremental or differential backup. Remember, doing a full (normal) backup resets all of the archive flags. The only files that will be backed up after that are ones you have changed since the last full or incremental backup. Let's take a quick look at each of the types of backups.

Full (Normal) backup

You won't want to do a full backup to floppy disks. Depending on the amount of data you have, it might take several hundred, or even several thousand disks. That means you need to have either a tape drive or another hard drive (preferably on another computer that you have connected as part of a workgroup). The easiest way to perform a full backup is to use the Backup Wizard, and select the choice of backing up all of your data, and then choosing which drive it will be backed up to. Again, depending on the amount of data you have, this may take several minutes or several hours. A full backup should be performed on a regular schedule (weekly or monthly) and incremental or differential backups completed on a daily basis. A full backup copies all files on your hard drive, regardless of the setting of the archive flag, and then clears all flags. This tells the backup program the next time it is run that there are unmodified copies already stored on a backup device. If you install a new program or change files, the archive flags are turned on again, showing the files that have been modified, and, therefore, a copy of these changed files is not part of a previous backup. This tells the backup utility which files have changed and need to be backed up again in order to have all files up to date with the current state of your computer.

Copy backup

Copy backups are seldom used. This feature copies all selected files using the backup utility, but does not change any of the archive flags. This option is useful if you have only a few files you want to back up but you don't want the archive flags reset. If the archive flags were reset, that would mean that in order to do a total restore, you would need the normal backup, the incremental or differential backup, *and* the Copy backup. This makes one more thing that can go wrong, and keeping the lowest number of component backups is the best way to make an efficient restore when the need arises.

Daily backup

Similar to the Copy backup, the daily backup copies all files changed on that particular day, but doesn't reset the archive flags. Again, this can cause problems when a full restore becomes necessary. Remember, the key here is to make complete restoration of your drive as quickly as possible.

Incremental backup

Once you do a full backup, all of the archive flags are reset. Only newly created files, modified files, or newly installed software will be backed up during an incremental backup. Since the incremental backup resets the archive flag, each file that is new or modified is backed up only one time (unless you modify it again). On succeeding incremental backups, only files modified, created, or installed since the last full backup *or* the last incremental backup are backed up. For example, after performing a full backup, if you create Document1.doc and Document2.doc on Monday, these two files will have the archive flags set, and only those two files will be backed up. The incremental backup clears the archive flag, indicating the files have not changed since the last full or incremental backup. On Tuesday, you create Document3 and Document4. An incremental backup backs up only these two files (not the two from Monday) and clears the archive flag. If, on Wednesday, the only changed file is Document3, only that file is backed up (and the archive flag cleared). This is very different from the way things work with a differential backup.

 After installing any new software application, do a full backup. This will reset the archive flags for newly created files as well as all the files installed by the software application. If you don't do this, all of the application files will have to be backed up every time you do a differential backup or the first time you perform an incremental backup. If the files are large and/or numerous, this can take a lot of time and extra drive space to back up.

Differential backup

After performing a full backup, completing a differential backup the first time is exactly the same as an incremental backup. On succeeding differential backups, only files modified, created, or installed since the last full backup are backed up (unlike incremental backups because the archive flags are *not* reset). For example, after performing a full backup, if you create Document1.doc and Document2.doc on Monday and do *not* have the archive flags reset, only those two files will be backed up. Because the differential backup does not clear the archive flag, Document1.doc and Document2.doc indicate that the files have been changed since the last backup. On Tuesday, you create Document3 and Document4. A differential backup backs up all four files. If on Wednesday, the only changed file is Document3, Documents 1 through 4 are all backed up again, without resetting the archive flag. Each incremental daily backup backs up more and more files, resulting in additional time being added every day.

Advantages and disadvantages of the backup types

Normal (full) backups are a requirement if your data is meaningful to you. Backing up only your data can be a quick path to extended downtime, and maybe even leading to a computer that won't restart after installing the operating system for a second time. If you've only had your computer a few days, this isn't as critical as if you have had it for several months. Think of all the software you have added and any individual settings you've made since you got the computer. Having to do a complete installation, including all of the software and getting all the software to run the way you want can be a major challenge. So, I suggest that however old (or new) your computer is, you immediately do a full backup. A reasonably priced backup tape generally holds about 8 GB of data. If your drive has more than 8 GB of data, you may find you need more than one tape to do a full backup. The software will tell you when to insert another tape if needed.

An 8-GB tape is capable of holding only 4 GB of data. The tape assumes that your software will compress the data at about a 2:1 ratio, and that's why the tape is rated at 8 GB. Depending on the files you are backing up, you may find more or less than the 2:1 ratio. If many of your files are MP3 (audio files) or JPG (graphics files) or application files other than data, you might not get that kind of compression, since those three file types are usually already compressed. No additional compression can be made by the backup software.

Differential and incremental backups each have advantages and disadvantages. One is better used to back up files, the other more efficient for restoring them. Using an incremental backup means that only the files you haven't yet backed up are written to the backup file. In many cases, you can use a floppy to accomplish an incremental backup. However, when the time comes to restore your data, you need to have access to your full backup, and individually restore each backup set. If one of the disks is bad, it may be that you cannot restore later incremental backups.

Differential backups have their major disadvantage when backing up files, since a complete backup is made of all files backed up since the last *normal* backup. Each day, the backup takes longer. The advantages come when restoring data. You need only your full backup and the last differential backup you have made. If your last differential backup set is corrupted, you can go to the previous differential backup set. This not only means a shorter time in restoring your data, but also basically gives you backups to your backups (since each backup set is complete in itself).

I do a full backup once a month, unless I install a new software application, at which time, I do another full backup. I do daily differential backups because I consider my data to be important, and I don't want to lose it because of a single disk of an incremental set being bad. If I find that a daily backup is taking too long, I do another full backup and continue making my differential backup.

Verifying your backup

When you back up your data, there is an option for verifying the backup. All this actually does is make a bit-by-bit comparison between what is being backed up from the drive and onto the recording media. Although it takes nearly twice as long to verify all data, it is a good idea to use this feature.

Just because you have verified your backup set, doesn't mean that you are able to restore the data. You must do a test restore, covered in the next section, in order to make sure that at least some files are capable of being restored.

Starting the Windows XP Backup or Restore Wizard

The first time you run the Backup Utility, the application begins by looking for any known backup devices connected to your systems. Start the Backup Utility by clicking Start ➪ All Programs ➪ Accessories ➪ System Tools ➪ Backup.

After a few seconds, the opening screen of the Backup or Restore Wizard is displayed, as shown in Figure 18-3.

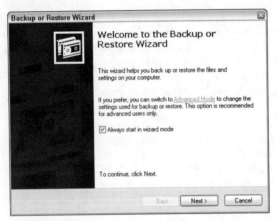

Figure 18-3 *The opening screen of the Backup or Restore Wizard is displayed the first time you run the backup program.*

In the first screen, you can make two choices. Clicking the Advanced Mode link closes the Backup or Restore Wizard and takes you to the Backup Utility. If you do not want to run the Wizard each time the application begins, remove the checkmark from the Always start in wizard mode option box. Otherwise, click Next to continue using the Wizard.

Before you can restore data, it must first be backed up. The second Wizard screen, shown in Figure 18-4, asks if you want to Backup files and settings (the default), or Restore files and settings. When you have made your selection by selecting the appropriate option, click Next.

The third screen of the Backup or Restore Wizard, shown in Figure 18-5, allows you to choose between one of four options. The default is to back up My documents and settings. The second option is Everyone's documents and settings. This option is used if more than one person has an account on the computer. (You will learn more about adding users in Session 27.) The third option is to back up all data on this computer. Finally, you can choose Let me choose what to back up. After you have chosen, click Next to continue.

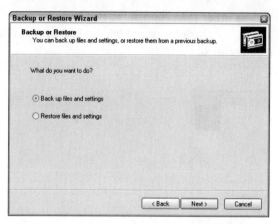

Figure 18-4   *The second screen of the Backup or Restore Wizard allows you to choose between backing up files and settings or restoring files and settings.*

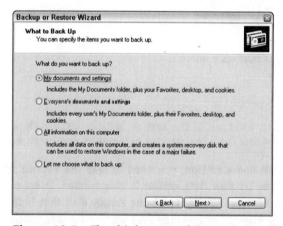

Figure 18-5   *The third screen of the Backup or Restore Wizard allows you to choose which groups of data you want to back up.*

The fourth screen, shown in Figure 18-6, doesn't allow you to choose the type of file backup you want to accomplish. (The default backup type is Normal.) Backup types are discussed in the next section. Here, the backup type is grayed out, and a complete backup of the My Documents folder, plus your Favorites, desktop, and cookies are all backed up (if that was your choice at the third screen). You can choose to back up your data to one or more floppy disks (depending on how much you have to back up), and a reference name for the backup. You may find that you need to make several backups over time, and naming them will help keep straight what is contained in each backup file and when the backup was performed. Clicking Next starts the backup process. If you are backing up your data to floppies and more than one is needed, you will be prompted to insert more disks.

If you want to do a backup type other than Normal, at the first screen, choose Advanced Mode. Choose Tools ⇨ Options and on the Backup Type tab, choose the type of backup you want to perform.

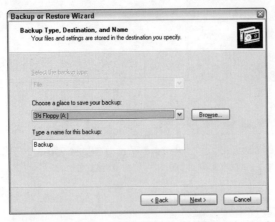

Figure 18-6   *The Backup Type, Destination, and Name window allows you to choose the storage destination and give the backup a name.*

Performing a sample backup

In this section, you'll do a backup of a file, and then in the Restore section, you'll restore it to a different directory. That way you know that both the backup and restore functions work.

If you are using Windows XP Home Edition, you need to load the backup program as described in Backing Up Your Data earlier in this session. Users of either version of Windows XP must have at least one floppy disk that is formatted and empty. See the *Formatting a Floppy Disk* section for information on preparing the disk. You can also choose to back up data to a different location on your hard drive (not a good idea, because a hard drive failure could corrupt both your original and backed up data), or to a different hard drive.

Creating a sample file to back up

To create a file to do a simple backup, complete the following steps:

1. Make sure you have a floppy disk in the drive.
2. Open WordPad by choosing Start ⇨ All Programs ⇨ Accessories ⇨ WordPad.
3. Type **This is a test**.
4. Click File ⇨ Save. At the Save As dialog box, click the My Documents icon in the left pane.

5. Save the file as Test18.rtf.

6. Close WordPad. If it asks you if you want to save the document, just click Yes.

Backing up a sample file

To back up the file to a floppy, follow these instructions:

1. With all applications closed, choose Start ⇨ All Programs ⇨ Accessories ⇨ System Tools ⇨ Backup.

2. In this case, we won't use the Wizard. When the Wizard opens, click Advanced Mode. The Welcome to the Backup Utility Advanced Mode is displayed. Notice there are four tabs, and each has several options. You could run the Advanced Backup Wizard from here, but instead, click the Backup tab. The Advanced Backup screen is displayed, as shown in Figure 18-7.

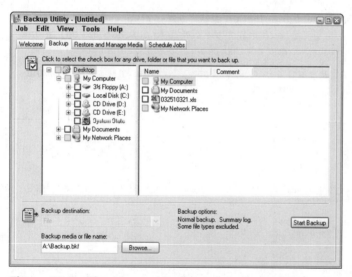

Figure 18-7   *The Advanced Backup tab in the Backup application allows you to choose the files you want to back up, set a file destination, and specify the type of backup you want to use.*

3. Notice in the left pane that drives, folders, and files have a plus to the left of the name. Clicking a plus expands the folder or device. Since the file is in the My Documents folder you will want to select it.

4. If you place a checkmark in any option box, that entire drive, folder, and all the subfolders and files will be backed up. In the right pane, if you put a checkmark in the My Documents folder, all subfolders and files within those subfolders will be backed up. This is not necessary in your case. Double-click the My Documents folder in the right pane (not the option box!). If necessary, scroll down until you find the Test18.rtf file. Place a checkmark in the option box next to the option. Check Backup Media or File Name and make sure it is saving to the A: drive.

5. From the Menu Bar, choose Tools ➪ Options. Click the General tab. Turn on the third option (verify after completion). Click OK.

6. Now you are ready to begin your backup. Click Start Backup in the lower-right portion of the dialog box. The Backup Job Information dialog box is displayed as seen in Figure 18-8.

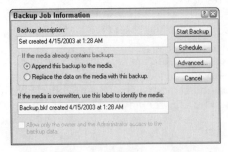

Figure 18-8 *The Backup Job Information dialog box is displayed. This gives you a Backup description, which can be changed; the ability to append (add on) to any existing backup on this media; and another chance to change the backup name.*

7. Click Start Backup. After a few minutes, you see a message that backup is complete. See Figure 18-9 for a sample completion screen.

Figure 18-9 *The Backup Progress dialog box shows the progress of the files and folders being copied.*

8. When the computer is finished, close the Backup application.

9. Use My Computer to verify the contents of the disk. You should see an icon and a file ending with .bkf. The is the backup file, and it has been verified.

10. Close My Computer.

Restoring Your Data

As the final task for this session, you will restore the file you backed up earlier to a different directory. (If you have modified the file *after* the backup, restoring it to the same folder would write over the file, destroying any changes made since the backup.)

1. With all applications closed, choose Start ⇨ All Programs ⇨ Accessories ⇨ System Tools ⇨ Backup.

2. In this case, you won't use the Wizard. When the Wizard opens, click Advanced Mode. The Welcome to the Backup Utility Advanced Mode opens.

3. Click the Restore and Manage Media tab. Your screen should be similar to the one shown in Figure 18-10.

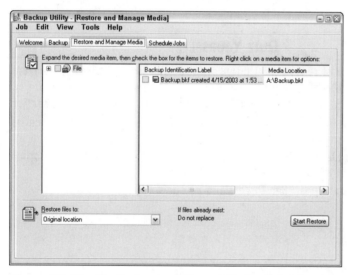

Figure 18-10   *The Restore and Manage Media dialog box is used to select which backup sets you want to restore.*

4. In the left pane click the plus sign. In the Backup option (also listed in the left pane) click the plus on the Backup name. Place a checkmark in the C: drive check box.

5. In the Restore Files to drop-down box, choose Alternate Location. In the Alternate Location text box, leave the setting at C:\.

6. Click Start Restore. You are asked to confirm what you are doing. Click OK to begin restoring the file. After a few seconds, you will see a Restore Confirmation dialog box. Click Close.

7. Close the Backup Utility.

8. Browse to your C:\ drive, and you should see the restored file. If you don't see it, you probably want to try it again.

Done!

REVIEW

- At some time in the life of your computer, you will almost undoubtedly have a loss of data.
- Microsoft includes a Backup program in Windows XP.
- Running the Backup or Restore Wizard is a simple way to back up your data.
- File attributes indicate whether the files have been backed up.
- Although Windows XP includes the ability to verify your backup, it must be turned on. It is off by default.
- There are five different types of backup, each having its own advantages and disadvantages.
- You can also use the Backup Wizard to restore your data.

QUIZ YOURSELF

1. Name three examples of reasons you might want a full disaster recovery program. (See *An Overview of Disaster Planning* section.)
2. What is a file with an .msi extension used for? (See *Backing Up Your Data* section.)
3. Which file attribute indicates that a file has or has not been backed up since last modified? (See *File Attributes* section.)
4. What happens if you leave a floppy disk in the computer, and you try to boot the computer? (See *Performing a sample backup* section.)
5. Name the five backup types. (See *Understanding backup types* section.)

Session Checklist

✔ Creating an e-mail account

✔ Installing Outlook Express

✔ Customizing Outlook Express

✔ Creating e-mail

✔ Using Outlook Express as a newsgroup reader

O utlook Express (included with Windows XP), as the name indicates, is a "lighter" version of Outlook (included when you purchase the Microsoft Office suite of applications). Although Outlook Express is missing many of the more advanced features of Outlook, it is a solid e-mail application and offers the advantage of being able to access newsgroups and retrieve mail directly from Hotmail accounts (such as john@hotmail.com or john@msn.com). Many users prefer the simplicity of Outlook Express to using feature-rich Outlook. In this session, you'll learn the basics of e-mail, as well as using Outlook Express as your e-mail application and news reader.

Setting Up an E-Mail Account

**30 Min.
To Go**

Before configuring Outlook Express, you must have an e-mail account. In all likelihood, the company that provides your Internet access (called your Internet Service Provider, or ISP for short), will provide you with one or more e-mail accounts. In some cases, users prefer the anonymity of a free e-mail account from a free service, such as hotmail.com or yahoo.com.

Finding an ISP

Deciding on an ISP is a very personal preference. If you only have a modem, you have many different choices. Many people opt for a pay service, such as America Online (AOL). AOL has local phone numbers throughout the world, so you can generally find a local number to call if you are traveling. For those staying nearer to home, a local ISP may be slightly less expensive. One way to find a listing of these is to look up Internet Access Providers in the yellow pages. If you are in a large city, you might want to pick up a free copy of *Computer User* magazine. This magazine generally offers many local providers of Internet services. (To see if your city has a local edition of *Computer User*, go to www.computeruser.com. Actually, this is a good site to get updates on computer news, too.) The last option is a free ISP. These have many disadvantages, including few lines for calling in, local access only in large cities, and a tendency to go bankrupt or start charging for their services.

When you open an account with an ISP, you will get the information needed to set up your e-mail account on your computer, such as the e-mail server name and type.

Before you set up your e-mail account, you must have at least three pieces of information. First, you need to know the type of server your ISP provides. There are five options from which to choose: Microsoft Exchange Server, POP3, IMAP, HTTP, and Additional Server types. Your ISP will provide you with the correct setting. Next, you need to have the name of the server that receives your e-mail. Finally, you need to have the name of the server from which your mail is sent. The most popular type of account to receive your mail is POP3. For example, a good POP3 address would be mail.*myisp*.com or pop3.*myisp*.com, where *myisp* is replaced with the name of your ISP. Similarly, an address for sending mail might be smtp.*myisp*.com. There are variations on these names, so you need to check the Frequently Asked Questions (FAQs) list posted on your ISP site, or check with technical support for your ISP to get the correct settings. Write all three nuggets of information down on paper. You will need these shortly. You might also want to write down your username and password (these are the ones for logging on to your ISP, not the one used for logging on to your computer, if you are part of a network).

Installing Outlook Express

If you did a Normal install when you installed Windows XP, you won't need to install Outlook Express. However, the icon for it will not be on your desktop. You can find the icon for Outlook Express by clicking the Start button and choosing E-Mail (Outlook Express) from the top-left portion of the Start menu. If Outlook Express is not installed on your computer, you can install it by clicking Start ➪ Control Panel ➪ Add or Remove Programs ➪ Add/Remove Windows Components and placing a checkmark in the Outlook Express option box. Click Next. Wait until the Wizard is finished and click Finish. Outlook Express is now installed.

To create an Outlook Express shortcut on your desktop, follow these steps:

1. Double-click the My Computer icon.
2. Click the C: drive icon.
3. Choose Program Files ⇨ Outlook Express.
4. Right-click msimn.exe. From the context menu, click Send To ⇨ Desktop (create shortcut). You now have a shortcut for Outlook Express on your desktop.

The first time you open Outlook Express, you will see the Internet Connection Wizard, shown in Figure 19-1. Enter the name you want others to see in the From field of your e-mail.

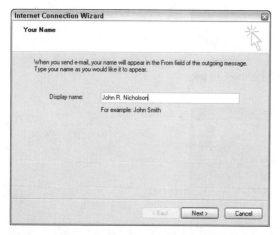

Figure 19-1   *Put the name you want others to see on your Sent or Reply e-mails.*

 If you have already opened Outlook Express and cancelled the Installation Wizard, you can get back to the Internet Connection Wizard dialog box by choosing Tools ⇨ Accounts ⇨ Mail ⇨ Add ⇨ Mail. This will display the Your Name window shown in Figure 19-1.

Click Next to continue. In the Internet E-mail Address window, shown in Figure 19-2, enter the e-mail address that others will use to send e-mail to you. This will be the one you registered with your ISP.

 Many users may have more than one e-mail account that they use for different reasons. If you fall into this category, just run the Wizard again to set up another account.

Clicking Next again brings you to the E-mail Server Names window. Here, you first have to tell the Wizard what type of incoming mail server you have. Next you enter the name of the Incoming mail server, followed by the Outgoing mail (SMTP) server name, as shown in Figure 19-3. Remember, this is information you get from your ISP.

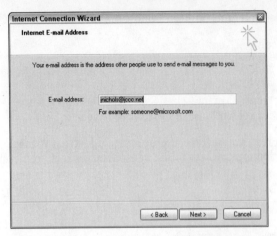

Figure 19-2 *In the Internet E-mail Address window, add the exact e-mail address you want other users to use to send e-mail to you.*

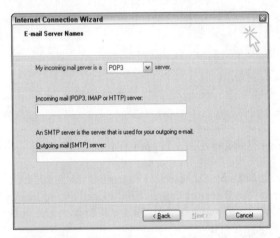

Figure 19-3 *Enter the name of the incoming and outgoing mail servers as supplied by your ISP.*

Click Next to display the Internet Mail Logon information window, shown in Figure 19-4. Here, you enter your account name and password. The account name is usually the name part of an e-mail address. For example, if your e-mail address is jnichols@jccc.net, the account name would be jnichols. In a few cases, you might find that you are required to put in the entire e-mail address.

Figure 19-4   *In the Internet Mail Logon window, you enter the account name you created and the password you have chosen.*

Your password can be simple or very complex. If your password consists of a real word, such as spouse or pet name, chances are excellent it can be broken by a very simple program. If the password is overly complex, you may find it necessary to keep a copy of it written down by your computer. Either of these options defeats the purpose of having a password, which is to keep your files private. A good password will consist of 5 to 8 characters, letters, special characters, and numbers. The password is case-sensitive, meaning both upper- and lowercase letters can be used. Since one type of program checks for all words in an enhanced dictionary, you should make sure that any word you use is not recognizable. For example, I could use my first name, reversed, with a capital letter in the wrong place, a special symbol, and one or more numbers. For example, a password for me might be nHoj&30. While not a totally secure password, it would be difficult for a dictionary program to break.

Clicking the Next button displays a Congratulations windows. This indicates that all required information has been entered, and an account is now created. Clicking Finish displays the Outlook Express default view, shown in Figure 19-5.

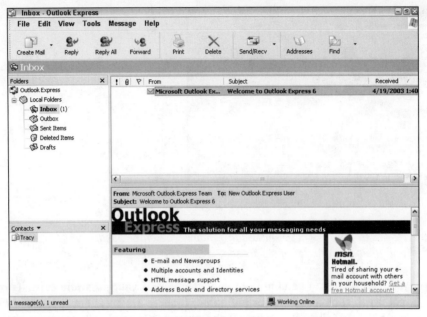

Figure 19-5 *The default Outlook Express window is displayed.*

Customizing Outlook Express

20 Min. To Go

Once you have installed Outlook Express, you may find that the default settings don't suit your taste. This section discusses two of the many ways to modify Outlook Express.

Using the Options dialog box

Open the Options dialog box by choosing Tools ⇨ Options. The General tab of the Options dialog box is displayed as shown in Figure 19-6.

As you review each of the General options, remember that they are enabled if there is a checkmark in the option box and disabled if no checkmark is present. Some options may be disabled. For example, in the Default Messaging Programs pane the two options are grayed out and unavailable. If you also installed Outlook (from the Microsoft Office suite of programs), the options in this pane would be available for you to choose your default mail-handling application.

Another option you might want to change is to add a signature line to each e-mail you create or reply to. To do this click the Signatures tab. In the Signatures pane click the New button. The tab now appears as shown in Figure 19-7.

Figure 19-6   *The General tab of the Options dialog box allows you to change the way Outlook Express operates.*

Figure 19-7   *The Signatures tab allows you to create multiple signatures to add to the bottom of each e-mail you send.*

You can now create a basic signature in the Text box. You might want to insert one or two blank lines by pressing Enter for each line. Your signature can consist of just your name, or it can include additional information about you.

Many users like to add a short saying, either funny or serious, to the end of the signature. It should not be offensive and be no longer than two lines. For example, I sometimes add, " You are not paranoid if they really are out to get you."

There are many other ways you can change how Outlook Express functions. Explore the Options dialog box at your leisure, or use the Help feature to learn more.

Changing the display of Outlook Express

When Outlook Express is first installed, the Inbox is displayed in the upper-right pane. The Inbox shows you a list of the e-mails that you have already read but not deleted, or that are waiting to be read for the first time. Immediately after installation you will find a single message in your Inbox. It is a message welcoming you to Outlook Express. The upper-left pane is a list of default folders that can be used to organize your messages. The lower-left pane is used to display contacts from your address book. The final quadrant display is a portion of the message highlighted in the upper-right pane. If several messages are visible in the upper-right pane, only the selected message will be displayed in the lower-right pane. There are many viewing options you can modify from the View menu on the main toolbar. Try some of them to see which fit you best.

The vertical bar between the inbox and message screen is adjustable. Move the mouse pointer over any portion of the vertical line dividing the two areas, and the cursor changes to a double-headed arrow. Press the left mouse button and drag the line to the new position.

Composing an e-mail message

Composing an e-mail is a simple task. Simply click the Create Mail button on the toolbar. An empty e-mail message is displayed, as shown in Figure 19-8.

**10 Min.
To Go**

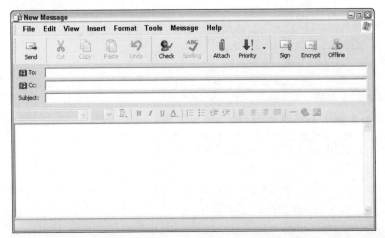

Figure 19-8 *Composing an e-mail is as simple as filling in the blanks.*

Type the e-mail address of the intended recipient into the To: field. If the e-mail address is held in your contact list, you can click the book icon to the left of the To: box and select the desired name to enter the address without typing it. The same holds true if you want to send a CC: (in the typewriter days, that stood for Carbon Copy) rather than making the receiver the main recipient. There is also a box for Subject. You should carefully consider what you type in this box. It may induce the recipient to read the e-mail or delete it without reading it. Never use a general subject like, "You gotta see this," because that is exactly what e-mails containing viruses say, and your message may never get read. Be specific, both for the recipient reading it the first time and, if necessary, to find it again for later reference.

You can attach objects to e-mail by clicking the Attach button and browsing to the file location you want to attach. It is an excellent idea to compress large files with a program such as WinZip before attaching them. (You can download a shareware version of WinZip, complete with tutorial, from www.winzip.com.) Most attachments are sent with a .zip extension, in order to decrease the download time for the receiver of the message.

Many ISPs will not accept e-mail with attachments over 1 MB. This is particularly true for free e-mail accounts. You might want to check with the recipient on the file size maximum before sending large attachments.

The large, open area is where you type your message. Give your message some thought. Remember that the recipient has no nonverbal cues to tell if you are serious about a specific comment.

When the cursor is outside of the message area, you can press Tab to move to the next field, or Shift Tab to move to the previous field. Also, you can move to a new field by pointing at it with the mouse cursor and clicking.

When you have written (and formatted, if desired) your message, you can click the Send button. Although e-mail used to be a nearly instantaneous form of communication, it can take an hour or more for the server to process the message, depending on how busy it is doing other things.

Not all e-mail reader programs can handle formatting. You should make sure which e-mail reader the recipient is using before including special formatting in your message. Outlook Express and Outlook can easily read special formatting applied by the other application, but other e-mail readers may not be able to display the special characters.

Organizing incoming mail

As you learned in Sessions 10 and 11, when you get too many files you need to organize them into folders. The same idea applies to e-mail. When you get too many, it is easier to organize them into folders. See Figure 19-9.

The Local Folders are the *root* (first-level) folders. To create another root-level folder named, for example, Business, follow these steps.

1. Right-click Local Folders and choose New Folder. The New Folder dialog box is displayed.

2. Type Business in the Folder Name box and click OK. This adds the Business folder beneath the Root folder.

Figure 19-9 *Outlook Express creates several default folders, but you can easily add more.*

To create a new folder beneath an existing one, right-click the folder name and choose New Folder. Type the name of the new folder, and it is created beneath the folder you selected. This is particularly helpful in the Save folder. I have hundreds of e-mails I have saved for reference purposes, broken down into about a dozen subfolders. This makes finding things much easier when the need arises. You can delete a piece of e-mail by dragging it to the Deleted Items folder, or by selecting it and clicking the Delete button on the Toolbar.

If you drag the message to the Deleted Items folder, or select it and click Delete, the message stays in the Deleted Items folder until you delete it from there. To delete a message permanently, so it doesn't take up room on your hard drive, select the message, press Shift, and click Delete. You will be asked if you want to delete this item. If you click OK, the e-mail cannot be recovered. You can also empty the Deleted Items folder by right-clicking the icon and choosing Empty Deleted Items Folder.

Using Outlook Express as a Newsgroup Reader

Newsgroups are an area on a computer network, especially the Internet, devoted to the discussion of a specified topic. There are newsgroups to cover every topic imaginable. Some are moderated, which means that an individual or small group decides which messages are worth posting to the newsgroup. Although there is some censorship involved, most moderators are fair. In unmoderated groups, you get everything that anyone decides to post, and you may have to wade through hundreds of messages a day in the more popular groups.

Each server will have a listing of available newsgroups. Not all servers subscribe to all newsgroups. One way to begin setting up Outlook Express as a newsgroup reader is to choose Tools ⇨ Accounts and select the News tab. Click the Add button. You will need to provide some personal information, and then the name of the newsgroup server. Usually, this will be news.*myisp*.com, where *myisp* is the name of your ISP. If you truly want to become a newsgroup addict, you can go to www.newsgroups.com, which offers choices from over 90,000 newsgroups for a monthly or yearly fee.

Spam: The non-meat

Spam is e-mail that you have not requested. Spam is like bulk *snail mail* (snail mail is the term for mail sent via the U.S. Post Office), but multiplied millions of times. Once you sign up for an e-mail account, you will get spam for selling merchandise, improving yourself, announcing political messages, and, most of all, spam for pornography. Any time you order something via e-mail, or put your e-mail address into a contest, or do nearly anything else that announces that the e-mail account address is active, you will be placed on spam lists, and seemingly forever receive more and more spam.

Don't ever reply to spam to remove your address from the spam list. That confirms that the account is in fact active and therefore can be sold to other spammers for a premium price. Instead of being removed from a spam list, you will multiply your spam received many times. Although spam is defined as *unwanted* e-mail, it is quite acceptable to remove your e-mail address from a newsletter you have requested to receive.

Only sign up for a single newsgroup at first. See how many messages you get, and how helpful they are to you. Add one at a time, making certain that each is one you want to monitor on a regular basis.

Done!

REVIEW

- Outlook Express, an e-mail and newsgroup reader, is provided free with Windows XP.
- An e-mail account must be provided by your Internet Service Provider (ISP) or some other company.
- You should know the addresses of your ISP e-mail outgoing and incoming servers before attempting to install Outlook Express.
- You can use the Options dialog box to adjust many settings in Outlook Express.
- You can click Tools ⇨ View to change the way the screen is displayed.
- Outlook Express can be used as a Newsgroup Reader.
- You can easily create additional folders for organizing your e-mails.

QUIZ YOURSELF

1. What do you need to have before configuring Outlook Express? (See *Setting Up an E-Mail Account* section.)
2. What is the most popular account type to receive e-mail? (See *Setting Up an E-Mail Account* section.)

3. If Outlook Express was not installed during the installation of Windows XP, how can you install it? (See *Installing Outlook Express* section.)

4. What is the Options dialog box used for? (See *Using the Options dialog box* section.)

5. What is a Newsgroup? (See *Using Outlook Express as a Newsgroup Reader* section.)

SESSION

20

Instant Messaging

Session Checklist

✔ Accessing the Windows Messenger

✔ Sending an Instant Message

✔ Talking to others using the Windows Messenger

✔ Sending a file using Windows Messenger

✔ Pros and cons of sending instant messages

I f you plan to use your computer as a tool for keeping in touch with friends, family, and coworkers, one of the most useful tools included in Windows XP is the Windows Messenger. This handy utility allows you to see when your contacts are online and then send them messages that are delivered in real time. Windows Messenger also allows you to transfer files and photos to other users and even use your computer's microphone and sound card to speak with other users just like talking on the telephone.

This session begins by showing you how to access the Windows Messenger and create a new Passport account. Once connected to the Windows Messenger, this session proceeds to demonstrate how to send an instant message, set up the voice communications, and transfer files.

Accessing the Windows Messenger and Creating a Passport Account

**30 Min.
To Go**

Before beginning to use Microsoft Messenger, you need to have a Passport account from Microsoft. The easiest (and free) way to sign up for one is to go to www.passport.net/ and follow the prompts to sign up for a new account. If you already have one, you just need to know your account name and password.

You need to have an e-mail address, but you can sign up for a free Hotmail account at the same time you are registering your passport. As with most elements of Windows, there are a couple of ways to access the Windows Messenger. The most common method of accessing the messenger service is to Choose Start ⇨ All Programs ⇨ Windows Messenger. An alternative method, however, is to add the Windows Messenger icon to the Quick Launch bar. To add Windows Messenger to the Quick Launch bar:

1. The Quick Launch bar is immediately to the right of the Start button. Make sure it is unlocked by right-clicking any empty space on the Task Bar. Choose Properties. Make sure the Show Quick Launch option is checked. Also, make sure the Task bar is not locked.

2. Click Start ⇨ All Programs. Click the Windows Messenger icon and drag it onto the Quick Launch bar.

3. You can move the Quick Launch icon to another position on the Quick Launch bar by dragging it left or right.

There is no difference between Windows Messenger for the Home Edition of XP and the Professional version.

Once you have opened the Windows Messenger, follow these steps to create a Passport account:

1. If this is the first time you have opened the Windows Messenger, you will receive a message, similar to the one shown in Figure 20-1.

2. Click the link, and the .NET Passport Wizard begins. The .NET Passport system consists of a huge database, hosted by Microsoft, that allows you to use the same username and password to access items such as the Windows Messenger, Web-authoring features of MSN.com, and Passport-enabled sites such as eBay.

3. Click the Next button to begin the process. If you already have an e-mail address, click Next or choose to create a new address with MSN Hotmail and click Next.

4. Select Yes if you already have a Passport account, or No to register your e-mail address with Passport and click Next.

5. Follow the prompts and click Finish and Windows Messenger signs you on to the system.

Figure 20-1   *When accessing the Windows Messenger for the first time, you are asked to sign in.*

Adding Contacts

After you have created your account and are signed on to the Windows Messenger, you need to add the e-mail addresses for the people you want on your contact list. The easiest way to do this is to compile a list of e-mail addresses from your address book and create new contacts in the Windows Messenger. If you don't know the desired e-mail address, you can also look it up by name and location. To look up an e-mail address by name and location, choose Search for a Contact in the Add a Contact dialog box. From there, you can put in the person's name, city, state, and country. The person must have a Hotmail account for this method to work.

To add someone to your contact list:

1. Sign on to the Windows Messenger.

2. In the I want to . . . panel at the bottom of the Messenger panel, click Add a Contact.

3. In the Add a Contact dialog box, shown in Figure 20-2, choose whether you want to identify the person by e-mail address or search the directory. (The directory can be either your e-mail contacts or the Hotmail database.)

Figure 20-2 *You can select contacts by a variety of methods.*

4. If you chose to look the person up by e-mail address, simply type in his e-mail address and click Next. If, however, you chose to look in the directory, type the person's name and/or region and click Next. Whichever way you choose, you should receive a Success message. If the request was not a success, check the e-mail address and confirm that the other person has created a Passport account.

5. Click Finish and the person is now added to your contact list.

Sending an Instant Message

20 Min.
To Go

Let the fun begin! Now that you are signed on to the Windows Messenger and have someone to talk to, it's time to chat it up. To start using Windows Messenger:

1. Open the Windows Messenger and sign on.

2. In the I want to . . . panel, click the Send an Instant Message link or double-click any of your contacts who are online. (If a contact is already online, their username will show in the middle of the windows.)

3. In the Conversation window, type your message in the field below the button bar and click the Send button. When the message is sent, it is displayed in the message panel, as shown in Figure 20-3. When the other person replies to your message, her response is displayed in the message panel as well.

> **If the network is busy, you may find that it takes several seconds to have your message displayed to your contact, and to receive one in return. Rather than waiting, many users type multiple messages during the time they are waiting. With even two people chatting, you may find yourself looking at previous messages to figure out exactly what is being said. Adding additional users can result in a "free-for-all" that requires a level of multitasking that your brain may not be used to. Keep at it. Practice makes perfect!**

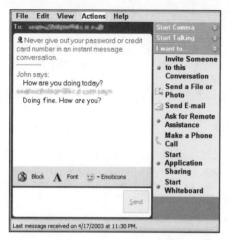

Figure 20-3 *Once you send the message, it is displayed in the message panel.*

4. If conversing with one person isn't enough, you can click the Invite Someone to this Conversation link and request that another person from your contact list join in.

5. To modify the font of your messages, click the Font button and choose a font, style, and color.

6. If you want to add a visual emotion to your message, click the Emoticons button and choose from the various emoticons shown in Figure 20-4. With the emoticon added to the message, click Send.

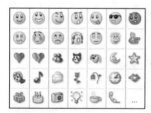

Figure 20-4 *Emoticons allow you to add emotions to your message.*

It is estimated that 70 to 90 percent of our communication is nonverbal. If someone is being sarcastic, it might come across as a serious message. This is cause for many misunderstandings. In addition to the Emoticons, you can use such text as <Grin> (or simply <G>). You might use <Smile>, or even <raspberries>. The choice is up to you, but make sure your communication partner knows what the symbols mean. One of the earliest text emoticons was :-) (a smiley face turned on its side). Using a semicolon instead of a colon can indicate a wink, such as with an inside joke or frisky comment. ;-)

Using Voice Communications within Windows Messenger

If your typing skills aren't what they used to be, or you would rather chat it up on the phone than type messages, give the Windows Messenger voice communications a try. Using a microphone, your computer's sound cards, and speakers (or better yet, a headset), you can talk to people on your contact list that have the same setup. To start a voice conversation, follow these steps:

1. Open the Windows Messenger and log in.

2. Right-click any of the users in your Online list and choose Start a Voice Conversation from the context menu. You can also start a voice session by choosing Actions ➪ Start a Voice Conversation from the Menu bar and selecting the user from the dialog box, as shown in Figure 20-5.

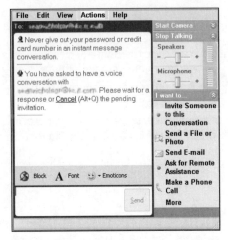

Figure 20-5   *Choose the user with whom you would like to converse.*

3. Once you initiate a voice conversation, the other user must accept the invitation to talk before the connection is established. When the user accepts, an indicator is displayed in the message panel and the Start Talking panel on the right side of the window expands. During the voice session the Speakers and Microphone indicators, shown in Figure 20-6, automatically adjust to the levels of a typical voice conversation.

4. To end a voice session, choose Actions ➪ Stop Talking from the Menu bar.

Figure 20-6   *The Speakers and Microphone indicators auto-adjust.*

Sending Files and Photos Using Windows Messenger

10 Min. To Go

Now that you are able to type instant messages and conduct a voice session in Windows Messenger, how about being able to transfer files to others on your contact list? Gone are the days of waiting for that e-mail attachment to be sent, processed by the sender's e-mail server, processed by your e-mail server, and finally delivered to your inbox and downloaded. Instead, you can transfer files instantly from your computer directly to another user's computer. To transfer a file, follow these steps:

1. Open Windows Messenger and log in.
2. Right-click the online user to whom you would like to send a file and choose Send File or Photo from the context menu. In the Send a File dialog box, shown in Figure 20-7, browse to the file you would like to send and click the Open button.
3. Before the file is transferred, a message is displayed in the message panel indicating that the system is waiting for acceptance from the receiver.
4. Once the file transfer has been accepted, the file is transferred directly to the other user's My Downloaded Files folder and you receive a confirmation that the file was accepted, as shown in Figure 20-8.

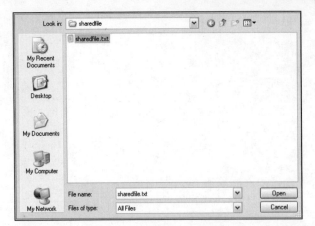

Figure 20-7 *Use the Send File or Photo dialog box to transfer a file to another user.*

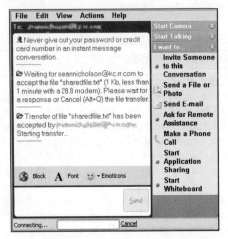

Figure 20-8 *The file has been transferred successfully.*

5. If another user sends a file to you, you have the option of accepting or rejecting the file as well. If you choose to accept it, Windows Messenger provides a reminder, shown in Figure 20-9, that some files might contain viruses. Remember to run a virus scan on any file you receive prior to opening it.

Figure 20-9 *Be sure to scan any files that are transferred to your computer.*

Done!

REVIEW

- Windows Messenger allows you to communicate with other users via text messages and voice messages.
- You can add contacts to your contact list by either using the person's e-mail address or looking up his or her name and region.
- You can open a voice session and speak with other users using a microphone, speakers, and your computer's sound card.
- Sharing files is easy over Windows Messenger, but the other user has to accept the file before it can be delivered.

QUIZ YOURSELF

1. How do you add a contact to your contact list? (See *Adding Contacts* section.)
2. What button do you push to transmit your message to other users? (See *Sending an Instant Message* section.)
3. What button do you click to begin a voice session? (See *Using Voice Communications within Windows Messenger* section.)
4. When sending files, what should you do after you accept the file and before you open it? (See *Sending Files and Photos Using Windows Messenger* section.)

PART

IV

Saturday Evening
Part Review

1. What are three ways of opening the Computer Management Console?
2. When in the Event Log, what is the most important piece of information you can get if you are going to get a support professional to help you troubleshoot an error?
3. Which category allows you to create accounts so others can use a computer or combine individuals into a group and apply settings and control access based on being a member of a group, rather than on an account-by-account basis?
4. By default, is the Performance Logs and Alerts category enabled or disabled?
5. In which feature is the Services and Applications category?
6. What is the name of the Microsoft backup utility file?
7. What is the file attribute called that tells the backup program that a file needs to be backed up?
8. What is another name for a Normal backup, which backs up all of your hard drive?
9. What type of backup copies all files created or changed since the last normal or incremental backup and does *not* reset the archive attribute?
10. What part of the backup utility do you use to reload files that have been damaged?
11. Where do you get your primary e-mail account?
12. If Outlook Express is installed normally, is there a shortcut to it on your desktop?
13. What would comprise a fairly safe password?
14. How can you tell if an option in a dialog box is enabled?
15. Which utility program might you use to compress a file you are sending as an e-mail attachment?
16. What type of account must you create in order to use Windows Messenger?
17. What might cause a delay between the time a message is sent and the time you receive it?
18. What are the icons called that can be included with a message in order to demonstrate nonverbal cues?

19. What three things are required to use Windows Messenger to send audio communications?

20. What two types of objects can be sent easily to another user of Windows Messenger?

☑ Friday

☑ Saturday

☑ **Sunday**

PART

V

Sunday Morning

Mastering Media

Session Checklist

✔ Accessing the Windows Media Player

✔ Playing media-based audio files

✔ Playing Web-based audio files

✔ Playing video files

✔ Using alternative media types

I n the not-too-distant past, many home computers weren't equipped with sound cards or speakers, and the possibility of playing video files was nonexistent. Processors were just too slow, the hardware was too expensive, and the files were too large to store on a small hard drive or transfer over a 14.4-bps modem connection. As hardware has become more advanced and less expensive, however, sound cards (or at least their functionality included on the motherboard) and speakers have become a staple feature included in most of today's computer packages. In addition, increased dial-up speeds and the introduction of broadband Internet access has made large file transfers much easier to accomplish. Because of these advances, computer users are now able to listen to their favorite music, record and watch videos, and enjoy streaming media all from the comfort of their computer.

This session shows you how to use the Windows Media Player to access a variety of media-based and Web-based content. In addition, you learn about alternative media types and the players used to access them, such as QuickTime movies, Flash Web sites, and Shockwave applications.

Accessing the Windows Media Player

The Windows Media player can be accessed from the Start menu by choosing Start ⇨ All Programs ⇨ Accessories ⇨ Entertainment ⇨ Windows Media Player. Alternately, you might have to choose Start ⇨ All Programs ⇨ Windows Media Player. The media player also is configured to automatically open when certain types of files are accessed, such as CD-ROM audio tracks or some types of video files.

To explore the functionality of the Windows Media player, follow these steps:

1. Open the Windows Media Player, shown in Figure 21-1, by choosing Start ⇨ All Programs ⇨ Windows Media Player or through Start ⇨ All Programs ⇨ Accessories ⇨ Entertainment ⇨ Windows Media Player.

Figure 21-1   *The Windows Media Player is used to access a wide variety of audio and video files.*

2. In the Windows Media Player, choose the Now Playing tab. This view allows you to see which files are currently available on your playlist and start, stop, and pause the playback using the buttons at the bottom of the window.

3. Click the Media Guide tab. The content in this view is updated when you access the Internet and provides access to information such as top music and news headlines, movie reviews, and even information about sporting events. Be sure to scroll down to view all of the content on the page. In addition, click the various submenus located at the left side of the main window. Each subcategory allows you to view information about that specific topic.

4. Select the Copy from CD tab. In the Copy from CD view, shown in Figure 21-2, you are able to transfer tracks from your audio CDs into a compressed format that is stored on your local hard drive. This makes it easy to listen to your favorite music while at your computer without having the CD loaded. Files transferred using this view are stored in your My Documents\My Music folder.

Figure 21-2 *Using the Copy from CD view, you can transfer music from a CD to your computer.*

5. Choose the Media Library tab. When accessing this view for the first time you are asked if you would like the Media Player to search your hard drive for various media types. As you add or remove media, the Media Player updates the locations of the files on your hard drive.

6. If you prefer to listen to the radio and are connected to the Internet, choose the Radio Tuner tab. Using this view, you can search for and listen to hundreds of stations that are streaming broadcasts on the Web.

7. Click the Copy to CD or Device tab to transfer audio or video files that are currently stored on your hard drive to a CD or portable device such as an MP3 player.

8. Finally, choose the Skin Chooser tab, shown in Figure 21-3, to customize the way the Windows Media Player looks. If the default skins don't strike your fancy, click the More Skins button at the top of the window to download more skins from the Web.

One thing to note when copying large numbers of music or video files to a CD is file size. Most CDs only accept 650 to 720 MB of recordings. If you select files that together ultimately are too large for the recording space, you may not receive a warning message stating this until much later in the process when you're actually trying to write the files to a CD. Whenever you're copying more than a few such files this way, try to keep an eye on total file size.

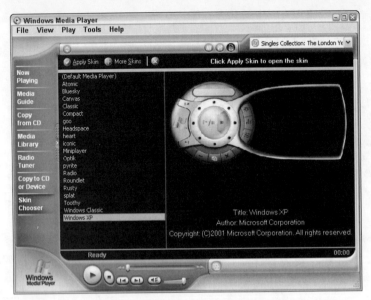

Figure 21-3   Customize the Windows Media Player using skins.

Playing Media-Based Audio Files

**20 Min.
To Go**

Media-based audio files are usually those stored on a CD-ROM although you can often find other audio files you've downloaded previously if you click Media Library in Windows Media Player. The first time you use this tool, it performs a search of your files looking for types of media it can play. You can also press the F3 key on your keyboard or open Tools ➪ Search for Media Files to add items to your playlist. Double-click any item on your playlist to play the selection.

The easiest way for you to play CD-based audio files is to simply insert the disc into your CD drive and close the drawer. Once Windows recognizes the disc as an audio disc, it can be configured to launch the Windows Media Player and start the first track automatically.

To see how easy it is to listen to CD audio on your computer, follow these steps:

1. Insert an audio CD into your CD-ROM drive and close the drawer. As shown in Figure 21-4, Windows XP recognizes the media as a music CD and asks what task Windows XP should perform. Choose Play Audio CD using the Windows Media Player and check the button that says Always do the selected action. The Media Player launches and track 1 begins.

2. At the bottom of the Windows Media Player, click the Pause button to pause the playback. You can resume the music by clicking the Play button.

3. To move to a different track, use the Previous and Next buttons. You can also double-click a track in the playlist to activate that song.

4. To control the volume of the media player, adjust the volume slider by clicking and holding the slider and moving your mouse to the left or right.

5. To stop the playback, click the Stop button on the button bar.

Figure 21-4   *Choose what Windows XP should do when a music CD is inserted.*

Note that if you experience low volume or off-balance problems when you use Media Player after you've adjusted the player's volume setting, you should check the volume control on your speakers to be sure it's turned to a sufficient level to hear it properly. You can also check Windows' speaker volume settings by following these steps:

1. Open the volume control by choosing Start ➪ Control Panel ➪ Sounds, Speech, and Audio Devices ➪ Sounds and Audio Devices.

2. Select the Volume tab.

3. Adjust the settings for Device Volume by moving the slide switch to the right (to increase it, or to the left to decrease it).

4. Click the Speaker Volume button and then use the slide switch again to adjust left and right speaker volume.

Playing Web-Based Audio Files

Playing Web-based audio files using the Windows Media Player is almost as easy as playing music from a CD. The only additional item that you need is an active Internet connection, and the faster your connection is, the more smoothly your audio will stream. To use the Windows Media Player to listen to streaming audio, follow these steps:

1. Open the Windows Media Player by choosing Start ➪ All Programs ➪ Windows Media Player.

2. Choose the Radio Tuner tab, shown in Figure 21-5.

3. Double-click any of the radio stations in the Featured Stations panel and choose Play from the submenu that appears when you make your selection.

4. To pause or stop the playback, use the control buttons at the bottom of the player.

Note that even with a fast Internet connection, you may notice slowdowns and even slight pauses in the radio play. This is not uncommon and is typically caused by a high volume of Internet traffic.

Figure 21-5 *You can easily listen to Web-based music using the Windows Media Player.*

Playing Video Files

10 Min.
To Go

Playing video files in the Windows Media Player is almost as easy as playing audio files, but requires a much more robust Internet connection. If you are connecting to the Web using a dial-up modem, expect a bit of a wait while accessing Web-based movies. If, however, you are using broadband (such as cable or DSL) to access the Web, playing movie files is usually a snap. To see how easy it can be to view movie files, simply:

1. Open Internet Explorer and type http://movies.yahoo.com/trailers in the address bar.

2. Choose from any trailer and allow Yahoo to detect your computer settings.

3. In the Media Helper, shown in Figure 21-6, choose the Windows Media Player and your connection speed and click Accept Settings.

4. Once your player and speed are configured, Yahoo! automatically plays the movie trailer in your browser using the Windows Media Player ActiveX control.

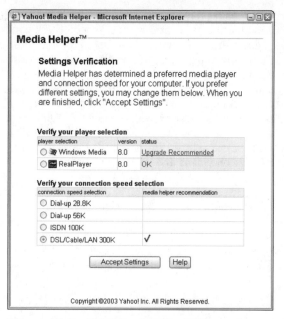

Figure 21-6 *The Yahoo! Media Helper assists you in choosing a player.*

Alternative Media Types

Now that you see how easy it is to play music and video on your computer using the Windows Media Player, it's probably a good idea to discuss some other media formats that you might encounter. Over the last few years, the MP3 format has rapidly grown in popularity due to its ability to compress music files into sizes that are significantly smaller than the format used to store audio on CDs. Microsoft has included support for playing MP3 files into the Windows Media Player, so feel free to digitize your audio collection and store them on your hard drive. Just remember that although MP3s are smaller in size, they still can fill up your hard drive quickly.

When it comes to video, the most common alternative format you will probably encounter are files using the Apple QuickTime format. To view QuickTime files, you need to download the QuickTime player from Apple's Web site at `www.apple.com/quicktime/download/`. You'll be prompted to choose your operating system (select Win98/NT/Me/2000/XP) and your language. To register your download (optional), you are asked to enter your e-mail address, first and last name, and your country. Then click the Download QuickTime button. When prompted to save the file, note its location. When the download is finished, if the installation does not start automatically, click Start ➪ Run, browse to the folder where you downloaded the file, and select QuickTime Installer. Click Open and the installation begins. Once installed, QuickTime will automatically play any movies that you encounter using the QuickTime format.

Along with audio and video, dynamic Web pages have grown in popularity as well. A company called Macromedia has led the way in creating applications that develop these content-rich Web sites and has produced several add-in browser components that allow you to enjoy sites that employ technologies such as Flash and Shockwave. To download the Shockwave player for your browser, visit http://sdc.shockwave.com/shockwave/download/download.cgi?P1_Prod_Version=Shockwave. To download the Flash player, visit www.macromedia.com/shockwave/download/download.cgi?P1_Prod_Version=ShockwaveFlash. Once you have these two add-ins installed, you can enjoy a wider variety of Web content that ranges from movies to games. For a sample of Flash and Shockwave–driven content, visit Macromedia's ShockWave Web site at www.shockwave.com. This site uses the ShockWave technology to allow you to listen to music, watch videos and even play games.

Done!

REVIEW

- The Windows Media player can be accessed using the Start menu by choosing Start ⇨ All Programs ⇨ Windows Media Player.

- You can configure Windows XP to automatically play music CDs using the Windows Media Player.

- Use the search function under Media Library or from the Tools menu to search for other compatible media files on your PC that may be added to your playlist.

- You can download and install other players, such as Apple QuickTime, to handle alternative formats for media that Media Player doesn't handle.

- From within the Windows Media Player, you can listen to streaming audio, watch video files, and even transfer music to your computer's hard drive.

- Using the Skins chooser, you can customize the way the Windows Media Player looks.

QUIZ YOURSELF

1. How do you access the Windows Media Player? (See *Accessing the Windows Media Player* section.)

2. Which view allows you to listen to streaming radio stations? (See *Playing Web-Based Audio Files* section.)

3. When playing a music CD, how do you change tracks? (See *Playing Media-Based Audio Files* section.)

4. Name two alternative media formats that you might encounter on the Web. (See *Alternative Media Types* section.)

Adding and Configuring Hardware

Session Checklist

✔ Understanding Plug and Play hardware

✔ Configuring hardware devices

✔ Installing, modifying, and removing drivers

✔ Learning about ports

✔ Getting port information

✔ Using Troubleshooters

Without the right hardware, Windows XP won't even install for you. But once you have Windows up and running, you will need to make only minor adjustments to your hardware. Usually, you will only need to deal with hardware when you make a change such as adding an additional or larger hard drive, replacing your video card, or adding a piece of hardware you have convinced yourself you can't live without any longer.

This session gives you advice on making hardware decisions, configuring new hardware, and gives you some answers to common hardware problems. You begin with a lesson in a type of hardware technology called Plug and Play.

You can find an article offering basic information on computer hardware at the companion Web site for this book, located at www.wiley.com/compbooks/nicholson.

Plug and Play Hardware

Plug and Play (PnP) devices are automatically detected and configured by Windows XP. This is made possible because hardware designers use the standards set forth by Microsoft to produce devices (and their associated installation software) that Windows can immediately recognize and work with. Most devices sold today are equipped with this technology and/or capability.

Windows XP has eliminated many of the Plug and Play problems that plagued earlier Windows versions and has made this feature relatively trouble-free. Often, this type of hardware installation is accomplished without any effort on your part. Other times, you may be prompted to insert the CD (or sometimes, a floppy disk) that came packaged with your hardware.

For example, install a new Plug and Play modem into your PC's motherboard (which requires your PC to be off and disconnected from power) and when you next turn on your PC, Windows will report that it has detected new hardware and will install and configure it. Likewise, if you plug a new printer into your USB port (discussed later in this session) while the PC is turned on, Windows immediately recognizes the new hardware connection, installs it, and makes it immediately available for your use.

Configuration and drivers

Each piece of hardware installed to your PC and Windows has a specific identity (think of this as a unique inventory ID) and is able to send information on specific "channels" that allow it to communicate with the PC's central processing unit (CPU). *Configuration* is the process by which a hardware device is adjusted to work properly with your system and to fit your specific needs. Some of this configuration is performed by Windows and your new PC automatically, while other aspects of configuration can be modified by you. For example, when you install a new video card, it may be automatically set to display a certain number of colors over a specific screen size or resolution such as 800×600 or 640×480. You can then configure the video card through options in Windows to increase or decrease the number of colors and screen size used.

But before a device can be configured, it must be seen by Windows and able to communicate with your PC. The control mechanism used to facilitate this process as well as the normal use of the hardware device itself is called a hardware *driver*. A driver is a program that controls a device. Every device, whether it be a printer, disk drive, or keyboard, must have a driver program. Many drivers, such as the keyboard driver, come with the Windows XP operating system. For other devices, particularly new devices released after the introduction of Windows XP, you may need to load a new driver when you connect the device to your computer.

A driver acts like a translator between the device and programs that use the device. Each device has its own set of specialized commands that only its driver knows. The driver, therefore, accepts generic commands from a program and then translates them into specialized commands for the specific device.

Drivers normally come from one of four sources:

- The Windows XP operating system disk
- A disk supplied with the hardware
- An Internet download from the device manufacturer's Web site
- A Web site dedicated to providing hardware drivers for a variety of devices

Automated updates of Windows XP (discussed further in Session 24) often provide additional drivers for new hardware. The drivers supplied with the hardware are generally not the newest versions, but will work adequately. Your best source for new drivers is the product manufacturer's Web site. If you simply can't get your hardware to work with Windows XP, a last resort is often searching the Internet for an XP driver that works with your computer. One of the best-known sites providing access to nearly all known drivers is www.drivers.com. Although this site is free, you need to register in order to get access to driver information and downloads.

When you plan to purchase new hardware to install to your Windows XP system, you should visit the Microsoft Windows Hardware Compatibility List page at www.microsoft.akadns.net/whdc/hcl/search.mspx to check a device's compatibility with your operating system. There, you can type in the exact product name you want to purchase, or look at a list of all devices under a particular category (such as audio, monitor, or printer) to determine which are compatible with Windows XP.

This is an important step because it helps ensure that the hardware you buy will be detected automatically and work as you expect. A device that isn't listed here may still work with Windows XP, although it may require a special driver you obtain from the manufacturer or have special installation or use instructions. Check your hardware manufacturer's Web site for details.

Internal and external hardware device connections

Internal hardware devices are generally connected directly to the motherboard. External devices are connected to the computer by means of one of several types of ports. A *port* is a connection on the outside of the computer. The most common types of ports are

- One or two serial ports (most commonly used to connect older hardware, such as a modem, keyboard, or mouse). These can have 9- or 25-pin connections. These ports are identified as COM1 and, if available, COM2.

- One parallel port (most commonly used to connect printers or older scanners). Parallel ports have a 25-pin connection. This port is identified as LPT1.

- PS/2 ports (commonly used to connect newer keyboards and mice). Usually, there are separate PS/2 ports for the mouse and keyboard.

- Universal Serial Bus (USB) ports are generally located next to the PS/2 ports or possibly on the front of the computer. These are the preferred ports to use, for reasons discussed in the next section. A USB device plug to the computer is a small rectangle without visible pins.

- IEEE 1394 (also called Firewire, although that term is exclusively for Macintosh systems) ports are becoming increasingly more common. These are 6-pin sockets (4-pin sockets on laptops) usually located near the USB ports.

**20 Min.
To Go**

Port type selection

When you purchase an external hardware device, you must pay close attention to the type of port used to connect the device to the computer. Most port types are associated with an *interrupt*. An interrupt acts as a signal between a device, your operating system, and your PC's CPU to tell the system when that device needs attention. Typically, a device sends such a signal because some event is taking place. This event can be a key press, when you initiate a printing job, when you try to use your modem, or when a device malfunctions and produces an error.

These signals or interrupts — along with the replies to the hardware made through your system — are communicated through tiny wires on your motherboard called interrupt requests, or IRQs. However, there are only a finite number of these IRQs (16 in total) that must juggle all of the signals they receive. Many of the IRQs are devoted to devices already installed in your PC or added to it. For example, your COM1 and LPT1 ports each have an IRQ available to them. Often, when you first buy a new PC, you may only have one, two, or three IRQs still open to accept new hardware that can communicate through them. Additional serial ports and parallel ports can be added to support additional hardware, but this means configuring each port to share any remaining interrupts. If you are using older types of hardware (often called legacy, ISA, or non-PNP hardware), you can quickly run out of IRQs to support them. Serial ports can send data in only one direction at a time, resulting in slow performance of any device connected. Parallel ports are bidirectional, and are, therefore, faster.

Today, the port style of preference is the Universal Serial Bus (USB). USB ports do not require any specific interrupts. That is to say, it will take any free IRQ you may have. However, what's different about USB is that no matter how many USB devices you connect (and the limit is 127 devices), they can all share that single IRQ. The original version of USB (1.1) is used exclusively with slower hardware such as keyboards, printers, scanners, and digital cameras because its transfer speed is limited to a maximum of 12 Mbps. This is faster than serial and parallel ports but not as fast as today's USB 2.0 that supports a maximum transfer rate of 480 Mbps, suitable for high-speed drives, digital video cameras, and other uses. (If you want to use more than two or three USB devices, depending on how many USB ports are built into your computer), you will need to purchase a USB hub. Home-size USB hubs run a cable from a single USB port on the computer to a hub which supports two, four, or eight devices. USB supports Plug and Play installation and hot plugging (also called hot-swapping), meaning that devices can be added or removed without having to turn off the power to the system and reboot the computer.

 For faster speed, upgrade or purchase equipment that is USB 2.0 compatible.

 In order to take advantage of the high speed of USB 2.0, the device, hub, and computer connection must all be rated USB 2.0. If any one of these components is only rated USB 1.1, all devices will operate at the 12-Mbps transfer rate.

Today, most new devices are rated USB 2.0. But if it doesn't say USB 2.0 on the package, it's not. When you plug in a 2.0 device, if you are not fully compatible for any reason, Windows XP gives you a message to the effect that you are still only operating at USB 1.1 speed.

 If your computer doesn't have USB 2.0 ports, you can buy a card for a reasonable price to insert into your motherboard and make your computer 2.0 compatible.

IEEE 1394 is another external connection port very popular for connecting digital video equipment and high-speed external drives. Like USB, it has two versions: a slower one with a maximum transfer speed of about 400 Mbps and the current 1394b standard which supports a maximum transfer rate of up to 3200 Mbps. Also like USB, IEEE 1394 takes just a single IRQ regardless of how many IEEE 1394 devices are connected through its ports.

However, IEEE 1394 is still not included on all desktop and portable PCs, although it's more widely available than it was a few years ago. You can purchase an IEEE 1394/1394b adapter which you can install to an available expansion slot on your PC's motherboard to give you this connection capability along with two or three ports.

Checking Your Ports

It's smart PC practice to check your ports, along with other hardware, on a periodic basis. This familiarizes you with what hardware resources are being used and may potentially alert you to a problem before you notice an error later on.

1. Click Start ⇨ Control Panel ⇨ Performance and Maintenance ⇨ System. If you are using the Classic menu, you can choose Start ⇨ Control Panel and double-click the System icon. The System Properties dialog box is displayed, as shown in Figure 22-1.

2. Click the Hardware tab.

3. At the Hardware tab, click the Device Manager button in the Device Manager pane. The Device Manager is displayed, as shown in Figure 22-2. At this point, the hardware items are displayed by categories. Clicking the plus sign next to a category reveals one or more devices assigned to that category.

You can also get to the same dialog box by right-clicking the My Computer icon on your desktop, and choosing Properties from the displayed context menu.

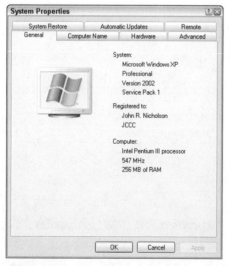

Figure 22-1   *The System Properties dialog box is used as the starting point for checking out your system.*

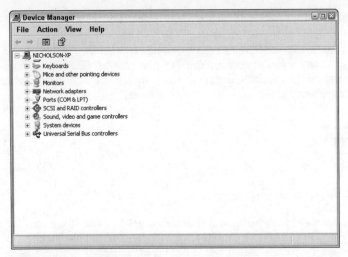

Figure 22-2 *The Device Manager dialog box displays all hardware categories currently being used by your computer.*

4. Click the plus sign next to Ports.

5. Right-click Communications Port (COM1) and Choose Properties. The General Tab is displayed, as shown in Figure 22-3. Notice that in the Device Status pane, the message that the device is working properly is displayed. Also notice the Troubleshoot button just beneath the message. You will be working with the button shortly.

Figure 22-3 *The General Tab of the Communications Port (COM1) Properties dialog box displays an overview of the device.*

6. Click the Port Settings tab. This displays the Device Settings, and will contain information on the selected device.

7. Click the Driver tab. As the name implies, this tab shows information about the Driver currently being used. A sample of this dialog box is displayed in Figure 22-4. Your information may differ. In addition to the Driver Version, you can update the driver to a newer version. If you have just installed the current driver and it doesn't work properly in your system, and you prefer to go back to the previous version, click the Roll Back Driver button to install the previous version of the driver.

The Roll Back Driver option is most often used when you are viewing information about your video driver.

Figure 22-4 *The Driver Tab displays information about the driver currently being used by your computer, and allows you to make changes.*

8. Click Cancel to return to the Device Manager window. Do not close the window at this time.

Using a Troubleshooter

10 Min. To Go

A common problem that you might experience is that your printer stops working. Another common problem is that your modem is not working. But the steps for troubleshooting any hardware device remain the same. Make sure it is plugged in and turned on (this is probably the most common problem for external powered devices, yet the one most often overlooked). If there isn't power to the device, check that the power cord is firmly held at the device, and at the plug into your power strip (surge suppressor). Make sure the socket on the power strip is still active by plugging a lamp or other device into it. If you still don't have power, refer to Session 29 for additional help.

If there is power to the device, but it still isn't working properly, open the Device Manager window, as described in the previous set of steps. The Troubleshooter for each device is a series of statements and questions. Your answer to each question takes you, in hierarchical order, from the most common cause to the least common cause.

As practice, take a look at the Troubleshooter for the mouse, another common problem.

1. The Device Manager window should still be open from the previous steps. Click the plus sign next to Mice and other pointing devices.

2. Right-click the description of your mouse. Choose Properties. The Mouse Properties dialog box is displayed as shown in Figure 22-5.

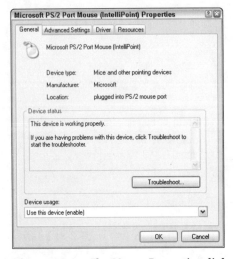

Figure 22-5 *The Mouse Properties dialog box is the place to begin if your mouse is not working properly.*

 Unless you have a Microsoft Optical Mouse connected to a PS/2 port, your display information will probably be different from that shown in Figure 22-5.

3. Click the Troubleshoot button. Figure 22-6 shows the first screen of the Mouse Troubleshooter.

4. Click the Next button. Explore the Troubleshooter at your leisure.

 For additional Troubleshooters, go to www.microsoft.com **and search for the term Troubleshooter. Choose the option offering Troubleshooters available for Windows. Then select the specific Troubleshooter you need.**

5. When you are finished, close down all open windows until you are back at your desktop.

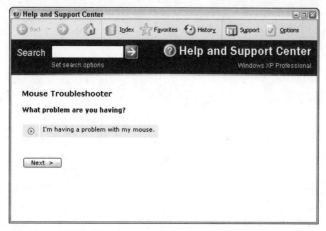

Figure 22-6   *The first step of the Mouse troubleshooter gets you started in solving a mouse problem.*

Done!

REVIEW

- Plug and Play devices are automatically detected and configured by Windows XP.
- Configuration refers to adjusting the settings through which the operating system recognizes and communicates with hardware devices.
- A driver acts like a translator between the hardware device and programs using the device.
- The four most common port types are serial, parallel, PS/2, and USB.
- Using the System Properties dialog box, you can obtain information about a variety of devices.

QUIZ YOURSELF

1. Describe the Plug and Play feature. (See *Plug and Play Hardware* section.)
2. What is a driver? (See *Configuration and drivers* section.)
3. What are the four sources from which you would normally obtain drivers? (See *Configuration and drivers* section.)
4. How many peripheral devices can be connected through a USB port? (See *Port type selection* section.)

Sharing Resources

Session Checklist

✔ Buying hardware

✔ Assembling the network

✔ Installing hardware

✔ Creating a workgroup

✔ Changing a workgroup name

✔ Sharing resources

✔ Adding resources to My Network Places

As you learned in Session 14, the purpose of a network is to share resources. Although Windows XP Professional is designed to be used as a domain model of networking, the Home Edition of Windows XP will not operate in a domain model environment. Regardless, both versions of Windows XP are quite capable of performing in a peer-to-peer workgroup environment, where resources are shared. In a workgroup some domain model features are unavailable, including a centralized database in which resource locations are recorded (called the Active Directory), the ability to log in from any computer, and enhanced security features.

This session examines the simplified ability to share resources within a workgroup. Before sharing resources with other computers and users, you must set up a workgroup.

Gathering the Required Workgroup Hardware

**30 Min.
To Go**

In order to implement a workgroup, each computer must have a minimum of a Network Interface Card (NIC) and an appropriate length of Category 5 (CAT5) cabling with RJ-45 connectors on each end (wireless requirements are found in the *Going the Wireless Route* section below). In addition, you must have a Network hub with at least as many connections available as you have workstations (computers in the workgroups). If you want to share an Internet connection among the computers, you should also purchase a router, again with at least as many workstation connections as you have computers in your workgroup.

For purposes of this session, when I refer to a network, I will be talking about a home network built on the workgroup model, which can be used to share resources using both versions of Windows XP.

A home network doesn't have to be expensive. The basic expenses, beyond the workstations themselves, involve about $20 (or less) for 10/100 MB for each NIC, another $25 for cabling, and $20 for a hub. A router will add about $75 for four ports.

You may also want to invest in an electronic KVM switch, which allows you to use the same keyboard, video display (monitor), and mouse for each workstation. Although a good one with cables runs about $100, it's a great investment.

The Network Interface Card

There are two things you need to know about NICs. First is the type of slot they require. You need to make sure your NIC type matches the slot on your computer. In a desktop computer that is less than about 2 years old, you will only have the newer PCI slots. The older slots are ISA slots and are much slower. If you purchase a new NIC, it will be PCI. Used NICs may be of either type.

The second thing to understand about NICs is that if you are using a notebook computer, you can purchase a wireless NIC (also called a wireless access card). However, doing so means that your other equipment must also be wireless. An NIC for a laptop is about the size and shape of a credit card. It might be identified as an NIC computer card, or, more commonly, instead of a computer card you may see it referred to as a PCMCIA card, short for Personal Computer Memory Card International Association.

Before buying any type of internal peripheral, make sure you have an empty slot to put it in.

The cabling

Category 5 (Cat 5) or the more expensive Category 6 (Cat 6) Ethernet cabling can be purchased in bulk or in individual lengths with connectors installed. Unless you have done Ethernet cabling before, don't try to save money by buying in bulk and adding your own connectors. This is a losing cause, and a single incorrectly placed wire can cause all kinds of problems. Each end of the Cat 5 or Cat 6 cable comes with an RJ-45 connector. This is similar to a standard telephone connection cable, although slightly longer and wider. The telephone connector is designated RJ-11. An RJ-11 connector will not fit snugly into an RJ-45 connection point.

The hub

Today, nearly all hubs need to be plugged into an electrical outlet. That means you must have enough room on your surge suppressor to insert a conversion adapter (which takes up the room of two regular plugs). Hubs usually come with either four or eight connections. If you think you might want to add more in the future, buy the larger one.

Hubs, like NICs, are rated at 10 Mbps or 100 Mbps, or both (designated as 10/100). (Newer equipment, which can handle 1 Gbps is not discussed here.) If you buy an NIC that is not rated as 10/100 Mbps, your hub must be capable of operating at the rated speed of your NICs. For this reason, it's a good idea to buy NICs that are rated at 10/100 Mbps.

Inexpensive routers

As mentioned earlier, you can buy an inexpensive router to use on your home or small business network. Routers can cost more than $10,000, but don't be frightened. An inexpensive one will work just fine to allow you to share one Internet connection among several computers. Like hubs, most routers come with connections for either four or eight workstations.

Assembling the Network

20 Min. To Go

Once you have purchased the parts for your network, putting it together should be fairly simple. If an NIC has already been installed in your computer, either by you or by the factory, the hardest work is already done. One of the ways you can tell if you already have an NIC installed is by looking at the back of your computer. An NIC connection looks like a phone cable but is larger. Also, an NIC will normally have small green and red or amber lights. Another way to tell is to right-click My Computer ⇨ Properties, click the Hardware Tab and click the Device Manager button. If you have a Network Adapters category, click the plus sign to the left of the text. If you have an NIC installed, you should see it listed, similar to the expanded line in Figure 23-1. If you don't have an NIC installed, you will not have that category.

Installing a Network Interface Card

If you don't have an NIC already installed, you need to add one. To install an NIC, you must first remove the cover of the system unit (the computer itself). Make sure you have an available (unoccupied) PCI slot.

As you look down on the motherboard, with the slots away from you, you may notice that the slot on the left is black and longer than the other slots. This is an ISA slot, and should only be used if you have a 10-Mbps NIC with the old-style plug-in. All other slots, other than the one holding your video card (which is generally the right-most slot) should be PCI slots.

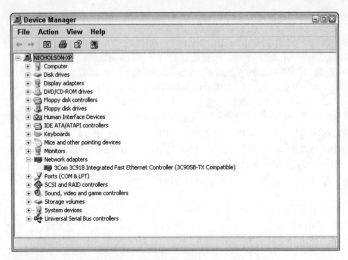

Figure 23-1   *The Network adapters category has been opened and displays the NIC information.*

Before ever removing a cover, you must know what you are doing. You must remove the power plug from the unit, as well as any other connections (such as the video and printer cables). Any stray voltage, particularly a static discharge from your body, can destroy the motherboard and other electronic parts. If you don't know what you are doing, you are taking a chance that could end up costing a lot more than you bargained for. You may want to review the article on computer hardware found on the companion Web site at www.wiley.com/compbooks/nicholson before attempting some of these tasks.

Installing the NIC is simple. Handling the NIC by its outer edges (not the bottom one where the connections to the motherboard are located), snap the NIC into the slot. You don't need to force it, but you may find that you have to press down firmly and evenly to get the card seated correctly.

After installing the NIC, it is advisable to replace the cover (although I don't put in the screws until I'm sure everything is working) before plugging the power cord into the system unit and *then* plugging the power cord into your surge suppressor.

Running the cables

Run an Ethernet cable from the NIC in each workstation to the hub. Don't plug in the hub until you have run all the cables, or even better, run one cable at a time, making sure the connection works; then unplug the hub while adding the next cable. When you plug in the hub, if you have a good connection between the hub and NIC, you should (normally) see a green light flashing on the front or back of your hub.

After all the cables have been installed at both the NIC and hub ends, you are ready to plug in the hub to the surge suppressor and see if things are working as they should.

At this point, other than the flashing lights of the hub, and a flashing light on the NIC, nothing is actually working. You must first create a workgroup, and then make sure there is at least one object on each computer that is shared.

Going the Wireless Route

You've just learned about the traditional way to set up a network. But what about a wireless network?

Wireless is a good choice when you want to avoid running lengths of cable throughout your home or office and want some flexibility in where you use a laptop, for example. Running a network cable out to your patio or deck probably isn't wise unless you can strictly control moisture and other conditions.

There are currently two major versions of wireless networking: standard and broadband (the latter is useful when sharing a broadband Internet connection with other computers on a network). The former has a maximum transfer rate of about 11 Mbps, while the latter boosts this as high as a maximum of 54 Mbps. Price differences between the two can be steep; if you go this route, compare prices carefully.

Different wireless networking packages offer a fair amount of variation in the hardware used and, to some degree, how it connects. Usually, what you need is a wireless-compatible NIC or wireless access card for each PC on a wireless network, with a device known as a wireless access point or WAP (also sometimes called a base station), which behaves as a central transmitter-receiver through which PCs on the network can communicate. This device replaces the cable that would normally have to run between each workstation.

The wireless access cards install the same way as the NICs you read about earlier. How the WAP connects can differ. Consult your product documentation to be sure yours is connected according to those instructions. You will find that most wireless networking hardware manufacturers include great Web-based instructions that supplement and enhance the printed documentation that ships with the hardware.

Verifying a Workgroup Association

Each computer must be a member of a workgroup. Follow these simple steps on each of your computers to verify that the computer is a member of your workgroup.

1. Make sure each computer is booted into Windows.
2. Right-click the My Computer icon and choose Properties.
3. Click the Computer Name tab in the System Properties dialog box. You should see a window similar to the one shown in Figure 23-2. By default, the name of the workgroup is WORKGROUP. (See the next section if you want to change it to something else.)
4. At this point, you can add an optional computer description in the open field if desired. The Full computer name was given when you installed Windows XP.
5. Click OK to save any changes you made to the description and close the dialog box.

Figure 23-2　*The Computer Name tab of the System Properties dialog box allows you to add your computer to a workgroup.*

What happens if one or more of the computers on your network do not appear as part of your workgroup? First, verify the workgroup name as you did in the previous steps. Each workstation must have the same workgroup name. Then recheck your network installation.

Changing the Workgroup Name

If you don't like the default workgroup name of WORKGROUP, it is fairly simple to change it. Although the tab you'll be working with says Computer Name, it's the workgroup's name that you will change in this exercise. Just follow these steps.

1. Make sure each computer is booted into Windows.
2. Right-click the My Computer icon and choose Properties.
3. Click the Computer Name tab in the System Properties dialog box.
4. Click the Change button. You see the dialog box shown in Figure 23-3, with the Computer name (not the Workgroup name) selected.

Changing the computer name itself rather than the workgroup name can cause unpredictable results, so use caution when changing it, and make sure you have plenty of time to troubleshoot any problems that might occur.

5. Highlight the Workgroup name.
6. Delete the current Workgroup name and enter the new name.

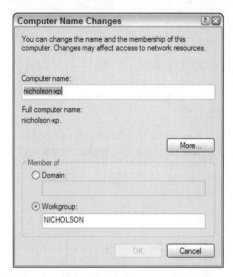

Figure 23-3   *The Computer Name Changes dialog box allows you to change the computer name or the workgroup name.*

The Workgroup name is entered in all capital letters, regardless of the status of your Shift or Caps Lock keys.

7. Press OK. You see the message shown in Figure 23-4 (with the new workgroup name you have entered).

Figure 23-4   *The message indicates that you have successfully joined a new workgroup.*

8. Pressing OK displays the message shown in Figure 23-5. The workgroup name will not take effect until after the computer is restarted.

Figure 23-5 *The warning reminds you that your computer must be restarted in order for the new workgroup name to take effect.*

9. Clicking OK again displays a message asking if you want to reboot the computer now. If you have any applications open, click Cancel, close the applications, and restart the computer.

**10 Min.
To Go**

Sharing Resources

Nearly any object or objects on your computer can be shared. You can share a printer or a folder. Each computer has a folder named Shared Documents. Dragging any file or folder into this folder will automatically make it a shared file or folder. In the next few steps, you learn to manually share resources. In this example, you share your My Documents folder.

1. Right-click the My Documents icon on your desktop. Choose Properties. Click the Sharing tab. The dialog box should look similar to the one shown in Figure 23-6.

Figure 23-6 *The Sharing tab of the My Documents Properties dialog box allows you to share the folder with other users or allows you to access it from another computer.*

2. In the Network sharing and security pane, make sure there are checkmarks in both Share this folder on the network and Allow network users to change my files option boxes.

3. In the Share name box, enter the name for the share. It should uniquely identify the object as to name and the computer on which it resides. When you are finished, press OK. You will see a hand underneath, holding any icon whose contents are shared.

Adding Resources from Other Computers

If you want to make shared resources located on another computer available to your current computer, the easiest way is by adding a Network Place. To do so, follow these steps:

1. Double-click the My Network Places icon. If it's not present on the desktop, click Start ➪ My Network Places.

2. In the left pane, click Add a network place. The Add Network Place Wizard is displayed, as shown in Figure 23-7.

Figure 23-7 *The first screen of the Add Network Place Wizard explains that you can create a shortcut to a Web site, an FTP site, or other network location.*

3. Click Next to continue. By default, the screen displays the option to select another network location.

4. Click Next to continue. Click the Browse button. You should see the names of all shared objects within your workgroup.

If you know the exact address of the shared object, you can enter it in the Internet or network address box. The format of this address is *computername**sharename**folder*.

If you have Windows Explorer, you can drag the object into the Internet or network address box.

5. Choose the shared object for which you want to add a network place. You might have to browse through several folder levels to find the one you want to add.

6. Click Next to continue. Type a short name you want displayed. Remember to make it specific, so that you can easily find exactly what you are looking for when you open My Network Places at a later time.

7. At the final screen of the Wizard, you can choose to display the network place now, or remove the checkmark from the option box so that it doesn't display immediately, and click the Finish button to close the Wizard.

8. To make sure that your new network place is available, double-click My Network Places. You should be able to see the newly added object.

9. Double-click the object to open it. You should now have access to an object on another computer.

Done!

REVIEW

- Use a workgroup to share computer resources without having a centralized server.

- For two or more workstations, an NIC and cabling, which are required for each, and a hub are the minimum required hardware items to share resources on a standard network. For a wireless network, you need two or more workstations, wireless access cards for each, and a wireless access point.

- Each computer to share resources must be a member of the same workgroup.

- You can create a network place, which is a shortcut to shared objects on another computer.

QUIZ YOURSELF

1. What are the minimum hardware items to share resources on a standard, cabled network? (See *Gathering the Required Workgroup Hardware* section.)

2. What type of NIC would you purchase for a laptop? (See *The Network Interface Card* section.)

3. What type of connector is used with Ethernet cables? (See *The cabling* section.)

4. What's the maximum transfer rate for the fastest wireless network? (See *Going the Wireless Route* section.)

5. Which Wizard is used to create shortcuts to resources on other computers? (See *Adding Resources from Other Computers* section.)

Updating Windows XP

Session Checklist

✔ Understanding the difference between hackers and crackers

✔ Explaining the difference between patches and service packs

✔ Updating Windows XP automatically, manually, or on a specified schedule

✔ Personalizing the Windows Update Internet site

✔ Understanding Product Key policies

E ven before a new version of Windows is printed on disc and shipped out on new PCs and to stores for retail sale, updates to that version are in the works. In general, these upgrades are small *patches*, generally implemented to fix problems in the operating system programming code, or occasionally to offer a very minor upgrade to a feature. Less frequently, such updates are made available to correct serious issues that may affect system performance or security flaws that may leave your PC vulnerable to infiltration by computer viruses or hackers.

To try to ensure that Windows XP can function optimally and remain operating in this fashion, it is very important that you keep your copy of Windows up-to-date — you must perform regular updates.

In this session, you will receive an overview of Windows security problems, learn the differences between patches and service packs, learn how to set Windows to automatically update itself or wait for you to manually update it, and review Microsoft's Product Key policies.

Hackers and Crackers

Windows XP contains over 50 million lines of programming code, so there is more than a little margin for errors and incompatibilities. Microsoft releases these fixes as quickly as possible. A major reason for the seemingly inordinate number of patches Microsoft has issued is the area of Windows security. As soon as Microsoft patches a security hole, someone figures out another way to breach security. There is a never-ending cycle between Microsoft and people who are trying to find security and other flaws in Windows XP. Some errors are found accidentally; others are purposefully manipulated.

Hacker is a slang term for a computer enthusiast who enjoys learning the technicalities of computer systems and is often considered an expert on the subject. Among computer professionals, depending on how the term is used, it can be either complimentary or derogatory, although it is becoming an increasingly derogatory term. The negative reputation of hackers is becoming more prominent largely because the popular press has co-opted the term to refer to individuals who gain unauthorized access to computer systems for the purpose of stealing and corrupting data. Hackers, themselves, maintain that the proper term for such individuals is cracker. Hackers have their own code of ethics, and they strictly adhere to it. However, a large part of hacker culture is devoted to discovering flaws in software products and making these flaws public. While the majority of these problems represent security concerns, others may illustrate a weakness in a software feature that needs attention.

When these flaws are noted in Microsoft products, Microsoft usually releases a patch to address the problem within a matter of days. You should consider allowing Windows to automatically download (the default setting) and install the upgrades. Occasionally, Microsoft patches affect other software in a negative way. Because of this, Windows always stores a rollback version on your hard drive, so that you can restore the system to the prepatched condition if necessary.

Patches and Service Packs

You should take advantage of Microsoft's regular upgrades to keep your system safe from intrusion and enhance stability. To some degree, the patches will often help stop viruses from destroying your data (although you still need a strong virus protection program, discussed further in Session 28). Think of a patch as a temporary fix to a problem.

If you reinstall Windows XP, you will need to download and install all patches again. This may take quite a while.

When there are many patches, and Microsoft has made significant changes to one or more modules within Windows, Microsoft issues a *service pack*. A service pack involves implementing all previous patches, and usually includes major changes to the code. One thing you may notice is that some of your applications may require an update or service pack within a period of time, often within a few months, after Microsoft issues a service pack. This occurs because the producers of some of your applications may find it necessary to upgrade their own code to reflect the changes made by Microsoft in its Windows service pack. You can easily find out what service pack(s) you have installed by right-clicking My Computer and choosing Properties from the context menu.. The General tab of the System Properties, shown in Figure 24-1, displays the service pack number, if any.

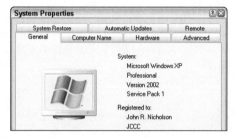

Figure 24-1 *The General tab of the System Properties dialog box displays the Service Pack number in the last line of the System information.*

As with patches, if you reinstall Windows XP, you must also add the service pack after the installation is complete. A service pack can be very large and take several hours to install if you are using a modem.

Updating Windows XP

To offer you maximum flexibility in when and how you update your operating system, Windows XP gives you three different methods you can use to perform those updates:

- Automatic
- Manual
- Scheduled

To change the update method, right-click the My Computer icon (or click Start ⇨ My Computer and select View system information from the context menu). Click the Automatic Updates tab. You will see a window similar to the one shown in Figure 24-2.

An explanation of each will follow to help you make your choice, but for now:

- To allow *automatic* updates to occur, click to select Download the updates automatically and notify me when they are ready to be installed. Then click OK.
- To perform updates on a *manual* basis, click to remove the check from the checkbox next to Keep my computer up to date (located at the top of this window). Click OK.
- To update on your desired schedule, click to select Automatically download the updates, and install them on the schedule that I specify. Then click on the drop-down list boxes below this option to set the date and time to perform this. Click OK.

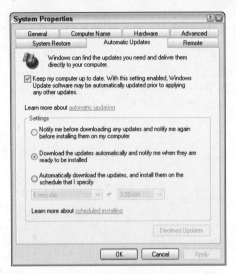

Figure 24-2   *The Automatic Updates tab of the System Properties dialog box allows you to choose either manual, automatic, or scheduled downloads of Windows updates.*

However, while the most important issue is that you do indeed update your system, it's also wise to choose the method that works best for the way you use your PC and the way you connect to the Internet.

Let's talk about that second part for a moment. Without an Internet connection available to a Windows XP system, you won't be able to use the Updating feature. Instead, you have to order update discs from Microsoft at a small cost or download these updates from a PC that has a connection and then copy these files either over your home or office network or burn them to a CD to physically install on the connectionless PC. Thus, it's generally easier all around if you can add an Internet connection to a Windows XP system.

You will learn more about the type and availability of your Internet connection as you read about each method.

Automatic Windows updating

By default, Windows checks for updates and downloads them automatically any time you are online. Also, by default, Windows downloads updates automatically and notifies you when they are ready to be installed. As shown earlier in Figure 24-2, you can also choose to be notified before any downloading occurs.

If your connection to the Internet is constant, in other words, you have a cable or DSL or high-speed satellite Internet connection, you are best suited to have Windows automatically check for updates (the default mode). Leave this default automatic update setting as is and any patches or service packs are automatically downloaded. When Windows has completed the download (in the background, so your work is never interrupted), a flashing icon appears in the Notification area of the Task Bar (the extreme right portion, where the time is located by default). Moving your mouse pointer over the icon displays a message that clicking the icon will begin installation of the updates. These updates can take anywhere from a few minutes to over an hour to install, depending on the size of the patch or service pack, and the speed of your computer.

Don't do an installation of updates until a time when you don't need the computer for a while, such as overnight. You should close all open applications before starting the installation. Following completion of the updates, Windows requires that you restart the computer to continue.

**20 Min.
To Go**

Before moving on to manual updates, it's important to appreciate that there are pros and cons to allowing Windows to update automatically without your active participation. For you, it should represent a savings in time and detail work because Windows is doing the job for you with the result being that your operating system is fully up-to-date.

However, there are downsides to this. For one, you could have several applications open as you work on your desktop and browse the Internet and wonder why your system and/or your Internet connection seem slower than usual. For another — and while this doesn't occur often, it does happen — not all updates go smoothly.

Here's an example. Using automatic update, Windows may try to upgrade your video driver and, in doing so, create a compatibility problem. Since the update happened automatically (unless you've specified that Windows should alert you before installing), it may come as a great surprise when you restart your PC later only to find Windows won't boot except in Safe Mode.

It's not that a bad driver or other problematic update only occurs when you update automatically. The same thing can happen if you go to your video card manufacturer's Web site and download a new driver. But because you aren't always fully aware that the update is happening, you may not realize that your update is the source of a problem that develops as a result of its installation.

If this last issue is of particular concern to you, even if you have an always-on high-speed Internet connection, consider manual or scheduled updating instead.

Manual Windows updating

You may choose to set your updates to occur manually, meaning that you initiate the check for updates to Windows and only select and download the ones you choose. This is the smartest choice when you're connecting via dial-up modem and your phone line when an Internet connection is not always available. It's also an option when you want to review information about a particular update component before it's installed onto your system.

Choosing the manual update route, however, means you must remember to check the Windows Update site, review your options, make your selections, and follow through on the installations. Should you wait a prolonged period of time between updates (more than 4 to 6 weeks, for example), you may find your update list very long and more difficult to weed through.

To manually update, you choose and install specific updates from the Windows Update Web site: `http://windowsupdate.microsoft.com`. When you view the Windows Update site, you see a screen similar to the one shown in Figure 24-3.

If you use this method , you will find that there are many Recommended Updates in the Windows XP area. While you will want to install some of the updates, others may be meant for equipment you don't own, to solve problems you don't experience, or simply be updates that you don't want. You can skip a listed update by not selecting it.

Figure 24-3 *The Windows Update Web site allows you to scan your hard drive for Critical Updates, Windows XP Updates, and Driver Updates.*

However, if you decide to skip an update for any reason, you will find that when you revisit the Windows Update site and your drive is scanned again to check for new updates, the update you skipped in your previous session or sessions will again appear in your list of available choices. There is, however, a way to stop this, so you don't have to sort though all the same unwanted selections on each revisit.

1. Open Internet Explorer and go to windowsupdate.microsoft.com.

2. At the Welcome screen, rather than clicking Scan for updates in the right pane, click Personalize Windows Update in the left pane. You will see a screen similar to the one shown in Figure 24-4.

3. Click the Scan for updates link.

Even if you have scanned for updates in a previous screen, entering the Personalize area requires another scan for updates.

4. After a few seconds, a screen similar to Figure 24-5 is displayed. In my sample screen, I only have Windows XP recommended updates. I have already downloaded and installed the Critical Updates and Service Packs, as well as the Drivers.

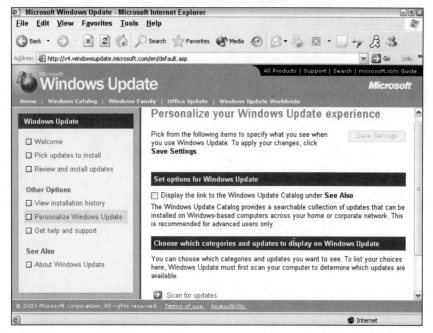

Figure 24-4   *The Windows Update Web site allows you to personalize the screen and determine which updates are displayed and which remain hidden, even though you haven't downloaded them yet.*

5. Remove the checkmarks from the option boxes next to the updates you do *not* want displayed on subsequent scans.

As Microsoft adds new updates, if you do not want to download them, and you do not want them displayed on subsequent scans, you must return to this screen and remove the checkmarks from the appropriate option boxes.

6. When you have made the changes you want to make, you *must* scroll to the top of the window and click the Save Settings button, or your changes will not be saved for the next time you visit the site.

If you are unsure of what a specific update does, there is a way to get more information. A knowledge base reference number is located just to the right of the appropriate option box. To find the article, write down the reference number (or better yet, copy it to the clipboard by selecting it with the mouse and pressing Ctrl+C) and then click the Search option in the upper-right area of the window. In the Search Microsoft.com box, type the reference number you want to search for (or press Ctrl+V to paste it from the clipboard). Click Go. Click the link that takes you to the reference number (there should only be one shown).

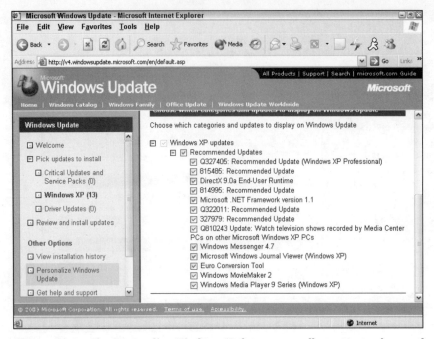

Figure 24-5   *The Personalize Windows Update screen allows you to change the settings for which updates are displayed when a scan is completed.*

Scheduled Windows updating

Rather than having Windows notify you when update files have been downloaded and are ready for installation, you can schedule the downloading *and* installation. You can choose to check for downloads and install automatically every day, or once a week on a specific day (for example, every Monday). You can also set the time for the download and installation to take place. Ideally, you would want to set the time for an hour your computer is normally unused.

You should only choose this option if you have a cable or DSL connection to the Internet. This is because there are often costs involved with prolonged connections on dial-up connections where downloads will go far more slowly than on a high-speed connection. Some phone companies charge you if your line is in use over a certain number of hours each month, while some Internet service providers charge extra if you spend more than a certain number of hours each month on their service.

Microsoft Product Key Policies

In order to install Microsoft Windows XP, you must have a unique Product Key (similar to a serial number). This key is a combination of 25 numbers and letters, and is on a sticker on the back of the CD case that the Windows XP disc came in.

Just in case your original CD gets separated from its case, you might want to write the Product Key on the label side of the CD with a soft-tip permanent marker.

Windows XP can only be installed on a single computer. If you try to use that Product Key on another computer, the Product Key will be rejected. Theoretically, you can install Windows XP an unlimited number of times on the same computer; however, reinstallation on the same computer can sometimes require you to reregister the product. Additionally, on occasion, installation of a service pack also requires reregistering the product. Changing the hardware on your computer may also require reregistration. If the Product Activation screen is displayed for any of these reasons, you can get a new activation number (see the instructions in the *Activating Windows XP after Installation* section of Session 2).

Although Microsoft, in some cases, allows the installation of a single copy of Microsoft Office on two computers [you must check the End User License Agreement (EULA) for further information], the Windows XP EULA allows installation of Windows on only one computer. You must buy a license for each computer on which Windows XP is installed.

Done!

REVIEW

- Windows XP has over 50 million lines of programming code.
- Hacker is slang term for a person who is proficient in the technicalities of computer programming.
- Crackers are users who gain unauthorized access to computer systems for the purpose of stealing and corrupting data.
- A patch is a programming code fix for a small problem. After many patches have been issued, they are combined into a single service pack.
- Windows can be set to update automatically or manually or according to a schedule you define.
- Installing a service pack may require that you contact Microsoft to receive a new activation key.

QUIZ YOURSELF

1. What is a cracker? (See *Hackers and Crackers* sidebar.)
2. What is a collection of many patches called? (See *Patches and Service Packs* section.)
3. Why is it wise to have an Internet connection available when updating your Windows XP PC? (See *Updating Windows XP* section.)
4. What are the disadvantages of using automatic updates? (See *Automatic Windows updating* section.)
5. How might a Service Pack affect the need for an Activation Code? (See *Microsoft Product Key Policies* section.)

25

Controlling the Windows Task Manager

Session Checklist

✔ Understanding the uses of Windows Task Manager

✔ Using the Applications tab

✔ Displaying application and Windows subsystems and services

✔ Measuring efficiency with the Performance tab

✔ Viewing network activity

✔ Fast switching between computer users

W hen an application locks up, and you can't get it to do anything, do you have any options other than restarting your computer? Yes, you do. While this process will lose any unsaved work in the offending application, you can open the Windows Task Manager and try to terminate the problem application. You should then be able to close the application and continue to work in other applications without loss of data in those. Windows Task Manager offers many features that will help you in operating Windows XP efficiently.

In this session you will explore the five tabs of Windows Task Manager. You learn the basics of each one and how they can help you while you are running Windows XP.

30 Min.
To Go

Introducing Windows Task Manager

Windows Task Manager has been around since Windows 95. Over the years it has matured into an extremely useful utility. You can open Task Manager in one of several ways:

- Press Ctrl+Alt+Delete.
- Press Shift+Ctrl+Escape.
- Right-click any empty area of the Taskbar and choose Task Manager.

In versions of Windows previous to Windows 95, pressing Ctrl+Alt+Delete caused the computer to restart. All data in all applications that had not been saved was lost. Often, a forced restart could cause corruption of application or data files. This caused many problems as well as a heightened level of frustration. In fact, Ctrl+Alt+Delete was often disabled when an application crashed. It was necessary to turn off the power, wait several seconds, and then turn the power back on.

Pressing Shift+Ctrl+Escape also opens the Task Manager. Windows is famous for the ability to use multiple key combinations to perform the same task. In some cases where Ctrl+Alt+Delete doesn't work, Shift+Ctrl+Escape will.

The third method of opening Task Manager is to right-click any empty area of the Taskbar and choose Task Manager from the menu. If your computer locks up and one method of opening Task Manager doesn't work, it won't hurt to try another method. However, if Task Manager doesn't respond to one, it's unlikely to respond to another. In such extreme cases, it may be necessary to power down your PC and then restart it. This, however, is an approach you take when Task Manager fails, rather than something you should do first.

As you'll see shortly, Task Manager does many things besides allowing you to recover from a crashed application. It is a program that is often overlooked by Windows users. Gaining proficiency in its use allows you enhanced control of Windows XP.

The first three tabs (Applications, Processes, and Performance) are visible on all computers. The Networking tab is only visible if a Network Interface Card (NIC) is correctly configured in the computer. The Users tab is visible only if Use Fast User Switching is enabled and the computer is a member of a workgroup or is a standalone computer. The Users tab is unavailable on computers that are members of a network domain. Figure 25-1 shows the Task Manager.

Figure 25-1 *The Windows Task Manager — the Applications tab displays currently active applications and their status, either Running or Not Responding.*

Regardless of the tab that is displayed, the area at the bottom of the dialog box displays the number of processes that are running, the percentage of the CPU's processing power currently in use, and some information about the system's current use of memory.

Task Manager normally runs in a resizable window that includes menu items, Title Bar, and tabs, as shown in Figure 25-1. Double-clicking an empty area of the Task Manager changes the display to a stripped-down, nondistracting, nonresizable version of the tab you are looking at. An example of the stripped-down version is shown in Figure 25-2. Double-clicking any empty area of the stripped-down version of the Task Manager restores the display with all features.

Figure 25-2   *Double-clicking an empty area of the Task Manager displays this stripped-down version of the window.*

Using the Applications Tab

20 Min.
To Go

Opening the Task Manager will normally display the Applications tab. In addition to displaying the applications that are running, this tab allows you to end a running task, switch to another task, or start a program. If a program has stopped responding, select that program and click End Task to close the application. You will lose any unsaved data in that application, but without data loss to other applications. Clicking the Switch To button allows you to switch to the highlighted application.

There are two easier ways to move between applications. Clicking an application icon on the Taskbar moves you to that application. If you have multiple applications open, press and hold the Alt key and tap the Tab key to move to the next application. Continuing to hold down the Alt key and repeatedly tapping the Tab key moves the icon selection one step to the right with each tap. When the desired application icon is highlighted, releasing the Alt key moves to that application. Pressing Alt+Tab displays the window shown in Figure 25-3. If you only have two applications open, pressing Alt+Tab toggles between them.

Figure 25-3 *Pressing Alt+Tab allows you to move easily between open applications.*

Clicking the Create New Task button allows you to type in a command, the name of a program, folder, document, or Internet Resource (such as www.microsoft.com), or browse to the object using a Windows Explorer style interface. A sample window is shown in Figure 25-4.

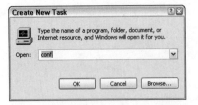

Figure 25-4 *Pressing the Create New Task button allows you to type a command, the name of a program, folder, document, or Internet Resource, or you can browse to the object.*

An Overview of the Processes Tab

The Processes tab shows information about the *processes* running on your computer. A process can be an application or a Windows subsystem or service that is managed by the operating system. A sample Processes tab dialog box is shown in Figure 25-5.

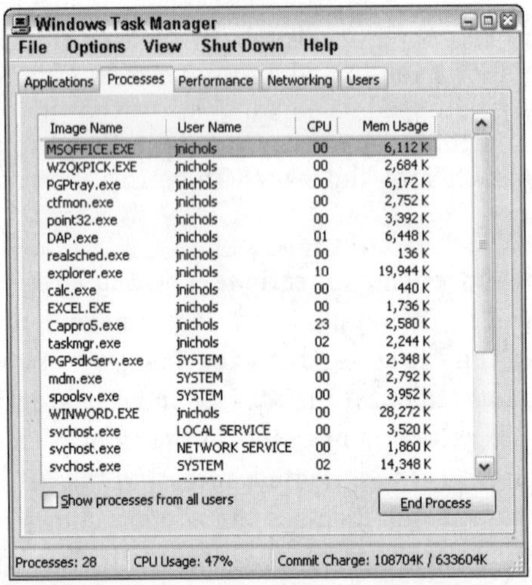

Figure 25-5 *The Processes tab of the Task Manager dialog box displays applications, Windows subsystems, and services.*

The Image Name column shows the name of the application or Windows subsystems and services. The second column displays the name of the user responsible for opening the item. The third column displays the percentage of CPU time each item is using at the current time, and the final column displays the approximate amount of memory used by the item.

This type of information can be useful when you're trying to troubleshoot a problem. Say Windows begins to behave as if it's being pressed into triple duty (it slows down and the drive seems to churn). First, you might close unnecessary applications to see if the situation improves. If it doesn't, you might close all open programs. Should that fail, you might want to look at the Applications and Processes tabs in Task Manager to see exactly what is running.

**10 Min.
To Go**

One thing you may notice looking at the Processes tab (glance back at Figure 25-5) is that you may occasionally see what appears to be duplicate entries. Certain applications and system processes run multiple versions of themselves as part of the operating process. For example, if you're running your Windows XP system on a home or office network, you'll typically see three or four occurrences of SVCHOST.EXE, one of the network services components. Look closer, and you'll see that each occurrence typically has a different username attached to it (system, local service, network service). This is normal behavior.

It's very smart to familiarize yourself with the processes running on your system when things are working well because it can make it far easier to spot a problem (example: something running that you simply cannot identify from past experience).

Checking Efficiency Using the Performance Tab

Although the Performance tab can be used to troubleshoot bottlenecks (slow areas of your computer), this feature is rather advanced, and I'll only touch on it briefly. Figure 25-6 shows a sample Performance tab. The Performance tab of the Task Manager dialog box displays graphs of CPU current usage, CPU usage history, current page file usage, and page file usage history. A page file (or paging file) is an area of your hard drive set aside to function as temporary RAM in case you have more applications and other items than can fit in RAM. Retrieving data from a page file takes the computer much less time than reloading it from the regular allotted drive area, but is much slower than if it is stored in RAM.

If you are having difficulties opening additional applications, you might want to check the amount of Physical Memory currently being used. If the Total and Available are approaching the same value, you either need to close some applications or get more RAM.

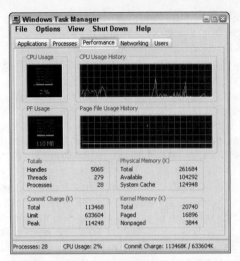

Figure 25-6 *The Performance tab of the Task Manager dialog box displays graphs of CPU current usage, CPU usage history, current page file usage, and page file usage history.*

Using the Networking Tab

As mentioned earlier, the Networking tab is only available if the computer has a properly configured Network Interface Card (NIC). This tab is available in both Windows XP Professional and Home Editions, even though the latter cannot be used if the computer is connected to a domain. The Networking tab reports on activity taking place on your network, including CPU and memory usage, percentage of network utilization (often at 0 percent when you're not actively working between two or more workstations), and the general state of the network connection (usually listed as operational). In Figure 25-7, I accessed the My Documents file located on another computer within my Workgroup, so the spike in the graph represents the time the NIC is in use accessing the other computer.

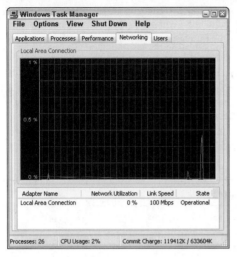

Figure 25-7 *The spike on the right side of the Networking tab indicates the time the NIC is used to connect to other computers.*

Controlling Computer Users

Do you frequently need to share a computer with one or more people in your home or office, requiring you to switch between different user accounts? If so, you should know about the Fast User Switching feature that can speed up the process. Instead of having to log off the system completely before the next person can log in, Fast User Switching sets up a situation whereby each of you gets logged in without anyone's having to log out (at least until the end of the session). This means you don't have to close programs you may have open to allow the next person to work.

However, for the programs to remain open, you need to specify this. Follow these steps:

1. Click Start ➪ Control Panel ➪ User Accounts ➪ Change the way users log on or off. By default, Use Fast User Switching is enabled (has a checkmark in the option box).

2. Select or remove the Use Fast User Switching check box by clicking it to toggle it on and off.

3. Click Apply Options to save your changes and then close the Users dialog box.

If this option is enabled, programs do not shut down when another user logs on to the computer. For example, if you are typing a report and your child wants to check e-mail, you can log off using Switch User, the child can log on, check e-mail, and then log off. You can log on and return to your report without losing your place.

To specify that programs shut down when users log off the computer, clear the Use Fast User Switching option box under User Accounts in the Control Panel. This takes up less memory, but means that users must actually log off, closing their programs, before another user can log on.

One thing to note about Fast User Switching is that while it speeds up the process of sharing a PC, it's slightly less secure. For example, if you do not have Windows set up always to require a password from you to log in, another person using your system can easily, even accidentally, log in as you. This situation exists regardless of whether you use Fast User Switching, but the latter makes you just a tad more vulnerable since you may have programs open and running that contain sensitive data.

Done!

REVIEW

- The most common way of opening Task Manager is to press Ctrl+Alt+Delete.
- The Applications tab of the Task Manager is used to review which applications are running.
- The Processes tab shows applications and Windows subsystems and services currently in use.
- Use the Performance tab of Task Manager to evaluate computer efficiency.
- The Networking tab can be used to monitor workgroup activity, such as viewing objects located on a remote computer.
- Users can quickly switch without logging off by using the Users tab. This tab is not available if you are on a domain-controlled network.

QUIZ YOURSELF

---

1. What happens in Windows XP if you press Ctrl+Alt+Delete? (See *Introducing Windows Task Manager* section.)
2. On the Applications tab, which two items of data do you see for each application currently running? (See *Using the Applications Tab* section.)
3. What is a page (or paging) file? (See *Checking Efficiency Using the Performance Tab* section.)
4. Where can you locate the option Use Fast User Switching to enable or disable it? (See *Controlling Computer Users* section.)

Preserving and Auditing Computing Performance

Session Checklist

✔ Handling issues in performance

✔ Checking performance settings

✔ Understanding Microsoft Management console (MMC)

✔ Opening predeveloped Administrative Tools

✔ Working with Performance Monitor

A t one time or another, computer performance is probably going to be an issue for you. You notice your system isn't functioning as robustly as it was. Yet how do you move from the subjective, "I think something is wrong" to identifying the exact problem or problems at fault?

In this session, you're going to learn about performance, how you can keep your performance at an optimal level, how to spot-check it, and how to use the Microsoft Management Console and its Performance Monitor snap-in to allow you to audit how different aspects of your PC operate. Another word for auditing is tracking. In this case, auditing computer performance can mean either looking at performance at a particular point in time, or tracking performance over a period of time. Microsoft provides several tools for evaluating computer performance at a specific time, or recording readings over a more lengthy time period.

Issues in Performance

The moment you buy (or build) a new PC and press it into service for the first time, its performance will begin to decline. Usually, that decline is a very slow process that you may not notice for many, many months. This happens because you tend to add special utilities such as antivirus programs, instant message and e-mail software, and other programs that tend to run all the time; because your hard drive begins to build up a lot of unnecessary temporary or unneeded files that clog speed; and because that brand new hardware begins to react to months of hard work.

In other situations, the overall speed and operating ability may take a sudden, sharp decline, usually because of a precipitating event (an electrical surge that occurs to your power line where your PC is unprotected by a surge suppressor, a stick of memory begins to fail, a drive no longer works properly, or you've made changes to Windows that don't work well). Other times, dust, dirt, or moisture may begin to slow down your drives or affect the overall operational ability of your hardware.

Many different things may begin to wear down your overall PC performance. Some of these you can address through the operating system; others may require additional efforts such as increasing your amount of installed memory (RAM) or your hard-drive capacity.

Since the best medicine is preventive, let's look at proactive ways you can approach your PC performance to keep it in good shape and hopefully hold problems and slowdowns at bay.

- Be sure you have sufficient memory installed; for Windows XP, you really want a minimum of 128 MB RAM and you may need 256 MB or more if you typically have many different files and applications open at the same time or if you work often with graphics or video (creating or editing). Check your installed RAM by clicking Start ➪ Control Panel ➪ Performance and Maintenance, click the System icon, and choose the General tab: Your installed RAM amount will show at the bottom of your information listed there.

- Do you have icons for programs or utilities you don't use in your System Tray? If so, remove any that you don't need. Each icon loaded in the System Tray represents a program loaded into memory while you work.

- Keep your hard drive free of unneeded files and applications. The more "junk" fills the drive, the more this may affect overall system performance.

- Regularly defragment (also called defrag) your hard drive(s) using the Disk Defragment tool under Start ➪ All Programs ➪ Accessories ➪ System Tools to help keep your drive(s) optimized, well organized, and running smoothly.

- Once the free space on your hard drive falls below 500 MB, consider cleaning the hard drive of unneeded files and applications. You also may want to think about either replacing the drive with a larger drive or adding a second hard drive to your PC.

- Since many types of Trojans and other viruses reduce good PC performance and can mimic other types of problems, regularly check your system using up-to-date virus-scanning software, as discussed in Session 28.

- If you install a new program and notice it doesn't behave well on your system, uninstall the program (through Add/Remove Programs in Windows Control Panel) until you can check with the program's publisher to determine the source of the problem.

- Don't tweak settings that others may recommend to optimize your computer; in most cases, it's best to let Windows manage your virtual memory and overall performance settings (more about this in the *Checking Performance Settings* section).

- Try always to operate your PC in a clean and dry setting where it is not subjected to extremes of temperature or exposed to high levels of dust and dirt, smoke, or situations where there may be grease (such as near a kitchen or active garage) or moisture in the air.

● Keep your drivers up-to-date, as recommended in Session 24. Outdated drivers can impede good performance.

Checking Performance Settings

Windows XP gives you the ability to check the performance settings currently configured for your setup as well as (in some cases) customize these settings. In this section, you'll learn about both with one caveat.

Under normal conditions, it's really wise to let Windows XP use the settings it judges to be best with what it knows about the hardware and software you have installed. While you're going to find numerous online and print PC articles suggesting that you tweak this or that setting to get a particular effect (usually, to speed something up), such recommendations often either don't work or can impact your performance badly (for example, the PC seems to run faster but is not stable).

Until you become more comfortable with how your PC and Windows work together, it's better to let Windows manage it. Thus, this section isn't going to tell you how to tweak for best speed, but what your default settings should be so you can return to them if they later get changed and you want to reset them.

To check your performance settings:

1. Click Start ➪ Control Panel ➪ Performance and Maintenance.
2. Click the System icon and then select the Advanced tab.
3. Under Performance, click the Settings button.
4. The Visual Effect tab opens automatically. The default setting to be checked is Let Windows choose what's best for my computer. The selected options are those which Windows selects for the best combination of appearance and performance..
5. Next, click the Advanced tab as shown in Figure 26-1.

6. Check to see that the following options are selected:
   ■ Under Processor scheduling, Programs is chosen.
   ■ Under Memory usage, Programs is chosen.
   ■ Under Virtual Memory, click the Change button and be sure System managed size is selected. Click Set. Click OK.
7. Click OK until you exit the System Properties dialog box section.

You must be logged in as an administrator to make changes (rather than simply view) your Performance settings. To learn about administrator accounts, see Session 27.

Figure 26-1   *Check that the settings are correct on the Advanced tab of the System Properties dialog box.*

Spot Performance Checks

You already learned about one way to check your system performance in Session 25 when you read about using the Performance as well as the Networking tabs in the section *Introducing Windows Task Manager*. For example:

1. Press Ctrl+Alt+Delete.

2. Choose the Performance tab as shown in Figure 26-2.

3. Look at CPU Usage, represented as a percentage. Normally, if everything is working well, your CPU usage percentage should be below 25 percent (often below 10 unless you've got active operations such as file copying going on at the same time).

If you regularly see a CPU usage of more than 50 percent, even at times when operations like file copying are not going on, you may have a problem with too little disk space (you need to free some up), too little memory or failing memory, or a misbehaving program or hardware that is demanding constant attention from your CPU.

Next, look at the Physical Memory settings. Your total installed memory amount (in K or kilobytes) is shown first. Under that is Available for what memory is still available for your programs and data to use. If the Available setting routinely falls below 4000 or 5000K, you may have the same types of problems discussed under CPU usage.

It's smart to familiarize yourself with the results shown under the Performance tab while your PC is running well so you have a baseline against which to compare future performance results.

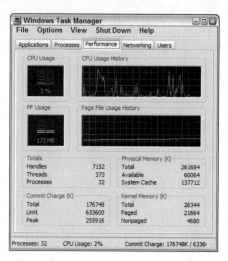

Figure 26-2   *The Task Manager's Performance tab shows your computer's performance statistics.*

In the next section, you're going to learn about the Microsoft Management Console and snap-ins you can use to help control and monitor your system. However, please be aware that this is advanced material normally used only by those with a solid background in configuring Windows for optimum use. You may not want to use such tools until you feel more comfortable in your overall knowledge of Windows.

Introducing Microsoft Management Console

While many standard tools in Windows XP are packed into options contained under Windows Control Panel or My Computer or found under the menu when you click Start ⇨ All Programs ⇨ Accessories ⇨ System Tools, other specialized utilities for managing your PC are somewhat hidden. These utilities — including a way to monitor the type of performance factors you spot-checked earlier in this session — are housed in something called a Microsoft Management Console (MMC), with each utility available for use with the MMC called a snap-in.

Note

MMCs come in two varieties: specific MMCs where the snap-in has been added by Microsoft, and blank MMC shells to which you can add all the snap-ins you use on a regular basis (if you come to do this) to create a customized MMC. Although many things other than snap-ins can be added to an MMC, these are advanced features, such as ones to handle Internet Information Services or IIS, a Web server available for Windows XP. If you are interested in additional MMC information, use the Help and Support option and search for MMC.

**20 Min.
To Go**

In Windows XP, the way you access MMC and these special snap-in utilities is through a special Administrative Tools folder available from the Control Panel. To access it, click Start ➪ Control Panel ➪ Performance and Maintenance ➪ Administrative Tools. If you have done a complete (rather than a minimum) installation of Windows XP, you should have seven snap-ins or utilities listed, as shown in Figure 26-3 (which includes an eighth file, desktop.ini, which is not part of the standard package).

Figure 26-3   *The Administrative Tools window displays seven available preconfig-ured MMCs with snap-ins (plus my desktop.ini file, which I store here but you proba-bly won't).*

Let's look at the seven built-in snap-ins and what they would be used for.

- **Component Services:** Provides management tools for data and financial transac-tions (such as when running a Web site where you reference a data source such as a database or use an online resource to update financial figures in a spreadsheet)

- **Computer Management:** Lets you configure settings for system tools, storage, ser-vices, and applications to more fully administer and control your PC

- **Data Sources (ODBC):** Used for managing connections between applications such as Microsoft Office and FrontPage with database and other data sources

- **Event Viewer:** Allows you to control special events (such as running Disk Defragmenter or scheduled Windows Updates) and how they run

- **Local Security Policy:** Is used for configuring and changing user access and tools on the local computer

- **Performance:** Offers tools for monitoring your system performance on a regular basis, discussed in detail under the section *Using Performance Monitor* later in this session

- **Services:** Permits you to view, add, and remove specialized services running on your system

As a newer user, there is very little here you will have any need to investigate, at least at this time. In fact, if you make the wrong changes with some of these management tools (for example, change a security policy so that it opens your PC files up to anyone who can get access to your system over a network), the result can be serious.

Thus, while you're free to look around, let's focus in on the one item here that may be useful for you when you want to keep a close eye on your system performance, such as when you're troubleshooting a sudden or growing slowness with your PC: Performance Monitor.

Using Performance Monitor

Performance Monitor is a powerful tool that can be used to identify bottlenecks (slow areas of performance). Understanding how to use this tool allows you to troubleshoot many areas of computer performance and tune your computer to operate at peak efficiency.

You've already had a taste of performance checking in the section *Spot Performance Checks*. But what happens when you want to do more than perform a spot-check of your system performance?

Spot-check results vary and are useful to a point. Check your system performance right this minute, and it may look wildly different than it will 10 minutes from now because you may be burning a CD during one check while your system is sitting idle for the next one. Which is right? They both are, but they're just a tiny piece of the information (just two tiny time slices) about what goes on within your system over the course of a day.

To get a better understanding requires a more consistent way of measuring times when your CPU usage may be high or your available memory is running low. The way to get that detail is to set up Performance Monitor which can perform regular checks for you, at intervals you set, over a time period you specify.

Before you get deeply into the tool, as you will in a minute, it's important to understand two important issues. First, using Performance Monitor too frequently or to monitor over long periods of time may actually slow your computer down. Second, if you don't know exactly how to interpret the results, you may find you make incorrect decisions and purchase parts or make changes based upon values received from Performance Monitor. As you work more with your Windows XP PC and increase your knowledge about PC hardware, you'll come to appreciate better what each bit of information really tells you.

You can easily start Performance Monitor by clicking Start ➪ Control Panel ➪ Performance and Maintenance ➪ Administrative Tools ➪ Performance. (You can also start this utility by clicking Start ➪ Run and typing perfmon. Click OK to continue.)

The basic Performance Monitor screen is shown in Figure 26-4. By default, the graph charts each item being measured, over a period of approximately one and a half minutes. If you are having difficulties seeing a specific object, you can highlight it in the bottom area of the screen and press Ctrl+H. This toggles highlighting on and off for a specific counter.

Objects, counters, and instances

New to Windows XP, by default, when you open Performance Monitor, three different objects are being monitored: Pages per second, Average Disk Queue Length, and Percent of CPU time. These are the three most helpful objects to monitor.

To open Performance Monitor, click Start ➪ Control Panel ➪ Performance and Maintenance ➪ Administrative Tools ➪ Performance. This opens the Performance Monitor dialog box.

The Administrative Tools menu is not added to the Start menu until you have created at least one customized MMC. To open an existing MMC before creating a customized one, use the Control Panel.

Now let's look a little closer at the tools available under Performance Monitor: objects, counters, and instances.

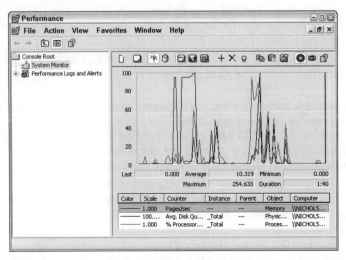

Figure 26-4   *The Performance Monitor dialog box allows you to monitor many performance measurements for troubleshooting system problems.*

Objects

As a system component performs work on your system, it generates performance data. That data is described as a performance object and is typically named for the component generating the data. For example, the Processor object is a collection of performance data about processors on your system.

Counters

Each object has one or more counters. Counters are data that represent how many times during a specified period that object is used, and what percentage of use is reached. For example, one counter that can be added to the graph is %Processor Time. This value, when plotted on the chart, illustrates when the Processor is being used and the percentage of CPU power being used.

Instances

Instances are used only when there are multiple objects that are the same. For example, you might have two hard drives. In this example, the first would be instance 0, the second would be instance 1. There is also a Total option. Selecting Total or Instance 0 is the same if there is only one object.

Performance Monitor graph icons

You can find out what each of the Performance Monitor icons do by holding the mouse pointer over the icon for about a second. A Tool tip pops up, giving a short explanation. The most important icons are the Plus icon (eighth from left, or press Ctrl+I), which opens the Add Counters dialog box, and the X icon, which allows you to delete the highlighted counter.

Test Driving Performance Monitor

Open Performance Monitor by clicking Start ⇨ Control Panel ⇨ Performance and Maintenance ⇨ Administrative Tools ⇨ Performances. Follow these steps:

1. Click the New Counter Set button (or press Ctrl+E) to clear all counters.
2. Click the Add Counter button (the Plus button, or press Ctrl+I). The Add Counters dialog box, shown in Figure 26-5, is displayed.

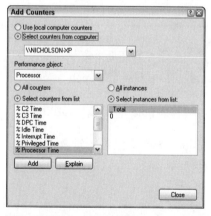

Figure 26-5 *The Add Counters dialog box allows you to choose specific counters to be added. When graphed, these counters give you a graphic overview of how your system is operating.*

3. By default, the Total (Instance) Processor (Object) %Processor Time (Counter) is selected. If you are unsure of what any Counter actually measures, select it and click the Explain button (beneath the list of Counters). Figure 26-6 shows a sample Explain box.

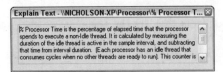

Figure 26-6   *The Performance Monitor dialog box provides details about what each counter can be used to measure.*

4. Click Total (Instance), Processor (Object), %Processor Time (Counter). Click Explain to view the Explain Text dialog box. This is probably the default, but check to make sure.

The Processor works 100 percent of the time. A *thread* is the smallest piece of code that the Processor can run. Most of the time, the Processor is running idle threads. The %Processor Time counter measures how much time the Processor is in use, and the percentage of CPU power that is being used.

5. Click Add and Close. Open a few applications, and see how this affects the Processor usage. Log on to the Internet and again refer to the Performance Monitor.
6. Close the Performance Monitor dialog box. You will return to this tool in Session 29.

Done!

REVIEW

- Many issues affect PC performance, including insufficient or failing RAM, a full hard drive or one that contains a large volume of unnecessary files and applications, infection by computer viruses, and operating your PC under unusual conditions.
- The Microsoft Management Console (MMC) is a shell for holding various utilities called snap-ins.
- Performance Monitor is an MMC snap-in which allows you to troubleshoot your system.

QUIZ YOURSELF

1. What is the absolute minimum amount of RAM you want installed on your PC for good average performance in Windows XP? (See *Issues in Performance* section.)

2. What should you do with a program that doesn't run well after you install it? (See *Issues in Performance* section.)

3. Why should you familiarize yourself with your PC performance rates while your PC runs well? (See *Spot Performance Checks* section.)

4. What do you call specific utilities that are added to an empty MMC? (See *Introducing Microsoft Management Console* section.)

5. What percentage of time is the CPU processing threads? (See *Test Driving Performance Monitor*.)

PART

V

Sunday Morning Part Review

1. What happens the first time you put a music CD in the CD-ROM drive if Windows XP Media Player is installed?

2. Besides music CDs, name two other types of media the Windows XP Media Player is capable of playing.

3. What type of Internet connection should you have if you want to play streaming audio from the Internet?

4. What is the main advantage of the MP3 format of file storage?

5. What is the most common alternative video format that you can expect to encounter?

6. What does configuration do in terms of your hardware?

7. Name two of the four sources from which you might obtain new drivers built especially for Windows XP.

8. What is an interrupt?

9. In what dialog box would you find a list of drivers used by your computer?

10. Some Troubleshooters are included with Windows XP. Where would you find additional Troubleshooters?

11. What does NIC stand for?

12. What two types of slots would you use to install a NIC in a desktop computer?

13. What are the three standard speeds for today's hubs?

14. How can you tell the difference between a NIC connection and a standard phone connection in a modem?

15. What is the default Workgroup name?

16. Between hackers and crackers, which are generally thought of as being the bad guys?

17. What is it called when a number of patches are combined and distributed as a single download?

18. What three ways can Windows XP be updated?

19. How can you find out what a particular update affects?

20. Where would you find the original Windows XP Product Key code?

21. Name two of the three ways for opening Windows Task Manager.

22. Which Task Manager tab would you use to stop a locked-up application?

23. What are the two easy ways to move between open applications?

24. What is the Processes Tab in Windows Task Manager used for?

25. What is a Page file?

26. What should you do when you install a new program that doesn't behave well under Windows XP?

27. Where can you find the settings for Performance under Windows XP?

28. Is it usually better to tweak your CPU's performance yourself even with little knowledge about how changes may affect your system or let Windows handle this automatically for you?

29. What tool would you use if you question whether a misbehaving program on your desktop is still running or is stalled (not running)?

30. In Performance Monitor, what is an item that performs work on your computer called?

PART

VI

Sunday
Afternoon

Managing Users and User Rights

Session Checklist

✔ Understanding differences between administrator and limited users

✔ Viewing the User Accounts dialog box

✔ Creating a new user

✔ Changing the way users log on or log off

✔ Changing users

✔ Understanding differences between domain and workgroup networks

E ven if you are the only user of your computer(s), you may want to create multiple accounts. There are several advantages to this. You can have multiple desktop layouts, ensure that only specific applications show when you log on as a particular user, and create separate My Documents folders for each account. If you have other family members using your computer(s), you can use multiple accounts to prevent others from messing up your workspace. By creating multiple accounts, you can also control access to specific files or tasks.

In this session, you will see the options of the User Accounts dialog box; learn to create, modify, and delete an account; and gain a better understanding of the two User groups included in Windows XP. Using information gained in this session, you will have even more control over your computer(s).

Administrator versus Limited Control Users

30 Min. To Go

When Windows XP is first installed, it sees two types of built-in user accounts (available under the Users icon in the Control Panel) by default: *Administrator* and *Guest*.

An administrator account is vital because someone needs to have the ability to control and change the PC at an operating system level. For instance, an administrator can make decisions and selections that control how others access and use the PC. In that capacity, he or she may decide that no one can log on to the PC without providing a password.

A guest, on the other hand, is treated as someone without a regular user account to access that PC, and so is given instead the ability to log in with limited rights to run applications and utilities. This is meant as a protection mechanism to limit either unintentional or deliberate privacy intrusion or damage occurring.

Once you have your system with Windows XP, you have the option of adding additional user accounts for yourself and others who may use your PC. When you do, you have two options available. You can make these accounts either *Computer administrator* or *Limited*.

As you work through this section, keep in mind that you only want to offer computer administrator access to trusted individuals who possess some understanding of working with Windows and a PC. Others should be assigned to limited accounts to reduce the risk that an unknowledgeable or malicious user can make unfavorable changes.

In fact, for good security, it's recommended that even you — if you're the primary or even sole user of your PC — not use an administrator account to perform your normal Windows tasks. If you always use the administrator account, you place your system at unnecessary risk. Fail to log off and you could find that someone else in your home or office comes along who may delete critical files, perform bad system changes, or have access to programs and information you may not intend others to use.

For this reason, you may want to create at least one additional account — even if you're usually the sole user of your PC — for yourself with limited rather than administrator access to use for your normal work. You will learn to add an account shortly.

It's also smart practice to:

- Disable your Guest account (especially if you don't use it) to make it nearly impossible for someone without a user account to access the PC
- Require passwords for login
- Use smart passwords (a combination of more or less random alphanumeric characters such as da66bo94k or sh841r2fla) and change them frequently
- Disable or don't enable Fast User Switching, discussed in Session 25.

But before you continue, it's important to understand that overall security in Windows XP Home Edition isn't robust, meaning that a person with some experience and a desire to break in to your PC can probably access it if he or she sits down at your keyboard. This is by design to try to prevent a situation where you get locked out of your own computer.

Observe good security practices, like those smart passwords, and you stand a better chance of keeping others out. Yet, if you find yourself wanting more security than Home Edition allows, you can consider moving up to Windows XP Professional or locating a third-party security utility to try to make it harder for others to access your PC.

Viewing the User Accounts Dialog Box

From the User Accounts dialog box, you can create a new user account, change the way users log on or off, or pick an existing account to modify. Using these options, you can adequately control who uses which computers, and which users receive specific rights to accomplish tasks. However, this option is only available to administrators; limited account users can only modify their own passwords or change the picture associated with the login window for the account.

Creating a new user account

**20 Min.
To Go**

All of the User Account changes are made from the User Accounts dialog box. This exercise gives you an opportunity to create an additional account for your computer. However, unless you're using an administrator account, you can only make changes to the password and picture for your own account and can't act on the accounts of others or create a new account.

1. Open the User Accounts dialog box by clicking Start ⇨ Control Panel ⇨ User Accounts. The User Accounts dialog box is displayed, similar to the one shown in Figure 27-1 (where the administrator account is my account "jnichols" rather than labeled with a default "administrator" title). Notice that near the bottom of the dialog box two accounts are listed. The account on the left is the one you use to log on, the one on the right is a guest account that has been disabled.

Figure 27-1   *The User Accounts dialog box allows you to create new users, make changes to existing users, and delete users.*

2. Under Pick a task, choose Create a new account.

3. For the name of the account, type NewUser (where this is the username you want to use). Click Next.

4. In the next step, you are asked to choose the type of account this will be. Select Administrator, and the new account has full rights over all user accounts in the Workgroup. Select Limited and you set up a normal account. In this case, click the Limited option button. Read the notification that is displayed, as shown in Figure 27-2.

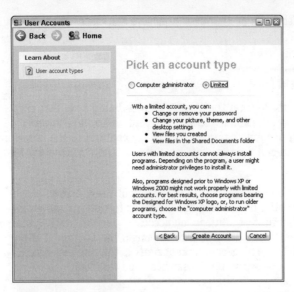

Figure 27-2 *The Pick an account type screen in the User Accounts dialog box allows you to create a new user with either Administrator or Limited privileges.*

5. Click Create Account.

6. Adjust the height and width of the window until you can see all of the information. Click the New User account you have just created. You should see the icon for the user as shown in Figure 27-3.

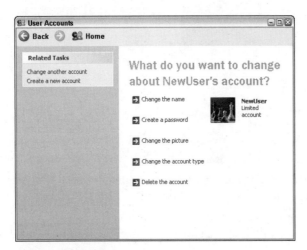

Figure 27-3 *The Change window allows you to change the properties of a specific user.*

7. Click Change the name. Type Limited in the New Name text box. Click Change Name.

8. Click Create a password. Remember that passwords are case-sensitive, and for a fairly secure site should include upper- and lowercase, special characters, and numbers. In this case, use passWord*1. Notice that the uppercase letter is not in what would be considered the normal position, at the beginning of the word. This helps defeat certain types of password-cracking programs. Press Tab and retype the password. If anything is different between the two, you will be asked to enter both again. Press Tab twice to move to the Hint text box. Type My Normal Password. You can type anything that is a reminder of your password, but the hint will be visible to all users. If necessary, scroll down until you see the Create Password button. Click it.

9. Click Remove the Password. If you click Remove Password, no password will be required to access the account. For now, click Cancel.

10. Click Change the picture. By default, you have a choice of 23 bit-mapped pictures. If you have another bit-mapped picture you would like to use, click Browse for more pictures. You can use a picture you have taken, one you have created, or one supplied on a clip art disk. Choose one from the samples, or select one of your own. Click Change Picture.

 You can use any picture that has a .bmp, .gif, .jpg, or .png extension. Most digital cameras take pictures in .jpg mode.

11. Click Change the account type. This is the screen you began with when you originally created the account. You can change the account from the Limited access currently assigned to Administrator access, or vice-versa. Click Cancel.

12. Clicking Delete account displays the screen shown in Figure 27-4. After viewing the screen, click Cancel.

Figure 27-4 The Delete User dialog box allows you to either keep some of the user's files or delete them all.

13. Click the close box in the upper-right corner of the window.

Change the Way Users Log In

When you, acting as an administrator, disable the Fast User Switching option and require account names and passwords to be used to log in to any and all accounts in Windows XP, you make it harder for someone else to simply walk up, sit down at your keyboard, and cause havoc (provided you remember to log out when you walk away). Only administrators can perform these changes.

In this exercise, you're going to accomplish three different tasks:

- Turn off the colorful Windows screen where you simply point to an account name and log in.
- Disable Fast User Switching.
- Require all PC users to log in using their account names and passwords.

Follow these steps:

1. Log in using your administrator account (if you haven't already).
2. Click Start ⇨ Control Panel and click User Accounts.
3. From the User Accounts window, under Pick a Task, double-click Change the way users log on and off.
4. Under Select logon and logoff options as shown in Figure 27-5, click to remove the checkmarks next to both Use the Welcome screen as well as Use Fast User Switching.
5. Click Apply Options.

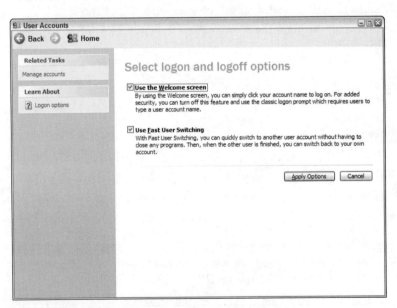

Figure 27-5   *Change the user logon and logoff options.*

One of the other smart practices recommended involves disabling the Guest account. To do this:

1. Click Start ⇨ Control Panel and click User Accounts.

2. When the User Accounts window opens, double-click the Guest account.

3. Under What do you want to change about the guest account, double-click Turn off the guest account.

Although you've just learned how to disable Fast User Switching, let's next discuss how your users can change accounts.

Changing Users

10 Min. To Go

Changing users is a simple matter, but can dramatically change the look of the screen. Each user's customized desktop is saved. By default the user's files are saved to C:\Documents and Settings*username*\My Documents. Desktop settings are kept in C:\Documents and Settings\ *username*\Desktop. When you first log on as a new user, you get a default desktop. You can then customize it in any way your account type allows. All changes are saved under the user's name, and the next time she logs in, the desktop will be exactly as she left it.

To change users without logging off, follow these steps. You should currently be logged in to your regular account, and have created the new user account.

1. Click Start ⇨ Log Off. You will see the Log Off box shown in Figure 27-6.

Figure 27-6 *The Log Off Windows box allows you to Log Off, closing all your existing files, or Switch User, leaving your files open for quicker access when you switch back to your original user account.*

2. Click Switch User. This takes you back to the sign-in screen. Notice that any programs you have running are still active. Click the Limited user icon. You are prompted for the password. Note that to the right of the password text box, there are two icons. The first (a right-pointing arrow) can be pressed after the password is entered. This starts Windows. (Pressing Enter accomplishes the same thing.)

If you want to quickly change users, just press the Windows logo key+L.

3. It will take several extra seconds while Windows builds a copy of the default desktop. Once the desktop is displayed, you can click Start ⇨ All Programs and see that all installed programs are still available to you.

If you have previously made customizing changes to programs, these changes will not remain in effect when a new user logs on. Each user has his or her own program settings.

4. To see an example of exactly how limited the current account is, click Start ⇨ Control Panel ⇨ User Accounts. Notice that you can only make changes within this account, unlike when you were logged on as an administrator. You cannot create a new account or delete an existing account.

5. Press the Windows logo key+L to go back to the log-in screen. Log in as an administrator.

6. Using the skills you have developed, delete the Limited account.

Account Differences between Domain and Workgroup Networks

If you are working in a workgroup, there are only two types of accounts available to you: Administrator and Limited. These offer little in the way of flexibility and security.

On a domain network, there may be dozens of different account groups. Users added to a specific group receive all the permissions assigned to that particular group. A user may be a member of multiple groups. This flexibility allows the administrator to assign users to groups, and then assign permissions to the group (such as permissions to create new accounts, have access to certain files, or use specific printers). Unless otherwise specified by the administrator of the network, only the administrator is allowed to create new groups, add users, or change group permissions. This makes for a much more secure working environment.

Although Windows XP Home Edition cannot be used on a domain network, Windows XP Professional works as an excellent client in a domain. So if you are going to be using Windows XP Professional in a domain environment, you might want to study how groups work in this situation. You will find that it is quite different from a workgroup environment, but shouldn't cause you very many problems. The most potentially serious aspect of this is that in a domain network, the network administrator (someone who has administrator rights over the entire network of computers) has complete control over your computer, even if you are the local administrator (someone who has administrator-level access on a single PC). The network administrator can control all aspects of your desktop, including the ability to install programs, change your desktop, or make changes to the way applications work. However, the network administrator can grant additional rights to a local administrator, if desired. If you have experience using Windows XP Professional at home and are used to doing whatever you want to your computer, and you move into a corporate environment using the same software on a domain network, you may be confused at first by the things you think you should be able to do, but are unable to accomplish. As long as you know this before you start, you won't have any serious surprises awaiting you when you begin your new position.

Done!

REVIEW

- From the User Accounts dialog box, you can create a new user account, change the way users log on or off, or pick an existing account to modify.
- Windows XP has only limited control over user accounts and groups.
- All of the User Account changes are made from the User Accounts dialog box.
- You can use a picture with a .bmp, .gif, .jpg, or .png extension for a user account. Most digital cameras take pictures in .jpg mode.
- By default the user's files are saved to C:\Documents and Settings*username*\My Documents.
- Windows XP Professional works as an excellent client in a domain.

QUIZ YOURSELF

1. Name at least two ways you can increase your user account logon security in Windows XP. (See *Administrator versus Limited Control* section.)
2. Which dialog box is used to create a new user account? (See *Viewing the User Accounts Dialog Box* section.)
3. What kind of graphics can be used to create pictures for user accounts? (See *Creating a new user account* section.)
4. What is the shortcut key for switching users? (See *Changing Users* section.)
5. Which offers more security features: a domain or peer-to-peer (workgroup) network? (See *Account Differences between Domain and Workgroup Networks* section.)

Protecting Your Computer from Viruses

Session Checklist

✔ Understanding the anatomy of a virus

✔ Catching a virus

✔ Identifying virus hoaxes

✔ Removing viruses

✔ Taking steps toward virus protection

✔ Selecting an antivirus program

There is only one perfect way to keep your computer virus free. Unplug all connections and encase it in concrete. For most users, this is not an acceptable choice, so you must do what is possible to minimize your exposure to viruses.

In this session, you take a brief look at the anatomy of a computer virus, how it spreads, the damage it can do to your system, and other important information. You'll get a brief overview of the three best-selling virus protection programs and links to virus-related sites.

**30 Min.
To Go**

Anatomy of a Virus

A *virus* is an intrusive program that inserts copies of itself into uninfected files or other parts of your computer. The copies are usually executed when the file is loaded into memory, allowing the virus to infect still other files, and so on. Viruses often have damaging side effects; sometimes intentionally, sometimes not. For example, some viruses can destroy all of the data on a computer's hard drive, or might take up memory space that could otherwise be used by programs.

The term *computer viruses* originated as a result of the resemblance they bear to biological viruses. Biological viruses get into the body and infect healthy cells. When this takes place, certain symptoms of infection will appear. A computer virus enters computers and infects files found on the hard drive. Just like biological viruses, computer viruses will carry out a number of actions once infection has taken place. In addition, viruses can replicate, thereby spreading infection to other programs and computers. Some viruses also have the ability to mutate, changing from their original state.

Not all viruses are truly viruses. *Trojans* are not viruses, as they do not replicate. Named after the Trojan Horse, they are in fact programs that are installed on computers and produce no immediate damage. Trojans are designed to open a back door on the victim machine, which makes it vulnerable to attack from a malicious user. A back door, as it's called, happens when a program is executed (such as you have with a Trojan) that creates the virtual equivalent of an unlocked door through which someone such as a hacker or cracker (see Session 23) — or more likely, software they've designed — may pass to explore your system, copy or maliciously revise key information, or run commands. All too often, this happens out of your view.

Among the actions that Trojans carry out, note the following: They capture screenshots, access confidential user information (including passwords), and open security holes in order to make the computer vulnerable to attacks, all of which can be sent to a remote computer immediately or at some distant time.

Another type of destructive, self-propagating program is called a worm. A worm is a program that replicates itself across computers, usually by creating copies of itself in each computer's memory. Rather than infecting healthy files, a worm usually duplicates itself in computer memory so many times that it causes the computer to crash.

Whether a true virus, a Trojan, or a worm, all of these are generally lumped under the term virus. Without an up-to-date virus-detecting protection program, your computer and data are at high risk. Realize that no virus, regardless of its category, can cause physical damage to your computer; rather, it can damage your data, open your computer to others, or cause your computer to crash. While these are not the only possibilities, they are the most common ones.

From this point on, I refer to any type of computer infection as a virus. There is no need to deal with each category separately, since in many ways they are similar, and since any worthwhile virus-protection program offers protection from a wide variety of different virus types

Catching a virus

One of the questions I am most commonly asked is, "How did my computer get a virus?" This is a difficult question to answer, but it usually involves the Internet. The Internet is the number one propagator of computer viruses. They may come as part of an e-mail, as an e-mail attachment, or as part of an application or other computer file you download. They've been passed around — usually as files — in Internet chat rooms, and new delivery techniques are seen regularly.

Does this mean that you could unhook your computer from the Internet and be safe from viruses? Absolutely not! If you move files from one computer to another using floppy disks, cable transfer, Zip or Jaz disks, CD-ROMS, or by any other method used to share files, your computer is at risk.

Are you safe if you don't start Internet Explorer or other Internet browser? Probably not. As long as you're connected to the Internet in any capacity, you could be at risk. Also, the Web browser is just one of the things you're apt to use when you're online. For example, you may run an instant message utility, Outlook Express (or Outlook if you use Microsoft Office) to check your e-mail, or an online media player such as Windows Media Player, just to name a few. If you accept files in your instant message software or e-mail, your risk increases.

Exploring a real virus

Klez.I is a good example of how quickly a virus can spread as well as how little you need to do to "catch" one. This can be spread through e-mail, but it doesn't require you to actually open the file attachment to become infected. Just previewing the file in the Outlook Express preview pane can do it.

At any time, experts estimate that this virus is present on about 2 percent of computers worldwide. It steals and sends out confidential information, drops the *Elkern.C* virus (which affects only the Windows 98 and 2000 operating systems), kills processes, and deletes files. The Elkern.C virus tries to disable the permanent protection of some antivirus programs. Elkern.C infects files with .exe. and .scr extensions that are over 8 Kbytes in size. Then it infects all disk drives and the network drives that can be accessed from the affected computer. Klez.I sends itself to everyone in your Contacts file and is characterized by its ability to modify the subject lines of the messages it sends out. This makes it particularly difficult to identify the virus as it reaches the computer via e-mail. In order to generate the subjects of e-mails it generates, it uses the words included in its code and text found in files on the affected computer. Because it e-mails everyone in your Contacts file immediately and changes the subject words for each e-mail, Klez.I is extremely difficult to contain. The only way to contain it is by making sure each of your computers has a virus-protection program that is updated on a daily basis. Klez.I first appeared in April 2002, and because of the speed with which it spreads, attempts to curtail it have failed. Although most good antivirus programs can protect your computer from becoming infected, there are always new users who think an antivirus program is unnecessary, and thus the virus continues to spread at an alarming rate.

 It is currently estimated that there are nearly 75,000 viruses, and new ones appear each day. Most virus programmers are looking for notoriety or social recognition within their programming circle. Others like to amass information, such as captured IDs, passwords, and credit card numbers, to use or sell elsewhere. Some no doubt just want to create havoc for their own sake.

Common virus hoaxes

If you receive an e-mail and the subject is *Very Serious Virus Warning!!!*, what should you do? The correct answer is to forward it to *no one* and delete it immediately. Does this e-mail contain a virus? No. But it can cause just as many problems. Usually, the text will be a warning of a deadly virus circulating on the Internet, a reference to a credible source, such as *The New York Times,* and a plea to forward this e-mail to everyone you know. The result of this e-mail is to cause a logjam in the operation of the Internet. When you forward the message to everyone you know, and they do the same, the result is an exponential increase in Internet traffic and a slowing of servers on the Internet, as they try to handle the increased level of e-mail traffic.

In most cases, virus hoaxes are basically harmless to your computer and cause a minimal amount of damage, although they may increase your anxiety level. Sometimes, the writer of the virus hoax simply wanted to cause trouble, such as the case of the *Bud Frogs* virus hoax. In this case, the message warns you not to install the Budweiser Frogs screensaver, as it contains a virus. This is simply incorrect information; the Budweiser Frogs screensaver does not contain a virus.

E-mail tracking or Microsoft E-Mail tracking (they are the same hoax with different subject lines) tells you that Microsoft is running an experiment, trying to track the flow of e-mail as it moves across the Internet. The e-mail normally is accompanied by a testimony from a user who has just received a check from Microsoft, and an urging that you forward the message to everyone you know, so that you can start receiving money from Microsoft. Although this seems like the silliest scheme anyone has ever heard of, people constantly fall for it. I still occasionally see a copy of it turn up in my e-mailbox.

Any time you receive notification of a virus from an individual, before sending the notification on to everyone you know, check one of the big three antivirus sites (www.symantec.com **,** www.mcafee.com **, and** www.pandasoftware.com**), listed later in the** *Antivirus Protection Programs* **section of this session.**

20 Min. To Go

Basic Steps toward Virus Protection

Even without buying an antivirus program, you can take some steps to reduce the probability of getting a virus.

- Don't open e-mail from anyone you don't know and be very wary of opening attachments even from people you do know (they may not observe good protection practices).
- If you aren't sure of the subject of an e-mail from someone you do know, check with him or her on the phone, or even write that person an e-mail before opening the suspicious one.
- Encourage everyone you know to be very specific in the Subject line of each e-mail.
- Update Windows XP regularly. This will solve many of your problems.
- Configure instant messaging software you may use to automatically decline file transfers; you can always temporarily enable the feature when you're sure the sender is a safe source.
- Definitely avoid so-called hacker and cracker sites and those offering pirated commercial software (called *Warez*) for download; they sometimes like to practice on their clientele by exploiting browser insecurities to get access to your system or information.
- If you are using Outlook or Outlook Express as your e-mail program, be absolutely certain to check on regular updates for these.

Although these steps will help prevent catching a virus, there is really only one way to do so — buy an antivirus program.

It's Not Always a Virus

Users, particularly new users, tend to think "virus" every time the computer doesn't do what they expect it to do. Having worked with computers for nearly 4 decades, my experience has shown that what might appear to be a virus is often actually the result of using an application incorrectly, some flaw in the operating system, a defective application, or any number of things other than a virus infection. A good example is when you buy a computer with an operating system installed, and you upgrade the operating system without fully reformatting the hard drive first. Although Microsoft says this can be done with no problem, it simply isn't a good idea, as it can result in intermittent misbehavior problems. Often enough, issues some people attribute to virus infection — common ones such as program instability, a misbehaving keyboard or mouse, or a flaky Windows working environment — have nothing to do with a virus at all. Running a virus scan removes the doubt and lets you move on to more likely culprits.

Another problem experienced by all users is that of watching the computer too closely after a problem, such as a virus, has been eradicated. For example, when I go out to fix a user's computer, I expect a follow-up call from about half of my clients, saying that their computer now does something, or doesn't do something, and it isn't working the way it did before. In nearly all cases, this is because the user is paying much closer attention to the computer, noticing things he or she never noticed before. So it is with virus removal. Once you have a virus confirmed on your computer, you are much more sensitive to potential problems, even though you were not previously paying such close attention to the computer. Confirming a virus tends to make you more paranoid. It is like someone has invaded your house and purposefully damaged your personal possessions.

Antivirus Protection Programs

If you have failed to purchase adequate protection from viruses, you may find it difficult to remove one when you actually get it. (Notice I said "when," not "if.") For the more popular viruses, you will find many "fixes" that are free and downloadable from the Internet. In some cases, these mini-applications are able to actually remove the virus from the computer. In other cases, they might end up quarantining specific files. This might not have an effect on running your computer, but often many of your data files will no longer be available to you.

In the cases of viruses, though, the old saw of "an ounce of prevention is worth a pound of cure" is something to pay attention to. In some cases, getting totally rid of the virus can be as extreme as reformatting your hard drive (or multiple drives and tape backups if you have them). If you have infected backed-up files, doing a restore from backup will simply re-infect your computer. So think of virus protection as insurance. Hopefully, it will never be needed; but getting infected once can cost you hours or days of work, and result in loss of a great deal of data as well as a loss of income if you run a business.

There are dozens of antivirus programs available, but I'm just going to mention the big three here. You can always go to www.downloads.com or www.tucows.com to find other free and shareware programs. Nearly any antivirus program you purchase comes with *virus definition* updates for a specific period. A virus definition is simply a description of the programming used in identifying a virus. Virus definition updates are normally free for 1 year. If the software comes bundled as part of your computer, this time frame may be less. In some cases, you may find that you have to upgrade the version of the software, depending on how old it is.

 It is imperative that you select an antivirus program that is specifically designed for Windows XP. Other versions will not work, unless expressly stated on the package. So don't try to skimp on price, and buy a version for 2001, since it won't work with Windows XP. Plus, you would no longer be able to update the virus definitions.

Often, it is price that drives the purchase of an antivirus program. This is probably not a good place to try to save money since you want one that is frequently updated and well supported.

Several major antivirus programs such as Symantec's Norton AntiVirus and McAfee Associates ViruScan, and Panda Software's Antivirus can be purchased online, downloaded, and, following instructions they usually provide a CD so you can keep an additional copy offline (in case you later need to reinstall it). If your virus software is only stored on your computer, a computer crash could cause problems. Also, these and others typically let you download short-term trial versions so you can see how you like the software before you purchase.

Make sure you check the length of time for available updates, and explore what happens if a newer version of the software engine (the program itself) becomes available. These, of course, are all secondary considerations. The primary consideration is, regardless of cost, whether the program provides you with the level of protection you deem necessary for your computer. Figure 28-1 shows a sample screen from the Panda Antivirus program.

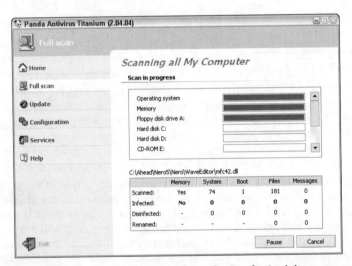

Figure 28-1 A sample screen from the Panda Antivirus program. These programs need to be regularly updated.

Protecting Your Computer from Unknown Viruses

You should be aware that, regardless of the price or reputation or frequency of virus definition updates, no antivirus program will catch all viruses as soon as they are made public. Ideally, antivirus programs should be able to detect, protect, and eliminate viruses before they are even known to the antivirus publishers. This is because many viruses have a similar *signature*, meaning that they use similar methods to infect your system, even though the exact virus may not have been found yet.

**10 Min.
To Go**

Norton AntiVirus

Norton (also called Symantec) AntiVirus (NAV), usually the best-selling of the commercial antivirus programs, can be downloaded from www.symantec.com or www.norton.com. Visit either Web site and you'll find links to NAV and how to download a 15-day free trial version. Remember, as with nearly all antivirus shareware or trial-ware, after the expiration date, the antivirus program is disabled and your system will no longer be protected.

NAV is a solid product, with years of expertise behind its development. In the past, some users have found that the NAV trial-ware did not work with their particular processor. Each year, Symantec requires that you purchase an update of the antivirus engine before it allows you to upgrade your virus definitions. Their thinking behind this is that virus engines are always evolving, so you need the latest available, plus regular virus definition updates.

NAV does have an annoying little problem in that you just can't remove it from your computer. You must first download a separate removal tool. This is free, but a minor irritation, nonetheless.

McAfee AntiVirus

Another long-time player in the antivirus arena is McAfee (www.mcafee.com). This program was used by educational sites for a long time because it was free. Like all companies, McAfee had to survive, so it took a double-pronged approach. The company began charging for its program but tried (and usually successfully) to make it a superior product in every way.

In many instances, McAfee includes its antivirus program with other security tools. This can save you quite a bit of money in the long run. McAfee has a good track record, and many users swear by it.

Panda Antivirus

New to the United States is the world's largest manufacturer of antivirus programs: Panda Software (www.pandasoftware.com.). Originating in Europe, Panda has been marketing hard in the United States for the past few years. Although comparatively unknown until recently, reviews have pushed sales to record highs. Once installed, virus definitions are updated automatically every day if you have a cable or DSL connection, or immediately upon connection, in the background, if you access the Internet from a modem. Also, if a dangerous virus is discovered during the 24-hour interval between normal downloads, immediate downloads are automatic.

Panda's Web site is also one of the easiest (in my opinion) to navigate. Getting information about virus hoaxes is simple. The virusometer (Panda's term for a meter that shows current worldwide threats, usually current within the last 15 minutes) is a help if you are paranoid about your computer getting a virus. A sample of the Web site is shown in Figure 28-2.

Figure 28-2 *One of the nice features of the Panda Web site is the virusometer in the upper-right corner of the page. It gives you instant information about virus threats and percentages of computers infected with specific viruses.*

A Final Few Words on Virus Protection

Virus protection is critical. I can't place a high enough emphasis on this. You must have updated virus definitions in order for the protection to be effective. Viruses can easily wipe out everything stored on your computer's hard drive or drives. The selection of an antivirus program is personal, but you should do research before buying one. The Internet is an excellent place to compare programs.

One other excellent source of virus information, although not a source of antivirus programs, is the CERT Coordination Center (www.cert.org). It is a center of Internet security expertise, located at the Software Engineering Institute, a federally funded research and development center operated by Carnegie Mellon University. This is the place for any security research.

Done!

REVIEW

- A virus is an intrusive program that inserts copies of itself into uninfected files or other parts of your computer.
- Although the Internet is the most common means of virus propagation, it is by no means the only one.
- A virus hoax is notification of a virus that really doesn't exist.
- After computer damage by a virus, you may find yourself paranoid about getting another one.
- Norton (Symantec), McAfee, and Panda are the three largest manufacturers of antivirus programs.
- www.cert.org is an excellent source of virus or any other security-related information.

QUIZ YOURSELF

1. Besides viruses, what other two types of programs are classified using the word virus? (See *Anatomy of a Virus* section.)
2. How frequently are new viruses reported? (See *Exploring a real virus* section.)
3. Why should you be careful in opening file attachments in e-mail even from people you know? (See *Basic Steps toward Virus Protection* section.)
4. What is the primary consideration when choosing an antivirus program? (See *Antivirus Protection Programs* section.)
5. Is it possible to protect your computer from an unknown virus? If so, how? (See *Protecting Your Computer from Unknown Viruses* sidebar.)

Basic Troubleshooting

Session Checklist

✔ Using Performance Monitor as a checking tool

✔ Troubleshooting hardware problems

✔ Troubleshooting software problems

✔ Troubleshooting operating system problems

✔ Troubleshooting browser problems

✔ Using System Restore

A wise, old computer technician once said, "It's not *whether* your computer will experience problems, it's *when* your computer will experience problems." Unfortunately, being a computer owner is not always peaches and cream. Hardware failures, buggy software, and plain old user error sometimes place computer users in a state of immeasurable frustration. Luckily, Windows XP has a few tools and utilities that can help you identify, and sometimes fix, problems with your computer.

This session shows you how to identify some of the more common problems that can occur with your computer. While it is not meant to replace a good computer technician, it might save you a few headaches (and even a few service bills).

Using Performance Monitor as a Troubleshooting Tool

In Session 26 you learned about the various issues that can negatively impact your overall system performance. You also saw how you can use Performance Monitor to perform an audit of your system performance by selecting various criteria like CPU usage to monitor over a period of time.

**30 Min.
To Go**

You can also use Performance Monitor when it's time to troubleshoot. Remember the counters discussed in Session 26? If you are trying to decide if something is seriously slowing down your CPU or processor (called in Performance Monitor the performance object Processor), for example, you might select counters such as %Processor Time (to see when your CPU is working overtime) or use the performance object Processor Performance and choose all three counters for a complete study as shown in Figure 29-1.

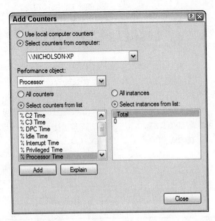

Figure 29-1 *The Add Counters screen in Performance Monitor can be used to study processor performance.*

If instead, you want to look at your memory because you may question whether you're underpowered for RAM or some may be failing, you can select performance objects such as Memory and select counters such as Available Bytes and Pages/sec (which tells you how fast "pages" are processed through your memory).

This is where the baseline you were advised to take in Session 26 can come in handy because it lets you compare results you took when the PC was operating well against the Performance Monitor results you obtain during the troubleshooting period.

Now let's turn to serious hardware troubleshooting.

Troubleshooting Hardware Problems

The first step in troubleshooting a hardware problem is to determine which piece of hardware is causing the problem. Sometimes, a single component such as a sound card or video card might be bad and other times, the hardware itself might be just fine, but it might be incompatible with your system or another component installed on your system. The first step in determining which piece of hardware is causing the problem is to check out the Device Manager. This utility allows you to easily determine if a piece of hardware is malfunctioning or is in conflict with another component.

Before you jump into Device Manager, you should understand that this tool will give you visual feedback when it does spot a problem. For example:

- A question mark icon on a device means that Windows can't tell what the device is (because, for example, it doesn't have the right driver, because the hardware is malfunctioning, and so on).
- A yellow warning sign indicates there is a problem with a device (the driver may be outdated or wrong), the device is trying to use the hardware resources of another device (see Session 22 which you should cross-reference often with this chapter).
- A red X indicates the device is malfunctioning or otherwise disabled.

The first thing you should do if you encounter such an issue is to attempt to update the driver for the device following instructions found in Session 22. If that doesn't work, another technique you can try is to remove the device by removing its entry from Device Manager and then restarting your system to see if Windows can rediscover the device and add it back properly. This can help sort out problems with hardware resource conflicts, for example, because Windows reinventories your hardware in the process. To do this:

1. Click Start ⇨ Control Panel ⇨ Performance and Maintenance ⇨ System ⇨ Hardware ⇨ Device Manager.
2. Click the plus sign next to each device category to expand it until you locate the device with the problem icon.
3. Double-click that device entry and select the Driver tab.
4. Click the Uninstall button as shown in Figure 29-2. You may be asked to confirm your selection. If so, click Yes or OK.

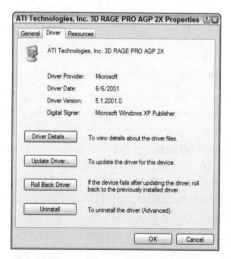

Figure 29-2 *Uninstalling the driver without physically removing the device tells Windows to try to redetect that device when you next restart your PC.*

5. Once complete, click Start ⇨ Turn off Computer ⇨ Restart.

20 Min.
To Go

If you want to troubleshoot the device without removing its driver as a test, you would follow these steps instead:

1. Click Start ➪ Control Panel ➪ Performance and Maintenance ➪ System ➪ Hardware ➪ Device Manager.

2. Click the plus sign next to the device category containing the device you want to troubleshoot.

3. The listing expands, as shown in Figure 29-3. Double-click on that device entry and select the General tab (it may open to this tab by default).

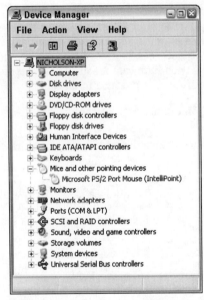

Figure 29-3   *After expanding a category, the individual devices are visible.*

4. From the General tab for this device (a mouse, in the example shown in Figure 29-4), click the Troubleshoot button and follow the prompts to resolve the problem.

Usually, the best place to start in troubleshooting the device is to restart your computer. If that doesn't work, try turning off the computer, reinstalling the device, and then restarting the computer. If the device still does not work, try updating the driver. Most manufacturers maintain the most current drivers on their Web sites. See Session 22 for more details.

Figure 29-4 *The Device Properties dialog box allows you to troubleshoot problems with the device.*

Troubleshooting Software Problems

Software problems are often the trickiest (and most infuriating) problems to troubleshoot. If a piece of software has a bug, it's usually difficult for the end user to determine. Instead, you might spend hours troubleshooting hardware only to find out that uninstalling a specific application resolves the problem.

One way to prevent this from becoming a problem is to monitor the behavior of new programs as you install them. As recommended in Session 26, you should uninstall any improperly functioning or unstable programs until you can determine the source of the problem. Taking care of this when you first notice problems with a new program can keep you from developing performance issues and system instability that, once time passes, you may forget started with the installation of the misbehaving software.

Likewise, you may also see this with older programs you've had installed for awhile. If so, uninstalling and then reinstalling such applications alone may resolve the issues you are experiencing.

Also, there are signs that might alert you to a problem with an application. The most prevalent symptom would be the unnecessary use of system resources. The best way to troubleshoot an application that has stopped responding or has become a processor hog is to use the Windows Task Manager.

To use the Windows Task Manager to troubleshoot an application:

1. Without trying to close anything on your desktop, press Ctrl+Alt+Delete, which opens the Windows Task Manager, shown in Figure 29-5.

2. In the Applications view of the Windows Task Manager, you can easily see whether a specific piece of software is running or not responding. If the program status is

Not Responding, select the application and click the End Task button. Be aware, however, that ending the task shuts down the application and any changes since your last save will be lost.

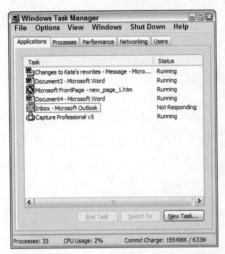

Figure 29-5   *The Windows Task Manager allows you to troubleshoot problematic applications. A Not Responding message, as shown here, indicates the program has become unstable and should be closed.*

Another way to use the Windows Task Manager to troubleshoot applications that are running but performing poorly is to click the Processes tab. In the Processes view, click the CPU column heading twice to sort the applications in descending order. Using this view, shown in Figure 29-6, you can determine which applications are using an unusually large percentage of the CPU. In this situation, Outlook (the application that wasn't responding earlier) really isn't attacking CPU utilization since it lists at 00 or 0 percent of utilization.

3. Close the Windows Task Manager.

In this case, there wasn't much to do except End Process to end the misbehaving program (Outlook) since it wasn't hurting anything but simply doing nothing. However, if another piece of software such as a game or word processor consistently shows Not Responding with a high CPU utilization, it's time to consider temporarily uninstalling the program (through Add and Remove Programs in the Control Panel) until you can determine the source of the problem. If necessary, contact the program's manufacturer or publisher. It could be that the program wasn't really written to work with Windows XP or it has a conflict with something else you may be running at the same time.

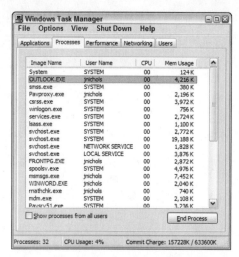

Figure 29-6   *Outlook.exe is currently using 0 percent of the CPU.*

Troubleshooting Operating System Problems

**10 Min.
To Go**

One of the most common complaints of computer users is that their computer is too slow. Even people with brand-new computers often find themselves feeling like the computer is not performing at the speeds expected. If you find yourself in this category, you could run out and spend a chunk of change on a faster hard drive and more memory which might solve your problems. Before you do that, however, consider making a few adjustments to your operating system that allow it to operate at peak performance.

To tweak Windows XP for best performance:

1. Open the System Properties dialog box by choosing Start ⇨ Control Panel ⇨ Performance and Maintenance, and clicking the System icon.
2. Choose the Advanced tab and under Performance, click the Settings button in the Performance panel.
3. In the Performance Options dialog box, shown in Figure 29-7, choose Adjust for best performance.

Using this setting removes all types of memory-hogging extras, including, for example, the smoothing of screen fonts. Allow Windows to try automatically adjusting the options for performance, and if you don't see a difference in speed, you can always go back to the dialog box and allow Windows to choose what's best for your computer.

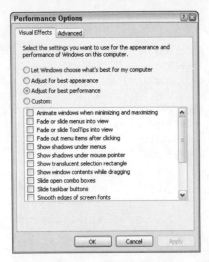

Figure 29-7 *Adjusting for best performance may increase the speed of your operating system.*

4. Next, click the Advanced tab in the Performance Options dialog box. Using the Advanced view, shown in Figure 29-8, you can specify whether your computer's processor should be tuned for applications or for background services. If your applications run fine, but background services like the backup utility or the disk defragmenter run slowly, consider checking Background services in the Processor scheduling panel.

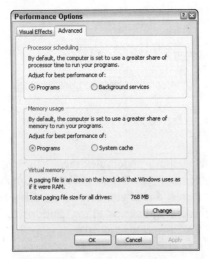

Figure 29-8 *The Advanced view allows you to configure your processor usage.*

5. Click OK to close the Performance Options dialog box and click OK again to close the System Properties dialog box.

Troubleshooting Browser Problems

Internet Explorer has become an integral part of the Windows operating system and there are several adjustments that you can make to the browser to enhance your Web surfing. The first step you can take to speed up your browser is to occasionally empty your browser cache. As you surf from site to site, the images and multimedia files are stored on your computer so that they don't have to be downloaded a second time when you visit that site again. These files add up, however, over time and can slow your browser down as they begin to congest your hard drive and impact virtual memory and desktop resources. Get enough of these files, and you may no longer be able to open up Web sites at all.

In addition to emptying the cache, you'll want to adjust the amount of hard drive space devoted to your browser cache based on the size of your hard drive. The more space you have, the larger cache you can afford to maintain.

Once your cache has been managed, you might take a look at some of the advanced features within Internet Explorer (IE) that can speed up the loading of Web pages. To see how to adjust your cache and tweak IE for best performance:

1. Open Internet Explorer and choose Tool ⇨ Internet Options from the menu bar.

2. In the Internet Options dialog box, shown in Figure 29-9, you can delete the files stored in your browser cache by clicking the Delete Files button in the Temporary Internet Files panel.

Figure 29-9   *The Internet Options dialog box allows you to adjust your browser settings.*

3. If you would also like to remove any cookies stored on your computer, you can also click the Delete Cookies button.

Deleting all cookies means that any information that is saved by a site, such as information needed to automatically log on to the site, is deleted. If you use Amazon's automatic login, for example, this will also be deleted by deleting cookies.

4. To adjust the size of your browser cache, click the Settings button. In the Settings dialog box, shown in Figure 29-10, adjust the slider based on the size of your hard drive. If you would like to view the objects currently stored in the Temporary Internet Files folder, click the View Files button.

Figure 29-10 *The Settings dialog box allows you to adjust the size of your browser cache.*

5. Depending on the way you browse the Web, there are also numerous adjustments to IE that can be made in the Advanced options. Return to the Internet Options dialog box and click the Advanced tab.

6. One of the more annoying features of sites built with Microsoft FrontPage is the page transitions that make the pages fade in and out or slide in from one side of the screen to another. Luckily, you can disable these page transitions by unchecking the Enable page transitions box. This is just one of the many tweaks you can make to IE to individualize your browser experience. If something goes wrong, you can always click the Restore Defaults button and return IE back to the state it was in when it was first installed.

7. Close the Internet Options dialog box.

Done!

REVIEW

- The Device Manager can assist you in troubleshooting hardware problems.
- When troubleshooting a hardware problem, be sure that you are using the correct driver for the device.
- The Windows Task Manager can help you determine if an application is not responding or if it is using a large percentage of the processor.

- If your operating system appears to be running slowly, try adjusting the performance options.
- In Internet Explorer, it is a good idea to properly manage your browser cache to avoid slowdowns.

QUIZ YOURSELF

1. How do you access the Device Manager? (See *Troubleshooting Hardware Problems* section.)

2. How do you access the Windows Task Manager? (See *Troubleshooting Software Problems* section.)

3. How would you delete the files in your browser cache? (See *Troubleshooting Browser Problems* section.)

4. How can you return Internet Explorer to its original state? (See *Troubleshooting Browser Problems* section.)

SESSION

30

Where to Go from Here

Session Checklist

✔ Using books and magazines as reference and learning material

✔ Determining the best book to fill your needs

✔ Using Microsoft sites

✔ Learning more about Windows XP

✔ Determining the job field you want to enter

Y ou've covered a lot of information in the first 29 sessions of this book. Now, you need
to take a look at what your next steps might be. You may feel comfortable enough with
Windows XP that you have all the training you need. It may be that you feel you need
additional resources, and that's what this session is all about. You probably won't want to take
the time to look at every resource listed here, but if you need them, they are here for you.

This session shows you how to take advantage of other resources to enhance your understanding of Windows XP, to solve potential problems, and, if desired, to get ready for a job
using Windows XP or another Microsoft application. This is by no means a complete list, just
a listing of some of the more popular resources you might want to check out. Some are free,
some costly. But with a little effort, you can find what you need.

Magazines — Printed and Electronic

**30 Min.
To Go**

In addition to printed periodicals, there are several *e-zines*, electronic magazines devoted to
computer topics that are generally free. A good selection of both is essential to your continuing education in the world of computers.

Listed here are a couple of my favorite print magazines, along with a few words about the subjects they cover. While they aren't Windows XP–specific, all cover the subject regularly and often in depth:

- **PC Magazine** (www.pcmag.com): The best bet if you like product reviews and keeping up-to-date on the latest in technological innovations.

- **PC World** (www.pcworld.com): Lots of reviews and hands-on tips and techniques. Very easy to read, and avoids most technical jargon.

- **Microsoft Certified Professional Magazine** (www.mcpmag.com): A high-level publication dealing with the various certification programs offered by Microsoft.

- **PC Gamer** (www.pcgamer.com): If you play a lot of games with your PC, this should be one to take a closer look at.

- **Computer Shopper** (www.cnet.com/computershopper): Find reviews and tons of ads for businesses that carry the largest, cheapest, or most esoteric items.

Nearly all computer e-zines are free. There is a virtual cornucopia to choose from. You can quickly become overwhelmed with the number of e-zines in your e-mail each day. Be very selective. Some are published daily, some weekly (the most common), and a few only once a month. Here are some you might take a look at. All of the ones listed below are free.

- **Woody's Windows Watch** (www.wopr.com): I find newsletters from Woody Leonhard to be extremely helpful. In addition to his Windows Watch, he also offers a newsletter for beginners, and a particularly helpful one on Microsoft Office.

- **Lockergnome** (www.lockergnome.com): Chris Pirillo and his gang have created several e-zines that are outstanding. Pay particular attention to Windows Daily (published each weekday).

- **Windows XP Magazine** (www.windowsxpmagazine.co.uk): A British magazine with an online edition.

- **Windows XP Technical Tips** (www.techrepublic.com): You must create an account, but that's just a matter of giving your e-mail address and a few other bits of information. Tech Republic offers over 30 e-zines from which to choose.

- **AnchorDesk** (www.zdnet.com): A daily offering of all kinds of computer information. Contains reviews, downloads, opinions, and lots of other information.

Books

There are hundreds of books on Windows XP. This one was a good starting place, but you may find that you need more advanced information on certain topics than this one contains. Here are some of the books I recommend.

 If you are considering buying a book to solve a specific problem, go to a large bookstore. You can also check online booksellers such as Amazon (www.amazon.com) to see their reader reviews to help make your selection, and get additional information about a title by visiting computer book publisher sites like Wiley's (www.wiley.com).

- *Alan Simpson's Windows XP Bible* by Alan Simpson and Brian Underdahl. Wiley (September 2001). Updated version of a long-time Wiley bestseller loaded with lots of details and tips.
- *Microsoft Windows XP Inside Out* (Deluxe Edition) by Ed Bott, Carl Siechart, and Craig Stinson. Microsoft Press. (2003). Weighing in at over 1400 pages, this is one of the most complete books for users of Windows XP. It deals with everyday problems you will have. Includes complete book on CD. Full Computer Dictionary eBook and Networking Encyclopedia eBooks are included.
- *Special Edition Using Windows XP Professional* by Robert Cowert and Brian Knittel. Que (December 2001). Again, a bulky reference book, about 1000 pages in length. Not as up-to-date as Ed Bott's book (above), but good material and easy to read.
- *Windows XP Secrets* by Curt Simmons. Wiley (January 2002). This one offers hundreds of secrets and workarounds for gaining more control of your system.

Microsoft on the Internet

20 Min. To Go

In this section, I look at some good sites for finding more information about Windows XP, including several that also offer areas where you can post questions and receive replies. Since some of the best details and help with Windows XP can be found with its manufacturer, I focus on some of Microsoft's Web sites.

Microsoft operates a number of different sites where you can get information on Windows XP as well as communicate with fellow users who share tips and solutions. You can start with one of two sites. First, there is the main Microsoft Support site (http://support.microsoft.com) shown in Figure 30-1, a central location for getting help with all Microsoft products including Windows XP. Or you can jump right to one of the most frequently used Microsoft support options, the Microsoft Knowledge Base (http://search.support.microsoft.com). This is a database of all known problems with Microsoft products and the appropriate solutions.

In a moment, you'll learn about the Knowledge Base site itself, but whether you realize it or not, when you search for a topic using Windows XP Help and Support, one of the references you check (if you're online when you perform your search) is the Microsoft Knowledge Base.

You'll see that this may be easier to use than the Web site itself if you follow these steps:

1. Click Start ⇨ Help and Support.
2. Point within the dialog box to the right of Search in the upper-left part of your Help and Support screen, and type a term you want information on-;, for example, passwords. Click the green arrow.

Your search will commence, and the results will show in the left-hand pane. Near the bottom of the results, you see that your last source option is called Microsoft Knowledge Base. Click this and it will expand to reveal the search results for the word you searched on from the Microsoft database, as shown in Figure 30-2.

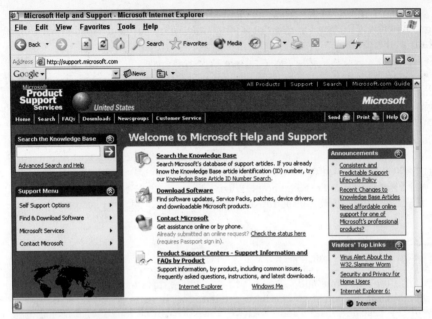

Figure 30-1 *The Microsoft support site offers a chance to search the Knowledge Base.*

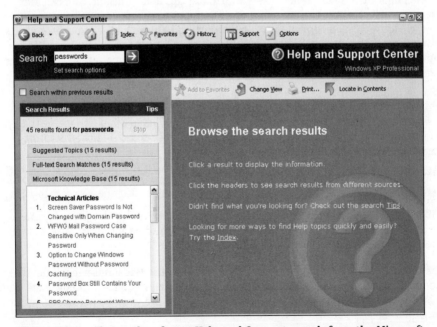

Figure 30-2 *The results of your Help and Support search from the Microsoft Knowledge Base.*

Figure 30-3 shows the search site for the knowledge base. First, you must choose the product (in this case, Windows XP). Next, enter the *keywords* for which you are searching. Keywords are the main words in a sentence. For example, in a sentence such as "are there problems with the defrag utility," problems, defrag, and utility would be keywords. After entering the keywords, you can choose to match any single keyword, the exact phrase as entered, or all of the words (although they may not be consecutive). You can also enter words using Boolean logic. Choosing AND shows pages that contain both of the words specified. OR shows pages that contain either of the words specified. AND NOT shows pages that do not contain the words specified. So a Boolean search might be "problem and utility and not defrag."

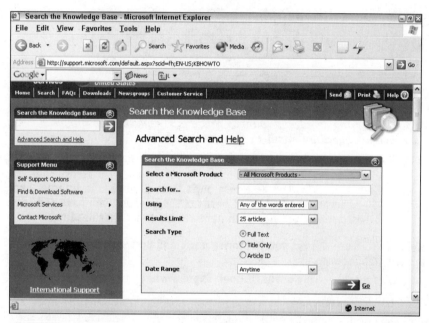

Figure 30-3   *The Advanced Search and Help screen allows you to search for topics of your choice.*

Also, directly through Windows XP, you can visit the Microsoft Expert (or XPert) Zone, a site where you can post questions to Web-based message boards (called Newsgroups)for usually quick (under 48 hours on average) help.

To use this feature, make sure you are connected to the Internet and then:

1. Click Windows Start ⇨ Help and Support.
2. From the Help and Support window, under Ask for Assistance, double-click Get support, or find information in Windows XP newsgroups.
3. Under Support, click Go to a Windows Web site forum in the left pane as shown in Figure 30-4.

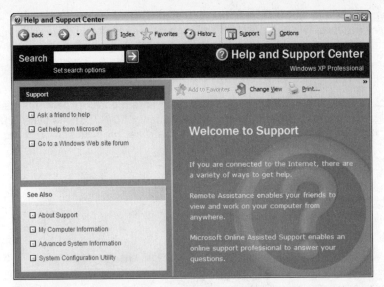

Figure 30-4 *Clicking here leads you into Windows XP–specific newsgroups where you can ask questions and get answers.*

4. In the right pane, click Go to Windows Newsgroups.

Once you finish Step 4, the Windows XP Newsgroup's main site opens in Internet Explorer, as shown in Figure 30-5. Locate the topic that best fits the question you have and then click either Use Web-based reader or Open with news reader under that heading.

- Use Web-based reader — Allows you to browse posts and post questions directly through your Web browser.

- Open with news reader — This opens Outlook Express which, besides handling your e-mail, can also handle newsgroups.

Click one of the options, and the newsgroup you've selected opens. Click a message to read it or click the New Post button to open a window where you can write a message to post on the newsgroup for others to see, as shown in Figure 30-6. This figure shows the screen when used with Microsoft Outlook Express as the newsreader.

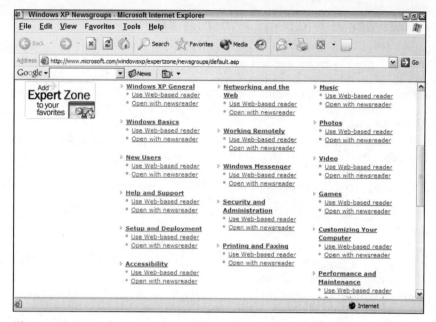

Figure 30-5   *Topics range from very general to very specific, such as Networking and the Web or Security and Administration.*

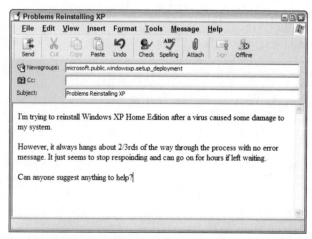

Figure 30-6   *In Outlook Express, type the topic, your question, and press Send.*

Learning More about Microsoft Windows XP

There are basically three ways of learning more about Windows XP: taking a formalized class, participating in self-directed study, and just playing with the program until you accidentally stumble across an answer. Although the last way is the most challenging and intriguing, it is also generally the slowest. A major drawback to learning an application this way is that you may not cover some of the basics, even though you end up with a very advanced knowledge of the product.

There are three major advantages to taking formal courses: You have somebody to help you when you have problems, it is a structured environment, and you have a record of completing the class. The best place (in my opinion) to take structured computer classes is at the community college level. Good equipment, small class sizes, and relatively inexpensive costs make these a good place to look for classes. Not all community colleges live up to all of these standards, but check out your local community college and try a sample class to see how you like it.

To complete self-study, you must be highly disciplined and motivated. There are two ways you can accomplish this. First, buy a book (like this one) and work your way through it. Second, try tutorial CDs, such as those in the Professor Teaches series. Check out these relatively inexpensive tutorials at www.individualsoftware.com. The books, however, tend to be more complete and give you more hands-on exercises than the CD tutorials.

Jobs

It's no longer enough to just say, "I want to work with computers." That's like going into automotive technology because "I want to work on cars." In each case, additional specificity is needed to determine the course of action you should take. Here's some directional advice I give my students. First, when people think about working with computers, they often think about programming. To be a computer programmer, you must be highly structured, good with repetitive work (until the program runs correctly and all of the bugs are out), and, in general, have a somewhat solitary nature. To get a job, you probably need a bachelor's or master's degree. And as is true in most of today's technology-oriented markets, you need lots of experience and good contacts at major companies.

A field I worked in for several years is information technology (IT). You may have heard of this as a field where jobs start at $100,000, you don't need a degree, and don't even have to have much experience. Well, that isn't true. IT students can start at about $40,000, but don't always need a degree. Again, the job market is tight for technology, so you need really good contacts. Most IT students work in Network Administration. This requires a skill set totally different from a programmer's. The network administrator must be people-oriented, customer service–oriented, extremely flexible, and have outstanding problem-solving skills. If you are taught 10 ways to solve a particular problem, none of them will work when you get into this field, so you also have to be invulnerable to frustration. Hours are long, and you may be on call 24/7 (24 hours per day/7 days per week).

Another field that has become popular is working with Microsoft Office. If you are working with Microsoft Word (the word processor), you will be competing against people with years of experience using this application. If you choose to specialize in Excel, most of the work will be in theoretical number manipulation (for example, what items do I have to increase prices on in order to compensate for a wage hike of 4 percent?). Currently, the biggest need is in database development (this is the Access part of Microsoft Office). Access is a database that is used in small- to medium-size offices, and there are few who are proficient at it, so that field might be worth another look.

Done!

REVIEW

- Magazines covering computer topics are available in printed format, or as e-zines.
- Books need to be chosen carefully, making sure they fit your needs.
- Microsoft Web sites are good resources for getting help with Windows XP.
- Three ways to learn more about Windows XP are to take a structured class, work in a self-directed environment, and learn through experience.
- To work with computers for a living, you must first identify the field in which you want to work.

QUIZ YOURSELF

1. What is an e-zine? (See *Magazines — Printed and Electronic* section.)
2. How would you go about choosing a good reference book for Windows XP? (See *Books* section.)
3. How could you use the Internet to help solve Windows XP problems? (See *Microsoft on the Internet* section.)
4. What are three job areas you could choose from if you wanted to work with computers? (See *Jobs* section.)

VI

Sunday Afternoon Part Review

1. Identify two smart practices when trying to improve Windows XP security.
2. What are the two types of User Accounts that can be created in Windows XP?
3. If User01 makes customized changes to the desktop, they are saved when the user logs out of the system. If User02 logs in, will the user see the customized desktop changes created by User01?
4. How do you force Windows XP to request a user's username and password to access Windows?
5. What command path do you follow to get to the User Accounts dialog box?
6. How can your computer catch a virus?
7. If you have a cable or DSL connection, are you only hooked up to the Internet when you open your browser?
8. What is a virus hoax?
9. If you are able to "remove" a virus, what potential problems do you still have?
10. Name two of the three big anti-virus manufacturers.
11. What is the first step in troubleshooting a hardware problem?
12. What is the most common problem experienced when a software application is not operating correctly?
13. How would you access the System icon in order to tweak your operating system for maximum performance?
14. In the Performance Options dialog box, which setting is used in order to make your computer operate at peak efficiency?
15. What is a cache?
16. What are the two types of magazines available to you to help you to learn more about Windows XP?
17. Name at least one e-zine that would be helpful to you in learning more about Windows XP.

18. What does Microsoft call the database that lists all of the known problems and potential solutions for Microsoft hardware and software?

19. How can you reach Microsoft newsgroups, where you can post questions about Windows XP?

20. What is a Web site where you can search the Microsoft Knowledge Base?

Answers to Part Reviews

Part I: Friday Evening

1. Windows XP is only a client operating system.
2. The Desktop Items dialog box is used to select which of the four most common icons that are displayed on the desktop.
3. Cable and DSL are the two types of fast Internet connections commonly found in home offices.
4. Internet Connection Sharing (ICS) allows multiple computers to connect to the Internet using a single Internet connection.
5. The Home Edition of Windows XP is capable of handling only one CPU and one Video Display Terminal (Monitor).
6. RAM is the single hardware component that would be the best investment to make your computer run faster.
7. The Hardware Compatibility List (HCL) is the Microsoft file that tells you whether your hardware should work with Windows XP or not.
8. The legal agreement that outlines your legal responsibilities in regard to Windows XP is called the End User License Agreement (EULA).
9. If an operating system is already installed, a full installation is the recommended type of installation for Windows XP.
10. The original Product Key that comes with Windows XP consists of letters and numbers.
11. The Start menu opens when you press the Windows Logo key.
12. The area of the Taskbar used to launch an application with a single click is called the Quick Launch bar.
13. In Windows XP, on the desktop you will find one or more small pictures representing applications, folders, or files. These small pictures are called icons.

14. Between "Windows" and "windows," "Windows" is the operating system and "windows" are the areas of the screen used to view information.

15. Right-clicking any empty area of the desktop and choosing Properties displays the Display Properties dialog box.

16. When doing a search in the Windows XP Help and Support Center, you can use keywords. Keywords are the important words in a sentence.

17. When saving a topic to the Favorites button, you use the Rename option when Windows uses a formal name for a topic, but you would like it listed using a name that makes more sense to you.

18. When doing a search, the maximum number of results that can be returned per provider is 999.

19. When a dialog box is displayed, you get general help by pressing the F1 function key, and specific help by pressing Shift+F1.

20. Three general components included in the term multimedia are graphics, music, and voice.

Part II: Saturday Morning

1. The Windows XP Control Panel helps you manage hardware, software, and applications that make your computer function.

2. To assist you in troubleshooting problems with common hardware peripherals, you would use the Printers and Other Hardware category of the control panel.

3. To connect your computer to a home network or Local Area Network, you must first have a Network Interface Card (NIC) installed in your computer.

4. Windows XP provides built-in tools for assistance to users with three different categories of disabilities: visual, audio, and mobility impairments.

5. If you want to clean up your hard drive, back up valuable data, and run the Windows Defragmenter to arrange the data on your hard drive in a manner that speeds up your computer, you would choose Performance and Maintenance in the Categories view of the Control Panel.

6. To display the list of installed Windows XP accessories, click Start ➪ All Programs ➪ Accessories if you are using the default menu. If you are displaying the Classic menu, click Start ➪ Programs ➪ Accessories.

7. The three ways of inputting data into the Calculator accessory are by using the mouse to click the numbers on the screen, pressing the number keys along the top of your keyboard, or (if you have one) using the numeric keypad on the right side of your keyboard.

8. If you need to add paragraph or character formatting, such as changing the font or adjusting the alignment of paragraphs, you would use WordPad rather than Notepad. Notepad is only capable of saving text. WordPad can save both the text and the formatting applied to it.

9. To insert an object, such as a graphic, into WordPad, choose Insert ➪ Object from the menu bar, and navigate to the object you want to insert.

10. Several reasons you might use Windows Explorer include creating new folders, moving folders to new locations, creating subfolders, copying and moving files or folders from one folder to another.

11. The four categories (subfolders) of accessories in a standard Windows XP installation are Accessibility, Communications, Entertainment, and System Tools.

12. www.microsoft.com/enable would be a good place to find out more about the accessibility accessories available in Windows XP.

13. To set up Remote Desktop you would use the Communication category of Windows XP accessories.

14. To change the volume control for your audio accessories you would use the Entertainment Accessories category.

15. To defragment your disk (put all of the files in order), you would use the System Tools category.

16. The two ways to see all of your desktop are minimizing all active programs, or by clicking the Show Desktop icon in the Quick Launch bar.

17. You might want to rearrange your desktop when icons are spread all over the screen, making a particular icon difficult to find.

18. If you want to arrange your desktop into groupings of similar types of files, right-click any empty area of the desktop, and choose Arrange Icons by ⇨ Type. This places all of the folders together, for example, all of the system files, all of the documents, etc.

19. You can manually rearrange your desktop icons by minimizing all active programs and dragging and dropping them into the desired location.

20. When you install a new program, Windows XP generally places the shortcut icon for the new program at the bottom of the Start menu.

21. A desktop theme determines the overall appearance of your desktop by providing a predefined set of icons, fonts, colors, mouse pointers, sounds, background picture, screensaver, and other window elements.

22. A problem that can occur to a monitor that sits unused for a length of time with the same image on the screen is called monitor burn-in. The built-in feature of Windows XP that can help reduce the chance of monitor burn-in is called a screensaver. You can use one provided with Windows XP or download dozens from the Internet.

23. You can add a password to your screensaver by clicking the On resume, password protect option box in the Screen Saver tab of the Display Properties dialog box.

24. Nearly all executable files have the three-letter extension .exe at the end of their names. This indicates they are an executable file, and double-clicking the icon will start the program.

25. If you are browsing the Internet and find a site so useful you want to add a shortcut icon to your desktop, you can choose File ⇨ Send ⇨ Shortcut to Desktop from the file menu.

26. In Windows, we often hear the term folder. In earlier operating systems, folders were often called directories. Both are a way of organizing your data, and they perform the same function.

27. You can easily determine the path to a folder by looking in the address bar. You can also find the path to a folder by right-clicking on the folder and choosing Properties from the context menu. In the Folder Properties dialog box, the Location value will display the path to the folder.

28. Windows XP only allows one file or folder name. If you try to name a folder or file with the same name as an existing folder or file, Windows XP displays an error message and asks you to provide a unique name.

29. You can move a folder from one folder to another by clicking the folder to be moved and dragging the icon to the new folder where it is to be located. This movement is called dragging and dropping.

30. When you copy a folder from one place to another all files and subfolders containing files are copied with it.

Part III: Saturday Afternoon

1. No. Windows XP Encrypted File System doesn't require a password. Instead it allows you to open the file (or denies your opening the file) based on your credentials assigned when you log on to the computer.

2. The FAT32 file system fragments your files (breaks them up into nonconsecutive sections on the drive) more than the NTFS file system.

3. No. You can convert your hard drive from FAT32 to NTFS without loss of data. However, converting it back to FAT32 requires reformatting your hard drive, resulting in total loss of data.

4. A typical floppy disk can hold approximately 1.44MB of data.

5. If you are trying to make a folder read-only, and a checkmark is already in the check box but the option is grayed out, it means that some files or subfolders within it are not marked as read-only. You fix it by clicking the check box once to remove the checkmark, and clicking it again to turn the option back on. At this point, all subfolders and files become read-only.

6. Yes. Windows XP automatically creates the My Documents folder in C:\Documents and Settings*yourusername*\My Documents.

7. The best place to store your images is in the folder C:\Documents and Settings\ *yourusername*\My Documents\My Pictures. This ensures that other users will not accidentally save images to the same folder.

8. The default view in the My Pictures folder is set to thumbnail. Although this is slower, it allows you to see a smaller version of each picture without having to open it based only on the name.

9. Other folders get added to the My Documents folder in one of two ways. You can add them manually to better organize your files, or, in some cases, installation of applications will automatically add subfolders to the My Documents folder.

10. The details view shows you the most information about files. It includes the filename, size, type, and date last modified.

11. The most common port where a printer is installed is to the parallel port, named LPT1.

12. If your printer came with a floppy disk or CD-ROM driver, when you reach the Install Printer Software page of the Add Printer Wizard dialog box, you should put the floppy or CD in the drive, click Have Disk, and browse to the correct file. The correct file will be listed in the installation instructions that come with your printer.

13. If you set the default printer preferences to print in Portrait mode (where the paper is taller than it is wide), you can temporarily change the settings from within an application to set the printer for landscape by opening the Print dialog box, and clicking the Properties button next to the printer. This setting remains in effect only for that application, and only until the application is closed.

14. You would choose a default printer if you had more than one printer available to your computer, such as in a workgroup or on a Local Area Network.

15. If you are successfully able to print a Windows XP test page, but a specific application won't allow you to print, the most likely problem is that the application is using its own printer driver, and you need to contact the software manufacturer to see if they have a new Windows XP printer driver.

16. The two basic models of sharing resources among computers are the domain model and the workgroup model. Windows XP Professional operates only as a client operating system in the domain model and Windows XP Home Edition will not work at all in the domain model. Both versions of Windows XP function fine in the workgroup environment.

17. Whether in a domain or a workgroup, a hub or switch connects the computers.

18. The two major disadvantages between a wired network and a wireless network are that a wireless network is more costly and may operate more slowly.

19. In Windows XP, whether in a domain or a workgroup, the TCP/IP protocol is used for communication between computers.

20. If you want to set up a domain network, in addition to components required for a workgroup, you will need to purchase a high-end computer and Windows 2000 or Windows 2003 Server software.

21. It is not necessary to type http:// into the address window of your browser. The Web browser automatically assumes that http:// is the protocol you want to use.

22. The Search button opens the search companion which allows you to find a Web site even if you don't know the exact address.

23. You might want to change your Home Page to a site other than the default if the default site takes too long to load, or if you have a specific site, such as CNN.com where you get your daily news.

24. Shortcuts to your favorite Web pages are also called bookmarks.

25. The four major functions you can perform from the Organize Favorites dialog box are Create Folder, Move to Folder, Rename, and Delete.

26. Web pages are developed in Hypertext Markup Language (HTML).

27. If you incorrectly set your Internet options, you can cause your browser to cease functioning.

28. If you want to control the level of language, nudity, sex, or violence, you would use the Content Advisor feature.

29. In order to use ICS, you must be connected as part of a workgroup or domain network. Otherwise, the ICS panel will not be displayed.

30. Cookies are small files that are usually placed on your computer by Web sites that you visit to store information about your browsing activities.

Part IV: Saturday Evening

1. There are three ways of opening the Computer Management Console. The shortest way is to right-click the My Computer icon on your desktop and choose Manage from the context menu. If you are in the default XP view (Category), click Start ➪ Control Panel ➪ Performance and Maintenance ➪ Administrative Tools ➪ Computer Management. If you are in the Classic view, click Start ➪ Control Panel ➪ Administrative Tools ➪ Computer Management.

2. In the Event Log, the most important piece of information you can get if you are going to get a support professional to help you troubleshoot an error is the Event ID.

3. The Local Users and Groups category allows you to create accounts so others can use a computer or combine individuals into a group and apply settings and control access based on being a member of a group, rather than on an account-by-account basis.

4. By default, the Performance Logs and Alerts category is disabled.

5. The Services and Applications category is in the Computer Management Console feature. The subcategories and tools located in this section allow you to perform three tasks: start, stop, and configure several different services, including Web services and the Windows XP Indexing Service.

6. The name of the Microsoft backup utility file is ntbackup.exe.

7. The file attribute that tells the backup program that a file needs to be backed up is called the archive attribute.

8. Another name for a Normal backup, which backs up all of your hard drive, is a Full backup.

9. The type of backup that copies all files created or changed since the last normal or incremental backup and does *not* reset the archive attribute is a differential backup.

10. The part of the backup utility you use to reload files that have been damaged is called Restore.

11. You get your primary e-mail account from your Internet Service Provider (ISP).

12. If Outlook Express is installed normally, there is *no* shortcut to it on your desktop. You must begin the program from the Start menu.

13. A fairly safe password would be comprised of 5 to 8 characters, letters, special characters, and numbers, as well as at least one of the letters having an abnormal case change.

14. An option in a dialog box is enabled if it has a checkmark in the check box to the left of the option name.

15. You might choose a utility program such as WinZip to compress a file you are sending as an e-mail attachment.

16. In order to use Windows Messenger, you must create a .NET account (also called a Passport).

17. A delay between the time a message is typed and the time you receive it is generally caused by a busy server.

18. The icons that can be included with a message in order to demonstrate nonverbal cues are called Emoticons.

19. The three things required to use Windows Messenger to send audio communications are a microphone, sound card, and either speakers or a headset.

20. The two types of objects that can easily be sent to another user of Windows Messenger are files and photos.

Part V: Sunday Morning

1. If Windows XP Media Player is installed, the first time you put a music CD in the CD-ROM drive you are asked if you want Windows Media Player to automatically play the music CD.

2. Besides music CDs, other types of media the Windows XP Media Player is capable of playing include Web-based audio files and video files.

3. To play streaming audio from the Internet, you should have a fast Internet connection such as cable or DSL. Although it is possible to use a modem, you may find a lot of stops and starts while the music is downloading.

4. The main advantage of the MP3 format of file storage is that it compresses the files into much smaller ones than are used to store them on a CD-ROM.

5. QuickTime from Apple is the most common alternative video format that you can expect to encounter on the Internet.

6. Configuration is the process by which a hardware device is adjusted to work properly with your system and to fit your specific needs.

7. The four sources from which you might obtain new drivers built especially for Windows XP include the Windows XP operating system disk, a disk supplied with the hardware, downloads from the manufacturer's Internet Web site, or downloads from an Internet Web site that specializes in providing hardware drivers.

8. An interrupt is a signal informing the operating system that an event has occurred, such as a key being pressed, or the mouse being moved.

9. You would find a list of drivers used by your computer in the Device Manager dialog box.

10. Some Troubleshooters are included with Windows XP. You can find additional Troubleshooters at www.microsoft.com.

11. NIC stands for Network Interface Card.

12. The two types of slots you would use to install a NIC in a desktop computer are ISA and PCI.

13. The three standard speeds for today's hubs are 10 Mbps, 100 Mbps, and a combination of 10/100 Mbps. Gigabit hubs are on the near horizon, but haven't found a large market at this time.

14. The NIC connection is slightly larger than a standard phone connection in a modem. A phone cable fits loosely in a NIC, and a NIC connector is too large for a modem connection.

15. The default Workgroup name is WORKGROUP.

16. Between hackers and crackers, crackers are generally thought of as being the bad guys.

17. When a number of patches are combined and distributed as a single download, it is called a Service Pack.

18. The three ways that Windows XP can be updated include manually, automatically, or on a scheduled basis.

19. You can find out what a particular update affects by going to the Microsoft Web site and searching for the Update reference number.

20. You would find the original Windows XP Product Key code on the back of the original CD case.

21. The three ways of opening Windows Task Manager include: press Ctrl+Alt+Delete, press Shift+Ctrl+Escape, or right-click any empty area of the Taskbar and choose Task Manager from the Context menu.

22. To stop a locked-up application you would use the Applications tab in the Windows Task Manager.

23. The two easy ways to move between open applications are by clicking the icon on the Taskbar or by pressing Alt+Tab.

24. The Processes Tab in Windows Task Manager is used to display the status of applications and Windows subsystems and services.

25. A Page file is an area of your hard drive set aside to function as temporary RAM in case you have more applications and other items open than can fit in RAM.

26. You should uninstall the program until you can get help to understand why it is not behaving on your system to reduce the risk it may cause other problems on your system.

27. Click Start ⇨ Control Panel ⇨ System icon ⇨ Advanced tab. Under Performance, click the Settings button.

28. Until you have a better sense of your system, it's better to let Windows manage performance for you.

29. To check the status of a misbehaving program, press Ctrl+Alt+Delete to open Windows Task Manager and look for the program listed on the Application tab.

30. In Performance Monitor, an item that performs work on your computer is called an object.

Part VI: Sunday Afternoon

1. Don't always log in as an administrator, disable your Guest account, require passwords and use smart passwords, and disable Fast User Switching.

2. The two types of User Accounts that can be created in Windows XP are Limited and Administrator.

3. If User01 makes customized changes to the desktop, they are saved when the user logs out of the system. When User02 logs in, the user will not see the customized desktop changes created by User01. All customized desktop settings are stored with the separate user account information.

4. Turn off the Welcome screen by opening User Accounts as an Administrator and selecting Change How Users logon and log off.

5. To get to the User Accounts dialog box, click Start ➪ Control Panel ➪ User Accounts.

6. Your computer can catch a virus by any means used to share files. Although the Internet and e-mail represent the largest threat, you can also catch a virus through any means used to make file transfers.

7. If you have a cable or DSL connection, you are connected to the Internet all of the time, whether you open your browser or not.

8. A virus hoax is notification that a potentially damaging virus exists when it doesn't. As you send notification to others on your mailing list, the Internet slows down in order to handle the excess mail generated by everyone sending the virus hoax to all their contacts.

9. If you are able to "remove" a virus, you still have the potential problem that one or more of your data files will be quarantined, and you will no longer have access to it.

10. The three big anti-virus manufacturers are Norton (Symantec), McAfee, and Panda.

11. The first step in troubleshooting a hardware problem is to determine which piece of hardware is causing the problem.

12. The most common problem experienced when a software application is not operating correctly is that the application is using too many system resources, particularly memory or CPU time used.

13. You access the System icon in order to tweak your operating system for maximum performance by clicking Start ➪ Control Panel ➪ Performance and Maintenance ➪ System icon (or Start ➪ Control Panel ➪ System).

14. In the Performance Options dialog box, select Adjust for best performance in order to make your computer operate at peak efficiency.

15. A cache is an area of memory or hard drive where uncommitted files are stored.

16. The two types of magazines available to you to help you to learn Windows XP are printed magazines and e-zines.

17. Four e-zines that would be helpful to you include *Woody's Windows Watch*, *Lockergnome*, *Windows XP Technical Tips*, and *AnchorDesk*.

18. Microsoft calls the database which lists all of the known problems and potential solutions for Microsoft hardware and software a Knowledge Base.

19. Choose Start ⇨ Help and Support ⇨ Ask for Assistance ⇨ Get support, or find information in Windows XP newsgroups.

20. The Web site where you can search the Microsoft Knowledge Base is found at `http://search.support.microsoft.com`.

What's on the Companion Web Site?

This appendix provides you with information on the contents of the companion Web site for this book, which you can find at `www.wiley.com/compbooks/nicholson`. Here's what you will find:

- The self-assessment test
- Links to additional resources
- Bonus material

The Self-Assessment Test

The self-assessment test helps you evaluate how much you've learned from this Weekend Crash Course. It will also help you identify which sessions you've perfected, and which you may need to revisit. Each question is taken from one of several general topics, so you can see where you need to do more work.

Links to Additional Resources

The companion Web site offers a list of links to help you locate other useful Web sites.

Bonus Material

This section offers an overview of hardware. You may find it useful to read this before beginning the individual sessions, or you may want to refer to it as questions arise.

Index

Continued

Continued